E-BUSINESS

PRINCIPLES
AND STRATEGIES
FOR ACCOUNTANTS

Second Edition

STEVEN M. GLOVER

STEPHEN W. LIDDLE

DOUGLAS F. PRAWITT

School of Accountancy and Information Systems
Marriot School
Brigham Young University
Provo, Utah

Prentice
Hall

Upper Saddle River, New Jersey 07458

Acquisitions Editor: Thomas Sigel
Editor-in-Chief: P.J. Boardman
Assistant Editor: Jessica Romeo
Media Project Manager: Torie Anderson
Marketing Manager: Beth Toland
Marketing Assistant: Christine Genneken
Managing Editor (Production): John Roberts
Production Editor: Renata Butera
Permissions Coordinator: Suzanne Grappi
Associate Director, Manufacturing: Vincent Scelta
Production Manager: Arnold Vila
Manufacturing Buyer: Michelle Klein
Cover Design: Bruce Kenselaar
Cover Illustration/Photo: © Eric Peterson, Conrad Representatives
Printer/Binder: Courier-Westford

Credits and acknowledgements borrowed from other sources and reproduced, with permission, in this textbook appear on appropriate page within text.

Pearson Education LTD.
Pearson Education Australia PTY, Limited
Pearson Education Singapore, Pte. Ltd
Pearson Education North Asia Ltd
Pearson Education, Canada, Ltd
Pearson Educación de Mexico, S.A. de C.V.
Pearson Education–Japan

10 9 8 7 6 5 4 3 2 1
ISBN 0-13-035915-7

Table of Contents

Chapter 1: Introduction 1

   E-Business Defined 2

   Benefits of E-Business..4

      Expanded Sales Opportunities 4

      Improved Communication, Customer Service, Feedback, and Loyalty..............6

      Lower Costs 8

      Supply Chain and Human Resource Management..9

      Benefits from a Customer Standpoint 11

   E-Business Benefits Not Easy to Achieve or Measure..12

   Risks 14

   How E-Business Affects Accounting Professionals 15

      The CPA Vision Process..15

      The Information Value Chain 16

      Career Differences Along the Information Value Chain....................................17

      Purpose of This Book...18

      Specific Effects on Accounting and Auditing...19

   Summary..20

Chapter 2: How the "E" Is Changing Business...23

   Disruptive or Sustaining Technology 23

      Early Reaction to the Internet..24

      E-Business Strategies 26

   History of E-Business: The Internet and EDI 28

      Development of the Internet...28

      Electronic Data Interchange 32

   Summary..36

Chapter 3: E-Business Models 41

   Comparing B2C and B2B...42

      Business-to-Consumer Models 42

      Business-to-Business Models...43

   Chapter Roadmap 47

   Online Stores, Marketplaces, and Services..47

      Small Businesses and Niche Providers Have a Home in Cyberspace................48

      Advantages of Online Stores..48

      Lessons to Be Learned 49

      Dell's Build-to-Order Model: A Lesson in Effective Communication...............49

      Amazon.com: Bookstore or E-Store? Staking a Claim in Cyberspace 52

      eBay: Immediate Profit in Creating a Virtual Marketplace for Consumers........56

      Eat or Be Eaten? Charles Schwab & Co. Does Both 59

   B2B: Supply-Chain Management...61

      Extranets...61

      B2B Auctions 62

      Automobile Industry Supply-Chain Management 63

Content Providers 64
    Publishers and Media on the Web...66
    Online Communities 68
Content Aggregators and Portals...68
Infrastructure Providers 70
Summary..72

Chapter 4: Identifying and Managing the Risks of E-Business 77
Risk..78
    What Is Risk? 78
    Risk in E-Business 78
Infrastructure Vulnerabilities: Risks and Controls 80
    Risks Associated with IT Infrastructure Vulnerabilities 80
    Controlling Risks Associated with Infrastructure Vulnerabilities 85
Falsified Identity: Risks and Controls 90
    Risks Associated with Falsified Identity...90
    Controlling the Risks Associated with Falsified Identity...............................93
Compromised Privacy: Risks and Controls...95
    Risks Associated with Compromised Privacy...95
    Controlling the Risks Associated with Compromised Privacy 98
Destructive Codes and Programs: Risks and Controls 99
    Risks Associated with Destructive Codes and Programs...............................99
    Controlling the Risks Associated with Destructive Codes and Programs..........101
Human Factors in E-Business..103
    People—The Weak Link...103
    Responsible Personnel 104
    Action Plan for Breach of Security 105
System Interdependencies 105
Anticipating and Managing E-Business Risk 107
Summary..108

Chapter 5: Implications and Opportunities of E-Business Assurance............................113
Financial Statement Assurance in an E-Business Environment 114
    IT Environment 115
    Other Financial Statement Risk Factors in E-Business.................................121
New Forms of Assurance to Facilitate E-Business..127
    Business-to-Consumer Assurance...130
    Business-to-Business Assurance 134
    Other Potential New Services to Facilitate E-Business.................................138
What E-Business Means for Accounting Professionals..141
    Application of Current CPA Competencies 141
    New Competencies Required of CPAs 141
    Competitive Environment 142
    Legal Liability Issues 143
Summary..143

Appendix A: Internet Technology...147

Appendix B: Web Technology...153

Appendix C: Encryption—Privacy and Authenticity....................................162

Appendix D: Firewalls and Proxy Servers..165

Appendix E: Getting a Small Business Online 169

Appendix F: Electronic Payment Methods 170

Index...175

Preface

To effectively add value in today's business environment, accounting professionals must understand the fundamental issues associated with e-business, whether functioning as financial adviser, assurance provider, or broad-based business consultant. This book is intended to provide a relatively nontechnical introduction to the fundamental e-business issues that today's accounting professional needs to understand. While accountants' comparative advantage with respect to e-business generally lies at the upper end of the information value chain (closer to decisions than to raw data, as discussed in Chapter 1), accountants need a working knowledge of underlying technology, current applications of e-business, and various e-business models. The first three chapters of the book provide the necessary background on e-business, and while these chapters are somewhat tailored to accountants, much of the information is equally relevant to other business disciplines. In these early chapters, readers learn about the historical development of e-business as well as the effect e-business is having on business. Coverage of the benefits and current usages of e-business make up a large part of Chapter 1 and the bulk of Chapter 3.

The speed with which "e" burst upon the business world has not permitted existing accounting, auditing, and information systems texts to address the important e-business issues accountants need to be aware of. The last two chapters and the technology appendices provide a good foundation of e-business terminology, strategic implications and important risks, threats, and opportunities, particularly with respect to the accounting profession. While the text covers fundamental information technology issues, this book is not intended to be an information technology "how-to" book.

In the two years since we wrote the first edition of this book, much has changed in the world of e-business. Of course this is what one would expect—change, and lots of it. April 2000 witnessed the bursting of the dot-com bubble. The tech-heavy NASDAQ stock index fell from its historic high mark of more than 5000 in March 2000 to well under 2000 as of this writing. Venture capital fled the e-business scene, and the mood went from exuberance and growth-focused to grim and profit-oriented. General recession and 9/11 have taken their toll as well. In this second edition, we have updated examples throughout the book and added new material to reflect the lessons and progress of the past two years. We remain convinced that even though e-business does change some of the rules, conventional business wisdom is still a vital factor in a company's success. We are glad to see much of the hype surrounding e-business has faded.

In collegiate settings, this book is primarily intended as a supplement to be used in existing accounting courses. It is appropriate for use in intermediate or advanced financial accounting courses, introductory or advanced auditing courses, and introductory accounting information systems courses. This book could also be used as part of a larger set of materials in a stand-alone e-business course for accounting students. While the book is targeted to accounting students, many consultants, business advisers, and CPAs will also find that the book provides a useful introduction to important e-business issues.

 We invite professionals, students, and faculty to visit our Companion Website, www.prenhall.com/glover, for additional resources such as links to the Web addresses referenced in this book, regularly updated references and links to current e-business articles, and more.

Acknowledgments

This book has been made possible by the support of many people and organizations. We thank all who have contributed to its development. We have enjoyed working with the Prentice Hall team and all others associated with this work. We thank our Acquisitions Editor, Thomas Sigel, who orchestrated the publication of this book. We also thank John Roberts, Managing Editor/Production; Renata Butera, Production Editor; Michelle Klein, Manufacturing Buyer; Bruce Kenselaar, Cover Designer; and Suzanne Grappi, Permissions Supervisor, who all worked diligently and carefully on this project. Thanks also to other members of the Prentice Hall book team, including P. J. Boardman, Editor-in-Chief; Beth Toland, Executive Marketing Manager; and Jessica Romeo, Assistant Editor. Finally, we thank Annie Todd who initiated and helped define this project. Without her we would not have written this book.

The Rollins Center for eBusiness at Brigham Young University has been generous and supportive in co-sponsoring this book. We are grateful to the Center's Director, Owen Cherrington, for his vision and support. We hope this will be the beginning of a long and successful collaboration with the Center.

We appreciate the contributions of the following reviewers for their helpful comments and suggestions:

> Mark Beasley, North Carolina State University
> Randy Coyner, Florida Atlantic University
> Paula Miller, Collin County Community College
> Scott Summers, Brigham Young University

We especially recognize Mark Beasley for providing extensive comments and going into great detail regarding ways to improve the manuscript, and Scott Summers for helping with end of chapter material.

We also acknowledge our research assistants, who were instrumental in collecting and organizing portions of the information presented in this book: Ryan Baxter, Brian Carini, David Mangelson, Ryan Oviatt, Kevin Smith, Joseph Van Orden, Brad Tingey, and Bill Tayler.

We gratefully acknowledge the American Institute of Certified Public Accountants for permission to use quotes and other materials from the accounting standards and from their Web site, including adaptations of the WebTrust and SysTrust principles and criteria. We also acknowledge the other companies and organizations mentioned in this book for permission to use information and screen captures from their respective Web sites.

We especially thank our wives, Tina, Melody, and Meryll, and our children for their support, love, and patience.

— S.M.G, S.W.L, and D.F.P.

The Rollins Center for eBusiness at Brigham Young University

E-Business: Principles and Strategies for Accountants is co-sponsored by the Kevin and Debra Rollins Center for eBusiness at Brigham Young University (BYU). The eBusiness Center, located at BYU's Marriott School, was established in January 2000 to be a leading influence in the study and development of e-business technology, strategy, and management.

e business
BRIGHAM YOUNG UNIVERSITY

The eBusiness Center fosters the study and teaching of how information technology is changing business management and impacting people. It serves as an intermediary between the high-tech business sector and BYU's faculty and students—forming new partnerships and undertaking joint research projects. The Center was also established to attract and maintain the highest quality faculty and staff, develop new course materials, expand the number of e-business classes at the University, and provide students with new employment opportunities, internships, and field study projects.

The eBusiness Center was founded in part by a generous contribution from Dell Computer Corporation Vice Chair, Kevin Rollins and his wife, Debra. "We all participate in an era where the Internet is allowing us to see and do more than at any other time," said Kevin Rollins, a Marriott School alumnus. "We have the responsibility to ensure technologies are used to benefit people's lives."

Dr. J. Owen Cherrington, Mary & Ellis Distinguished Professor of Accounting and Information Systems at BYU, is the founding director of the eBusiness Center. For more information about the center, we invite you to visit the Web site: ebusiness.byu.edu.

Chapter 1: Introduction

When asked how high the Internet was on General Electric's agenda, then-CEO Jack Welch responded, "Where does the Internet rank in priority? It's no. 1, 2, 3, and 4."[1] GE has invested $10 billion in information technology since 1998, and its digitization efforts are paying off. Online sales grew from about zero in 1998 to $7 billion in 2000. GE's e-business cost saving measures saved the company $1.9 billion in 2001 and are expected to save another $10 billion from 2002 to 2004.[2] Despite the recent dot-com collapse, strategic implications of e-business are still some of the biggest issues facing companies. E-business will have a particularly significant impact on operational effectiveness, with 2 deeper integration among service, sales, logistics, manufacturing, and supply chain.

The real key for business now is not only to improve operational effectiveness, but to carefully look beyond that to identify opportunities for e-business to create real strategic advantage. The Internet, the primary enabler of e-business, is a very powerful technology that will change the way business is done. We emphasize that the transformation is not yet complete—in fact, Internet-enabled e-business is still in its early childhood. Compared to other communication inventions, the growth and spread of the Internet is truly incredible. It took radio more than 35 years and television 15 years to reach 60 million people. In contrast, the Internet reached over 90 million people in just three years. The growth and reach of wireless devices capable of mobile e-commerce and the ability to use semiconductor technology to create connectivity between devices of all types promises also to be dramatic.

We wrote the first edition of this book when the buzz about the Internet and the "irrational market exuberance" was at its peak. Two years later, after many well-funded dot-coms are "dot-gones," the attitude toward the Internet has shifted so dramatically that for many the attitude is one of "irrational pessimism." At the writing of the first edition, we did not believe all the hype and at the time of writing this edition, we do not believe the doom and gloom. This is not the time for businesses to conclude that the Internet was a fad or a fluke. Many of the early e-business initiatives did not live up to the hype because they were not complete, sound solutions. These systems provided some capability to transact online, but the necessary information for good decisions was lacking and the business fundamentals were not in place. Furthermore, many early initiatives underestimated the difficulty of integrating e-business with existing cultures and the monumental task of linking outdated legacy systems. However, the fundamental value drivers of e-business are unchanged and still pervade both the basics and the future of business.

Evidence of irrational pessimism is the myth that online retailing or "e-tailing" is dead. Despite the highly publicized deaths of many major online experiments like Pets.com, eToys, and Webvan, "e-tailing" itself is not dead. Even in the declining economy, e-tailing grew 24.7 percent from mid-2000 to 2001.[3] Forrester research also predicts steady double-digit growth of online spending, and while not over 100 percent as in past years, growth is still strong. In an eMarketer report released in the Fall of 2001, business-to-consumer revenue is expected to grow to $156 billion, up from 38.3 billion in 2000. The population of Internet users is expected to reach nearly 185 million by 2003, compared to 116 million in 2000. Those that will actually make purchases over the Internet in 2003 will reach 130 million, compared to 79 million in 2001. Even in down economies, people will still buy products and they are increasingly buying online from trusted sources due to increased convenience.

The bad news for **pure Internet plays** is that most shoppers are heading to the Web sites of well-known retailers such as Wal-Mart and L.L. Bean. That explains, in part, why Amazon.com is forging relationships with established brick-and-mortar merchants like Circuit City, Toys "R" Us, and Target (see Chapter 3). It is also important to put the e-tailing growth and sales projections into perspective—current levels of online sales represent perhaps one percent of the $3 trillion retail economy.[4] Business-to-business transactions are also expected to dwarf business-to-consumer transactions. Worldwide business-to-business transactions were more than $430 billion in 2000 and are expected to grow to $1.9 trillion by 2002 and to $8.5 trillion by 2005.[5]

The most important lesson from the last few years is that for most businesses and industries e-business is complementary (i.e., another sales channel or a cost reducer) rather than contradictory or revolutionary. The underlying basics of good business, like knowing your customers and their customers, serving your customers, reducing carrying and processing costs, and planning for various economic futures, existed before the Internet and remain relevant in the face of improving technology. For some firms, the Internet will be used as a tool to facilitate and improve the execution of basic business strategies. For others, such as Dell, e-business will be a key strategic initiative that will dramatically impact business models to create real opportunity, value, and comparative advantage. Another important lesson learned is that leading-edge technology is not enough to overcome a poor business model. The old adage, "what we lose on every sale, we'll make up for in volume," did not work before the Internet and does not work with the Internet.

To function effectively as a valued adviser, consultant, or assurance provider, accounting professionals need to understand key issues associated with e-business. This chapter defines e-business, discusses the benefits and current usages of e-business, highlights the importance of e-business risk identification and control, and introduces some of the opportunities e-business offers to the accounting profession.

E-Business Defined

> **Electronic business** (**e-business**) is the use of information technology and electronic communication networks to exchange business information and conduct transactions in electronic, paperless form.

E-business leverages the power of information technology and electronic communication networks like the Internet to transform critical business strategies and processes. E-business minimizes traditional boundaries of time and geography and makes possible the creation of virtual communities of suppliers and customers. Our definition of e-business includes the exchange of business information that may or may not directly relate to the purchase or sale of goods or services. For example, businesses are increasingly using electronic mechanisms to improve company performance by facilitating collaboration and data sharing among employees and to provide improved customer support. Participants in e-business transactions and information exchanges may be individuals (consumers and employees) or automated agents (information systems that are programmed to perform with little or no human intervention). Transactions and information exchanges can take place within a company, between companies, between companies and individuals, and between individuals. Another term commonly associated with e-business is **e-commerce**, which we define more narrowly as the use of e-business to buy and sell products or services.

It is important to remember that e-business is not restricted to "high-tech" companies. For example, e-business helped Weyerhaeuser turn around its Wisconsin door factory (see Text Box 1.1). It is also important to understand that in the very near future there will not be a distinction between e-business and business in general. E-business is such a critical component of a successful business strategy that it will simply become a normal and universal aspect of business sometime in the future.[6]

Text Box 1.1 Weyerhaeuser Uses E-Business to Open the Door to New Profits

In the mid-1990s a Weyerhaeuser Co. door factory that cuts, glues, drills, and shapes customized doors according to each buyer's desire was on its last leg. Besieged by sagging sales, bloated costs, and poor morale, management determined to introduce e-business. The factory is profitable again and revenues are growing at a rate of 10 to 15 percent. The software, called DoorBuilder, is built on an Internet platform that includes communication networks and software for order taking and product tracking. DoorBuilder plugs into vast databases of information from the factory floor to supplier inventory and price lists.

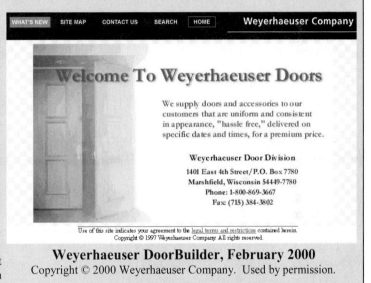

Weyerhaeuser DoorBuilder, February 2000
Copyright © 2000 Weyerhaeuser Company. Used by permission.

DoorBuilder improved the company's ability to track costs, develop pricing strategies, and identify the most profitable customer relationships. Order volumes doubled and return on plant assets went from 2 percent in the mid-1990's to 24 percent in 2000. Once key distributors were added to the network, Weyerhaeuser could offer faster turnaround and often lower prices than rivals.

DoorBuilder easily handles over 2 million different custom configurations. The system sorts through vast amounts of information to produce specifications and costs in seconds. Prior to DoorBuilder, orders often took weeks to finalize, and then the paper order would frequently be separated from the door in production, causing additional delays. On-time deliveries improved from about 40 percent up to 97 percent. DoorBuilder also drastically reduced the number of errors in production, ordering, and delivery. Weyerhaeuser was able to sell its Door Division to private investors in December 2000 for an estimated $50 million more than it otherwise would have worth without DoorBuilder's success.

Adapted from: Marcia Stepanek, "How an Intranet Opened up the Door to Profits," *BusinessWeek*, July 26, 1999. See also "The Value Growth Agenda," *Mercer Management Journal*, no. 13 (2001).

Information technology and the Internet are facilitating business process reengineering on a large scale. In today's competitive and innovative environment, companies are being pushed to improve their existing business processes. Organizations looking to improve may examine their transactions to ensure they are serving key customers in an effective and efficient manner. Evidence of the importance of integrating e-business with traditional business processes is found in mergers and joint ventures between Internet companies such as America Online with more traditional companies like Time Warner.

The DoorBuilder profile in Text Box 1.1 highlights the fact that companies wanting the most from e-business will take a critical look at the way they are currently doing business. In many cases, for established companies to benefit most from e-business, they must reengineer some of their processes. For example, in implementing e-business applications in sales and procurement, Sun Microsystems, Inc. realized the power of both the Internet and of outsourcing operations to third parties. As a result—for the first time ever—Sun required every division chief to explain their division's core competencies and defend the need for personnel and resources to determine if it is in Sun's best interest to keep doing business as usual, or move to an e-business solution developed in-house or outsourced.

Benefits of E-Business

The rapid growth in e-business clearly indicates that potential benefits greatly exceed costs. E-business transactions are generally completed faster, cheaper, and more accurately than more traditional transactions, which may translate to a competitive edge. This section provides examples of benefits companies are experiencing or expect to experience in the near future.

Expanded Sales Opportunities

- New sales channels to customers in all parts of the globe can be opened through e-business. For example, Landsend.com sells more clothing online than any other company. The industry-leading direct-mail catalog merchant leveraged its customer service and fulfillment process to add a front-end Web site—a digital version of its well-known catalog. The Internet has allowed Lands' End to extend its channel to the rapidly growing global online community—Lands' End 2001 online sales increased 59 percent over its 2000 sales.
- A new storefront added to traditional brick-and-mortar companies. For example, Office Depot hosts the number one office-supply Web site, OfficeDepot.com. The Web site, which is profitable today, offers service and convenience without undercutting brick-and-mortar store prices. While Web sites provide another sales channel to brick-and-mortar companies, in many industries online sales are not expected to make up a large percentage of total revenue. For example, Britain's largest supermarket chain, Tesco, is also the world's largest online grocer. However, Tesco's online sales channel accounts for $450 million in revenue which is about 1.5 percent of Tesco's total revenue (see Text Box 1.2).

- Providing product information, technical support, and order information online frees sales personnel from lower-value activities so they can pursue higher-value activities that generate new sales. Dell Computer is a good example of this (see Chapter 3).
- An e-business can be open all day, every day, and can be accessed from an Internet connection anywhere in the world.
- E-business can facilitate fast and flexible responses to market opportunities.

Text Box 1.2 Virtual Grocer

Britain's number one supermarket chain, Tesco, has watched British rivals and U.S. Webvan throw in the towel. Now Tesco.com is the world's largest and most successful online grocer. Started in 1996, it went slow by outfitting a single store to accept orders by phone, fax, and Web site. Tesco quickly limited orders to the Web because phone and fax orders were too costly and error-prone. By 1998, they had proved there was sufficient market demand for an online grocery business and they determined that picking from stores was cost effective. In 1999, Tesco.com rolled out the service to 100 stores and has since expanded its service to more than 250 outlets, over one-third of the chain's British stores. The business is on track to earn $450 million in revenues at a respectable operating margin of 5 percent, which is strong in a thin-margin business like grocery. That said, selling groceries over the Internet is expected to be small potatoes for the foreseeable future. The chain is expected to book sales this year of $30 billion, making online operations a mere 1.5 percent of total revenue.[7]

Despite advice to the contrary by high-priced e-business consultants, Tesco chose a decidedly low-tech approach rather than spend a fortune on a new distribution network outfitted with the latest technology. Fewer than two dozen employees are needed to pull products off the shelves in each store and schlep them in vans to customers in the neighborhood. They handle more than 3.7 million orders per year. Going slow with a viable business model is something many Net startups failed to appreciate. Says John Browett, CEO of Tesco.com, "You can't make a run for revenues and then work out the cost structure later." Tesco.com's strategy seemed all the sweeter after the failure of Webvan Group, one of the most richly funded ventures in history, in July 2001. Webvan devoured $1.2 billion in two years trying to establish a purely Web-based grocer in the United States. Webvan's strategy was vintage dot-com: It shot for the moon, aiming to build two dozen automated warehouses around the country, costing up to $35 million each. However, the numbers were terrible after building only three. Customer demand was too low. Analysts estimate Webvan lost $5 to $30 on an operating basis for every order it delivered. When depreciation, marketing, and other overhead were considered, the loss per order was a staggering $132!

Tesco has developed methods to organize, scan, assemble, and load orders efficiently. Each picking cart has a wireless touch-pad computer that plans the optimal route through the store and tells pickers which items to grab. Tesco's costs are approximately $8.50 per order, which are offset by higher margin purchases because online customers tend to be more affluent and buy more profitable products. Also, in contrast to Webvan's free delivery, Tesco charges $7.25 per delivery even though e-commerce "experts" said customers wouldn't pay the fee. The delivery charge almost covers the cost of driver and van and it ensures that the customer will be home during the delivery window (or they pay a redelivery charge). It also encourages larger orders: The average online order is three times the average in-store transaction.

In contrast with pure dot-com plays, Tesco.com also benefits from the parent company's advertising, branding, supply chain, and customer database. Tesco.com is not trying to create a standalone business. It is merely an additional sales channel that boosts revenue and pushes more products through the system.

Safeway has recognized the wisdom in Tesco.com's prudent approach to combining technology and brick-and-mortar and has partnered with Tesco to roll out its system of delivering groceries to online customers in Safeway's U.S. locations.

Adapted from: Andy Reinhardt, "Tesco Bets Small—and Wins Big," *BusinessWeek*, October 1, 2001.

Improved Communication, Customer Service, Feedback, and Loyalty

- Marriott International uses Net-based systems to track customer preferences, reward customer loyalty, and target marketing campaigns. Marriott's Internet-linked reservation system is credited with helping the company achieve hotel room occupancy rates of 81 percent while the industry average is around 68 percent. Marriott's system prices rooms based on the latest market data and Marriott.com makes it easy to find a hotel that matches traveler interests. Marriott plans to refine the customer data so it can cater to guests' idiosyncrasies and they believe e-mail marketing will add $10 to $20 million in revenue a year.[8]

- As Internet traffic expands, a successful Web site will continue to be an important means of developing and maintaining corporate and brand images.

- Company and product information is easily provided and maintained on the Internet.

- Searchable electronic databases containing previously asked and answered questions can be useful for both consumers and customer support personnel. In 1999, IBM's customer service Web site handled over 43 million online inquiries, which the company estimates saved $750 million over the cost of telephone customer service.[9] In a WorldCom survey, 63 percent of business Internet users say the Internet improves customer satisfaction.

- Direct and customized product promotion is possible. For example, Ticketmaster.com e-mails customers the play list from the most recent concert they attended with an offer to sell a concert T-shirt. The Boeing Corporation used to mail out technical aircraft manuals, parts lists, and other maintenance documents that each year equated to a stack of paper 130,000 feet tall. Boeing now offers airlines a Web site that contains technical information beyond what was previously provided, plus links to news sources, chat areas for discussing maintenance issues, as well as a means for two-way communication between Boeing and the airlines, which now allows Boeing to track changes made to airplanes after they leave its factories. The Web site is expected to improve record keeping, which should lead to improved safety.

- The electronic information that often accompanies e-business can be a treasure chest of data useful in tracking customer patterns and other marketing information. Twentieth Century Fox taps into the Internet to boost revenues and cut costs. Movie distribution executives are able to mine a huge database of more than 43 million box-office and movie records that go back for years. There, they have stored information on the number of tickets sold for films made by Fox and all its rivals—at every theater in any neighborhood. Fox developed a program to analyze the data to determine where to release films by targeting releases to theaters where similar films have played well. In addition, theaters use the Internet to send fresh data about how movies are faring so that executives can analyze the data daily. Recently, Fox determined that the movie *Titan AE* was flopping in some suburban areas, which allowed Fox to curtail planned advertising in those locales, saving $1 million. Text Box 1.3 (p. 8) describes how Pillsbury is leveraging its extensive electronic database.

- Twentieth Century Fox also creates interactive Web sites featuring online games, chat-room talks with stars, and even spoof news articles of mysterious events to promote movies and establish a new customer base to target during later promotions. By creating entertaining sites, Fox involves people emotionally, providing Fox access to new and large customer focus groups. Exit polls for the movie *X-Men: The Movie* indicated that 28 percent of those that saw the film had visited the X-Men Web site.[10]

- Corporate sponsored online communities allow "authorized eavesdropping." For example, in exchange for Hallmark gifts, 200 customers actively participate in Hallmark's online "Idea Exchanges" Web site. Participants say they love tuning into their online community. They chat among themselves, post pictures from home decorations at Hallmark's prompting (Hallmark breaks in to steer the conversation and conduct surveys), and answer the company's questions about products and ideas. Evidence from several companies suggests Americans are willing to invite corporations into their lives via online communities if the companies ask politely, protect people's privacy, and give incentives—sometimes cash, but usually gifts or coupons.

- Online customer service and administration. Reuters is a global supplier of news media with a wide range of products including real-time financial data, transaction systems, and access to numerical and textual historical databases. Reuters developed an online self-administration tool that seamlessly integrated with Reuter's information products and provides online access to order processing, billing, and customer service applications. The tool enables direct real-time communication between Reuters, its customers, and information providers. The system eliminated redundant and low-value-added processes, increased speed of processing and fulfillment, decreased reconciliation and discrepancies, and reduced "hands-on" involvement in customer and product administration.

- Online information and responses can be combined with human interaction. Leading e-tailers like Lands' End have learned the power of blending people and technology. For example, if you go to www.landsend.com you can access a "personal shopper" that suggests products that "best suit your unique taste, style, and preference."[11] Or if you have difficulty locating a shirt on the Web site that you previously saw in a Lands' End catalog, you can click a "help" icon and a salesperson can take control of your browser to lead you to a picture of the shirt. The salesperson might then use instant messaging to describe embroidery not visible on screen. As a result of this type of service, more than half of the people who put goods in a Landsend.com shopping cart wind up buying them, compared with just 22 percent at all consumer e-tail sites.[12] According to Jupiter Communications, over 90 percent of online customers prefer some form of human interaction during the e-business experience. Charles Schwab & Co., an online leader in financial and brokerage services, continues to open local offices because each time they open a local office they double the new business from that community. Even though most Schwab transactions are conducted online, the local office offers a security blanket to customers who are concerned about confusing Web sites or who want the option to meet in person.

- To most customers, e-business means "business my way, on my time, in my place." Companies who are able to adapt quickly to satisfy this new type of customer will be successful. In a survey conducted by PricewaterhouseCoopers, creating customer loyalty is a top priority of business executives. These executives recognize there is substantial evidence that loyal customers are more likely to spend more, provide more feedback, and refer more business than less-devoted customers. Furthermore, loyal customers are expensive to replace—it can be five times more costly to acquire new customers than to satisfy existing ones.[13]

- To stimulate and manage innovation, companies can set up "knowledge markets," which utilize various communication networks to connect small entrepreneurial teams that drive innovation. Once empowered, these small teams are relatively nimble and can function with a start-up mentality. Each week at Royal Dutch/Shell, several small teams, known as GameChangers, in the United States and the Netherlands meet to consider hundreds of ideas submitted by employees via e-mail. In recent years, four out of five top business initiatives at Shell emerged from their knowledge market. These projects are producing dollars. One idea resulted in a new oil-discovery method, which helped Shell find some 30 million new barrels of oil in its first year. Procter & Gamble has successfully used its "Innovation Net," a Web collaboration effort linking thousands of engineers, market researchers, and other pros that rarely teamed up before to share ideas and shorten product development cycles. P&G credits the rapid development of successful new products such as its dust mop "Swiffer" to the collaboration effort.

Lower Costs

- Internet-based e-business is not as expensive as paper-based transactions or even traditional electronic data interchange (EDI). For example, bank transactions involving tellers cost an average of $1.07 per transaction while ATM transactions cost just $0.39. Amazingly, online banking transactions cost only $0.01 each. IBM's online

---

Text Box 1.3 The Power of Pillsbury's Web Technology

Pillsbury developed Web-aware software called NetStat that helps analyze reams of data and change many aspects of the 133-year-old food giant, from the way it builds manufacturing plants and develops new products to the way it targets consumer preferences. With the NetStat software, Pillsbury employees have easy access to all sorts of data. For example, NetStat can analyze customer feedback that previously was manually typed into electronic databases and painstakingly analyzed by hand at company headquarters. NetStat results are posted to a Web page as a chart that can be accessed by marketing staff. NetStat is also expected to save Pillsbury up to $1 million per year in processing customer feedback.

Another example of the power of Pillsbury's Web technology involves the construction of new manufacturing facilities. Food-making equipment requires tedious and time-consuming adjustments. Before NetStat, facility test results had to be analyzed at Pillsbury headquarters. Because of the delay in testing and feedback, engineers would typically find problems in manufacturing equipment after a plant was running. Now with NetStat, test data from all points in the manufacturing process are captured and analyzed in real time, allowing engineers to easily measure food quality at every point on the conveyor belt. This has allowed Pillsbury to make plants operational much more rapidly.

NetStat also analyzes consumer preferences. Consumer products companies have found that people in different regions have different tastes. NetStat analyzes marketing and purchase data by zip code. On sales calls to grocery chains, Pillsbury representatives can use the Web-accessible database to bring up customer data and answer questions regarding sales and preferences. Access to such data provides a significant marketing advantage over the competition.

Adapted from: Roger O. Crockett, "Saving Dough with NetStat," *BusinessWeek,* September 18, 2000; and "Pillsbury: A Digital Doughboy," *BusinessWeek,* April 3, 2000.

procurement system has eliminated 5 million pieces of paper a year. In a WorldCom survey, 68 percent of business Internet users say the Internet reduces costs. Text Box 1.4 (p. 10) profiles how Kaiser Permanente is using e-business to reduce costs and improve effectiveness.

- Procurement costs are lower. IBM bought $13 billion of goods and services over the Internet in 1999, saving more that $270 million. General Electric is using online reverse auctions (see Chapter 3) to purchase basic supplies such as tape, brooms, and safety glasses. On purchases of $2.1 billion in 2000, the company reports savings of $234 million. Ford, GM, and DaimlerChrysler are reporting impressive cost savings on procurement managed through the automotive Web portal, Covisint (also described in Chapter 3). IDC Research projects savings from Internet commerce procurement will surpass $103 billion by 2003.
- Sales, marketing, and billing costs can be reduced. Southwest Airlines and Delta Airlines saved $80 million and $20 million respectively in 2000 in commissions and reservation-system fees by Web-enabling their reservation and ticketing processes. Savings are expected to grow significantly in the next few years. E-billing, the delivery of routine bills online, could save as much as 60 percent per bill. Most creditors pay about $2 a month per customer in bill processing, printing, and postage. Savings in billing functions for a large utility could be as much as $50 million per year.[14]
- Improved and less expensive consumer research. Kraft surveyed 160 panelists about frozen vegetables, then chose 24 to test a new product. Consumers sent responses via e-mail that were more detailed than traditional surveys. Research results came in 30 percent faster and 25 percent cheaper than a typical focus group. Moreover, the reach was nationwide rather than regional. General Mills, Inc. has moved 65 percent of its consumer surveys online, slashing costs by 50 percent and research time by 25 percent. Online bulletin boards, virtual focus groups, electronic surveys, and chats with companies are replacing those nagging phone calls that always seem to come at dinnertime. Companies spent $258 million, or 10 percent of consumer research to query shoppers online in 2000. That is expected to rise 70 percent to $439 million in 2001. Some predict that in 5 years most product concepts tests will be done online.[15]
- Hiring costs can be reduced. IBM has installed software that has cut the cost of hiring temporary workers by $3 million.
- Lowering defect rates. By leveraging Web technology, Miller Brewing Co. dramatically cut defect rates, such as broken bottles, from 5 percent to one-tenth of one percent, and revolutionized how it monitors its packing lines. Computers are attached to each of the lines to monitor machinery operations. Data is sent to a central computer that transforms the raw data into easy-to-understand diagrams posted immediately on the company's **intranet**.[16] The site also posts messages between operators and supervisors and pinpoints where there is a line problem. The system only took months and $100,000 to develop and yet it promises to save millions of dollars a year.

Supply Chain and Human Resource Management

Proper supply chain management is critical to successful business. Companies try to avoid overstocking inventory because it is expensive to store and overstocking increases

---

Text Box 1.4 Kaiser's Cyber-Cure

Kaiser Permanente, the country's largest health maintenance organization (HMO), used to keep virtually all its patient files on paper until 1998. To deliver files to the appropriate medical office or hospital, fleets of courier vans moved the paper files at night. Not only was it expensive, but also ineffective. Specialists with newly referred patients ended up without a patient's paper file 30 percent of the time. Then Kaiser launched a $2 billion project to move all its operations to the Internet to better serve all its constituents— 8.1 million members, thousands of corporate clients, over 350 hospitals and clinics, and 10,000 health care providers. Medical records are now electronic and accessible at any of its hospitals and clinics.

At kponline.org, HMO members can order prescription refills, book appointments, e-mail doctors, and ask pharmacists questions. Doctors can access the Permanente Knowledge Connection through Kaiser's site to retrieve clinical information and find journal articles. Doctors now pull up patient records on computer terminals in examining rooms. Doctors enter new information directly into the computer and write drug prescriptions online. In fact, the biggest cost savings thus far comes from better containment of pharma-ceutical costs because the system automatically offers physicians lower-cost alternative drugs when possi-ble. The system is also significantly reducing costly mistakes. Before the new system was in place, up to 15 percent of patient tests in some areas of the country had to be repeated because of lost paperwork.

Kaiser's Internet solutions also allow doctors and administrators to order everything from bandages to CAT-scan machines. While some companies are slashing tech spending, Kaiser upped its spending on e-business by 10 percent in 2001.

Adapted from: Douglas Gantenbein and Marcia Stepanek, "Kaiser Takes the Cyber Cure," *BusinessWeek*, February 7, 2000; and "Smart Business 50," *Smart Business,* August 14, 2001.

---

the chance of obsolescence and shrinkage. On the other hand, companies want to have items in stock to fulfill customer orders quickly. E-business allows retailers, manufactur-ers, and suppliers to share forecasts and information about current inventory levels, which allows for significantly improved control over inventory levels.

- The U.S. Department of Defense (DoD), previously burdened with cumbersome pro-curement practices, charged its Joint Electronic Commerce Program Office (JECPO) with accelerating e-business practices and improving its acquisitions processes. The challenge was that with multitudes of different DoD Web sites on the Internet, ven-dors often had difficulty finding the right sources of information about open and competitive solicitations. The DoD built a central Web portal to link the procure-ment processes and systems for the Air Force, Army, Defense Information Systems Agency, Defense Logistics Agency, Navy, and Marine Corps. Vendors now find they can locate requests and respond more quickly. The portal has decreased pro-curement lead times, decreased operating costs entailed in releasing solicitations, in-creased visibility of DoD Web sites, and increased both e-commerce and paperless communications.

- As noted above, General Electric is saving money by purchasing supplies online us-ing a reverse auction. The auction has allowed GE to reach a wider base of suppliers to negotiate better deals. Chapter 3 describes this concept in more detail.

- Online buying groups can result in significant discounts. The Internet has spawned large buying groups and consortia that pool their corporate purchases to get better deals and special treatment. For example, Comdisco Inc., a computer refurbisher, buys an estimated $1 million worth of circuit breakers and wiring each year. The company hopes to save as much as $200,000 by joining an online buying group purchasing equipment in huge volume. Vendors are happy to provide special treatment and quantity discounts because online groups lower vendor costs by supplying quick access to large, well-defined pools of buyers.

- Response time with suppliers and vendors can be improved because many more of the interactions are automated. And even for those interactions that are not automated, transmission of an electronic document through the Internet (e.g., e-mail) is much faster than sending a physical document via the postal service or even an overnight courier ("snail mail").
- Companies can leverage their purchasing power. IBM buys from suppliers who build only a small part of a machine. To ensure that IBM's various suppliers get IBM pricing from parts manufacturers, IBM wired 12,000 suppliers to a network. IBM uses data-mining software to determine whether, for example, the price charged to a supplier for a particular computer chip is the same price IBM would pay for the chip if it were ordered directly from the manufacturer. If IBM can buy the chip at a lower price than their supplier, IBM will go to the manufacturer and demand the same price for the supplier, who then passes along the savings to IBM.
- Suppliers can compete more effectively. Dell Computer provides its suppliers with scorecards showing their standing with respect to other competing suppliers. This helps suppliers know how they can better compete for Dell's business.
- Companies can improve their hiring and promotion processes. Home Depot recently automated its hiring and promotion processes by installing computer station kiosks in their stores. Job seekers apply for positions at the kiosks. The computer administers an extensive skills test and informs applicants when they are eligible for higher positions. For example, an applicant for a cashier position might demonstrate skills sufficient for a sales associate job; if so, the system makes this known. Applications are entered into a networked database so that managers at any Home Depot within commuting distance can access qualified personnel. Managers have reported that applicants tend to be more honest when completing applications at the kiosks compared with in-person interviews. Current employees also use the kiosks to apply for promotion. Managers consider at least 3 applicants for each position to be filled via promotion. The automated process has accomplished its main purpose—to ensure that a broader pool of applicants are considered for jobs.[17]

Benefits from a *Customer* Standpoint

- More efficient and convenient transactions. For example, electronic intermediaries or Internet middlemen, such as the auction site eBay.com, facilitate interactions between buyers and sellers that would otherwise be relatively difficult.
- Increased price competition between providers. Priceline.com allows customers to propose their own price for airline tickets and lodging reservations. Internet price-comparison services such as MySimon.com, DealTime.com, and Pricewatch.com give consumers better pricing information. Competitors can automatically scan one another's prices and make adjustments. For example, Buy.com automatically scans and undercuts Amazon.com's book prices.[18]

- Increased product and vendor selection. W.W. Grainger, the leader in sales of machine maintenance and repair supplies, used to provide customers a single option: page through a huge 4,000-page, 7-pound catalog listing 70,000 products. Now on the Grainger.com Web site, customers can search electronically through 3 or 4 times as many products in a fraction of the time and determine immediately whether a product is in stock. Grainger.com has successfully fought off the online marketplaces (see Chapter 3) that were supposed to run middlemen out of business. Grainger.com has over 1 million unique users per month.[19]

- Customization of information, product, and delivery to fit individual desires. For example, once a shopper locates a book at Amazon.com, he or she is also provided with recommendations for other similar offerings. Amazon also customizes its Web site for returning customers. Ticketmaster.com e-mails members news of future events that might be of interest. Many newspapers and magazines allow visitors to sign up for e-mail newsletters that are customized to the individual's interests.

- Improved service. As e-business makes vast amounts of data easier to capture, store, and analyze, companies do a better job of understanding what customers want, thus focusing on customers' real needs.

- Customized and personalized product feedback. Procter & Gamble's reflect.com Web site allows customers to design products for themselves. At the Web site customers answer a series of questions about eye and hair color, cosmetic usage, and many other dimensions that affect both the composition and color of their cosmetics. Based on this information, P&G creates unique products for their customers. At Landsend.com, the innovative "My Model" feature lets shoppers enter measurements and preferences to create a personalized 3-D manikin for modeling clothes (see Figure 1.1).

Perhaps it is not surprising that the benefits of online customer relations management have also increased customer expectations. Customers now want the ability to contact companies when they see fit, using whatever technology is convenient. To properly respond to high expectations marketing, sales, and customer relations must be linked so that each is poised to quickly respond to the customer's needs. Instead of just focusing on new customer acquisition, businesses must also work to develop long-term relationships with customers (create loyalty, cross-sell products and ideas). While using the Internet to replace human customer service representatives can result in immediate cost savings, it also introduces new challenges. For example, in a telephone encounter, a trained representative can ascertain a customer's frustration level and respond accordingly. However, it is not easy to know when the customer is navigating helplessly though a company's Web site.

E-Business Benefits Not Easy to Achieve or Measure

While the potential benefits of e-business are often easily identified, it is not always easy to reengineer processes, companies, or industries to take advantage of those potential benefits. A good example of this difficulty is the recent history in the health care industry. As originally envisioned by some, Internet companies were going to revolutionize everything from insurance payments to prescription drug refill, automating every stage of

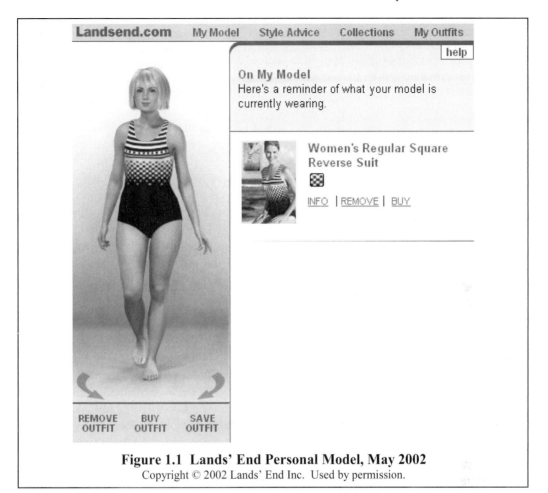

Figure 1.1 Lands' End Personal Model, May 2002
Copyright © 2002 Lands' End Inc. Used by permission.

the paperwork process and clearing away generations of stagnant bureaucracy. However, a wide range of problems has foiled the original grand dreams. Online companies underestimated the monumental difficulties of integrating the massively outdated systems for billing, insurance and accounting used to run the medical industry. To achieve the vision of "e-tizing" the industry, insurance companies and hospitals will need to open up their back-end systems and develop a front-end Internet interface that is kept in constant sync. However, historically hospitals and insurance companies have been reluctant to share patient information for privacy and competitive reasons. Further, despite their reliance on cutting-edge science, many physicians tend to resist change, including adoption of cost- and time-saving business technologies. For all its cutting-edge diagnostic and surgical technologies, the medical field remains largely in the dark ages when it comes to processing claims. Doctors say they have little time to learn new administrative tricks when it is difficult enough keeping up with scientific breakthroughs in their areas. Thus, despite isolated success stories like Kaiser Permanente (see Text Box 1.4, p. 10) and claims e-business would rapidly revolutionize the way patients, doctors, drug manufacturers and insurance carriers do business, little has changed.

Even when an e-business initiative is in place and yielding benefits, it is not easy to measure its overall success. One problem is that there are many different definitions of success measures such as Return on Investment (ROI), and companies have learned that if you ask an e-business project manager to report whether the e-business project is doing well, odds are the measures they choose to report will reflect positive results. Another problem is that some of the most important benefits of an e-business initiative, like customer relations and promoting brand, are very difficult to measure. It is even more difficult to determine how much improved relations or brand image have added to a company's bottom line. In fact, the biggest benefits of an online sales channel may not always be online sales. Bricks-and-mortar retailers are learning not to fret if consumers are not clicking the "buy" button online because a large percentage of consumers are now using a company's Web site to do research before they buy an item in the physical store. Surveys by Sears, Roebuck & Co. reveal that some $500 million worth of in-store appliance sales were influenced by customers researching items online first.[20] Some of the steps companies are taking to address these measurement difficulties are (1) carefully and consistently defining financial metrics like ROI rather than accepting "guestimates," (2) separating financial measures from "relationship" measures, and (3) not having an unrealistic expectation that every e-business initiative will result in fast profits.

Risks

The previous section paints a rosy picture of e-business in terms of its benefits and opportunities. It has been said, however, that, "risk is the mirror image of opportunity." Most potential benefits are generally accompanied by potential costs or risks. In Chapter 4, we devote significant attention to risk and potential mitigating controls because risk assessment, measurement, and management are important services provided by accounting professionals. Because the issues associated with e-business risk are a major component of later chapters, we provide only a brief discussion here.

Although many of the risks faced by e-business enterprises are common to all businesses, some are unique. For example, early in 2000, several of the largest Web-based e-businesses, including Yahoo!, eBay, E*TRADE, and Amazon, were temporarily brought to their knees by a massive onslaught of illegitimate requests for information from their Web servers. Such cyber-assaults are known as "denial of service" attacks. The dollars lost to Yahoo! and other e-business firms in forfeited revenues and other costs are every bit as real as if physical assets had been destroyed.

Special e-business risks can stem from an enterprise's information technology (IT) infrastructure, either through inherent vulnerabilities or through internal or external attacks. Further, vulnerabilities in IT infrastructure can create exposure to other e-business risks, such as those associated with compromised privacy, falsified authenticity, and destructive programs. System interdependencies can make an e-business enterprise vulnerable through the system of a business partner, even if the enterprise effectively manages the risks within its own boundaries.

The world of e-business is often uncertain, and e-business firms are experiencing considerable challenges as they grow and develop. We caution the reader not to get lost in the euphoria and "hype" so often associated with e-business.

How E-Business Affects Accounting Professionals

Business students specializing in accounting and auditing need an understanding and background in e-business to be comfortable in today's business world. E-business is rapidly taking hold and will affect virtually all firms in every industry. The e-business age is still in its infancy and the specific technologies supporting e-business are continuously evolving and changing. The Internet has spawned new companies, business models, and corporate structures—even new industries. It is a time of such commotion and confusion that few can agree on what is happening now, much less on what might come next.

In the short time since the World Wide Web exploded on the scene, much of what businesspeople thought they knew about business seems questionable. The bad news is that most "hot" technologies used for e-business today will soon be obsolete. The good news is that accounting and auditing professionals do not need to understand the intricacies of moving bits and bytes or of Web programming to be successful. But accounting professionals do need a good understanding of the key technologies underlying e-business in order to assess the benefits, risks, threats, and opportunities associated with e-business.

The CPA Vision Process

In the late 1990s, members of the accounting profession embarked on the Certified Public Accountant (CPA) Vision Process to develop a comprehensive and integrated vision of the profession's future with the goal of helping the CPA profession stay on top of important changes in the economy. With direct grassroots input from CPAs, educators, and students across the nation, and with support from the professional organizations that act on their behalf, the CPA Vision Process has created a comprehensive and integrated vision of the profession's future. This vision is intended to build awareness of future opportunities and challenges for all segments of the profession and to help CPAs leverage their core competencies and values. By focusing on the future, CPAs will be better able to plan for their own needs, as well as those of clients and employers in the next century.

The CPA Vision Team is an ongoing, independent group charged with overseeing the profession-wide implementation of the CPA Vision of the future. The CPA Vision statement is as follows:[21]

> *CPAs are the trusted professionals who enable people and organizations to shape their future. Combining insight with integrity, CPAs deliver value by:*
>
> - *Communicating the total picture with clarity and objectivity*
> - *Translating complex information into critical knowledge*
> - *Anticipating and creating opportunities*
> - *Designing pathways that transform vision into reality*

The Information Value Chain

The CPA Vision reflects a trend toward providing a broad range of value-added services focusing on knowledge and decision making. This vision is consistent with the American Institute of Certified Public Accountants' call for CPAs to focus on the knowledge level of the information value chain. The value chain is depicted in Figure 1.2.

The information value chain begins with observations or measurements of reality that result in data. For example, a business event or transaction is generally recorded as data in a database or a simple ledger. We convert data into information by placing it in a useful context. An analyst might filter and process data in a Web server log to determine, say, the number of unique visitors to a Web site in a month compared to a competitor's Web site for the same month. As this process continues, information is transformed into knowledge, and finally knowledge is used as an important input into decision making. As a result of transforming data into information, it is possible to answer useful questions and create knowledge, such as "the timing of marketing campaign A corresponded with an increase in Web site traffic and a 20 percent increase in sales to new customers, whereas campaign B showed no change."

From a decision maker's perspective, the product is more useful for decision making at each subsequent link in this information chain. A human intermediary makes information more useful by applying analysis and experience, and incorporating additional relevant data. CPAs can expand their role as information intermediaries by understanding the impact of new technological developments. Technological developments and training will provide new opportunities for CPAs to move closer to decision makers in the value chain. In order to capitalize on these opportunities, CPAs must understand how data, information, and knowledge affect decision-making activities.

For many organizations, data is captured, processed, and stored by computer programs designed by people who thoroughly understand the internals of hardware and software. While the capturing and the recording of raw data are at the front end of the value chain, this does not mean that these activities are unimportant. On the contrary, information systems are vital to a firm's operations, and are increasingly viewed as being strategic in their impact. Careers in programming, systems design, and administration are challenging and can be financially rewarding. However, the CPA profession has determined that this portion of the value chain is not where the profession's comparative advantage lies. And it is extremely difficult to develop and simultaneously maintain leading-edge expertise at both ends of the value chain.

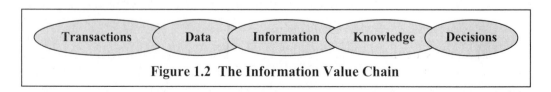

Figure 1.2 The Information Value Chain

Career Differences Along the Information Value Chain

Careers at all points along the value chain require the pursuit of life-long learning. However, careers specializing at the data end of the value chain are very different from careers focusing on the knowledge and decision-making end of the value chain. At the front end of the value chain, work and skills focus on an ability to perform given tasks in the context of technical processes. Activities at this level might include programming, bookkeeping, and preparation of financial statements. In the middle of the value chain, work and skills focus on the ability to identify and improve alternative systems. Another important skill is the ability to conceptualize multiple realities that exist within an environment and then capitalize on them. Examples of activities involved at this level include systems analysis, design, and integration, or business and strategic planning. At the decision-making end of the value chain, work and skills focus on an ability to integrate knowledge, conceptualize possible outcomes, make appropriate decisions, influence the direction of a company or industry, and lead an organization.

The information value chain can be compared to a professional sports franchise. Young, strong athletes with excellent coordination dominate the game. Coaches convert information about the strengths and weaknesses of their team and opponents into a game plan. But the coaching staff and top executives of the franchise are not physically capable of implementing the game plan—the players must do this. And though the players might beat the clock in a particular game, they cannot beat Father Time. Regardless of how well conditioned or experienced a player becomes, at some point the body can no longer perform at the necessary level and the player must retire. Just as the coaching staff focuses on applying its expertise to game plans, franchise executives focus on the strategic direction of the organization. The knowledge and skills necessary to be a successful player, coach, and organizational leader all differ. Current players must watch out for the next crop of inexperienced but extremely talented new players. Successful coaches and executives, on the other hand, develop skills and expertise that increase their value to the organization over time—even though their abilities to actually play the game are minimal. Certainly, without players there would be no team or franchise. But even the best players will not make a franchise successful without skillful knowledge, leadership, and good decision making at the coaching and executive levels.

In the world of high technology, just like professional athletics, young people who seemingly have an innate ability to understand new innovations in technology dominate systems implementation. Forty-year-old computer programmers do not worry about being displaced by the ability and drive of a sixty-year-old programmer; but they do worry about the whiz kid in his early twenties. Young technologists, like professional athletes, can often garner attractive compensation packages. Managers and executives of non-sport businesses, like coaches and executives of sports franchises, are typically unable to personally implement their "game plans" when it comes to technology and e-business because they simply do not have the technological skills to do so. Just as it is rare that a person can simultaneously be a top player, coach, and executive, it is rare that a person can simultaneously be a top programmer, information intermediary, and decision maker. With the speed of change in today's economy and with the degree of expertise required to be a top performer at any point in the information value chain, it is not practical to believe people can develop and maintain leading-edge skills at different points in the value chain. High-level executives do not have time to keep up with the nuts and bolts of new technological developments, and technology specialists do not have time to keep up on economic trends, capital markets, and important industry developments.

The importance of good decision making was very apparent in the market slowdown and "demise of the dot-coms" that occurred in 2000 and 2001. Many companies were at the leading edge of technology and e-business but failed to believe that good old-fashioned business "horse sense" would matter. The dot-com bubble blinded their view and caused them to see only skyrocketing trends and valuations. There was just an awful lot of "wishful thinking" going on. In running a successful business, no amount of technical training can compensate for poor business knowledge and decision making.

Interestingly, at the height of the dot-com boom there were calls for new financial and accounting valuation models. The traditional methods of financial measurement and reporting were alleged to be antiquated and irrelevant. Pro forma statements and valuations based on "eye balls" and multiples of revenues abounded. High-tech companies buried in losses used pro forma accounting to basically make up numbers they wanted and exclude numbers they did not want. Yahoo! Inc., for instance, reported pro forma earnings excluding the cost of buying Internet companies and of payroll taxes on stock options. In the aftermath of the meltdown and the economic slowdown, instead of calling "old fashion" broken, the press was calling for more of it—"It's time to get back to generally accepted accounting principles (GAAP), which have the virtue of transparency, comparability, and a decent dose of honesty."[22]

Purpose of this Book

Fortunately, to be successful at delivering value at the decision-making end of the e-business value chain, an accounting professional does not have to be an expert at the bits-and-bytes level. However, to be effective, accounting professionals certainly need a solid, but somewhat fundamental, understanding of the underlying technologies—including a historical perspective of the development of e-business and the disruptive impact e-business is having on traditional business. Chapter 2 and the end-of-book appendices or "technology toolboxes" are designed to provide the necessary technological background. The technology toolboxes cover key e-business technologies in more depth than in the text and are designed to be stand-alone units.

CPAs also need to understand the benefits and current business models associated with e-business. Chapters 1 and 3 are designed to provide this information.

While the first three chapters provide important foundational information for accountants, much of the information is not specific to accounting. In other words, the information in the first three chapters would be useful to a wide variety of professions interested in learning more about e-business. Once you have a basic knowledge of the technologies and business models enabling e-business, then as an accounting professional you must develop knowledge of e-business risk identification, control, testing, and assurance. With respect to the data and information levels of the value chain, accounting professionals must understand potential risks to the reliability and relevance of the data gathered. Chapter 4 addresses e-business risk identification and control. E-business is creating all kinds of new opportunities for accounting professionals, including expanded assurance services. Chapter 5 addresses e-business assurance. Business professionals with a solid understanding of the issues surrounding e-business will be well positioned to take advantage of opportunities and meet the challenges of the evolving online economy.

Specific Effects on Accounting and Auditing

Accounting firms are also tapping into the benefits of e-business. The Internet and the World Wide Web are new mechanisms that small and large accounting firms can use to advertise and sell services. Small firms can advertise and sell services across a wider geographic region. Large firms can use the Internet to leverage their expertise and extensive databases of knowledge. For example, Ernst & Young's www.eyonline.com Web site supports an online advisory service available for a fee to new and existing clients. Large international accounting firms can build virtual teams (teams with members across the globe that never meet face-to-face) to service client needs. For example, when one client in Hong Kong was involved in labor negotiations with an airline, the accounting firm had compensation professionals in London draft reports that were then revised by the client-service team in Hong Kong based on their knowledge of the client and the culture. When a counteroffer required additional expertise in pensions, tax, capital services, valuation, and accounting the firm was able to expand the virtual team to bring the right skills to the engagement even though team members were thousands of miles apart.

In addition to providing an effective and efficient new means of selling existing services, e-business presents new opportunities and challenges for accountants and auditors. We group the opportunities and challenges into two broad categories: consulting and assurance services.

Business Advisory Services

CPAs interested in developing a specialization in e-business will be in a favorable position to combine their understanding of business organizations, finance, systems, controls, and reporting with e-business consulting. Advisory opportunities include Web-site design (especially with respect to information flow and security), e-business strategy development, and helping clients integrate e-business systems with existing accounting and operational systems. Internet taxation represents another area of opportunity. Sales taxation is already complicated because of the plethora of sales tax schemes and rates employed by various cities, states, territories, and provinces. Internet sales taxation is even more complicated because the producer, seller, warehouser, and customer do not need to meet at any particular physical space. After a three-year Internet tax moratorium quietly expired in October 2001, what will happen with Internet taxes remains to be seen.

Assurance Services

In the mid-1990s, the accounting profession recognized that the core skills and competencies possessed by successful accountants and auditors could be leveraged to offer a wide variety of new services. The American Institute of Certified Public Accountants formed a special committee, commonly known as the Elliott Committee, to explore new assurance service opportunities. This committee developed the following definition for assurance services:

> *Assurance services are independent professional services that improve the quality of information, or its context, for decision makers.*[23]

"Context" includes the decision maker's decision process and the format in which the information is presented. Assurance-service opportunities related to e-business are numberless and include providing assurance that a Web site is secure and that the client's system produces relevant, timely, and reliable data. Assurance-service opportunities also include e-business industry benchmarking studies, providing assurance that new e-business trading partners are trustworthy, e-business-system control testing and enhancement, e-business risk assessment, and mitigation services.

Accountants have significant new opportunities to facilitate the conduct of e-business transactions. For example, consumers have concerns relating to their privacy and the security of their personal information when making purchases over the Internet. Assurance providers may be able to play a role in creating an environment in which consumers feel safer engaging in e-business transactions. As another example, enterprises involved in e-business transactions are often highly dependent on the reliability and security of their partners' IT systems, again creating the demand for independent, outside assurance. The potential for other kinds of e-business-related opportunities also exist for accountants who have an entrepreneurial outlook and are willing to develop new competencies. Chapter 5 discusses these issues in further detail.

Summary

In today's digital economy, developing and maintaining a successful e-business strategy is a top priority for virtually every company. E-business promises a multitude of benefits but also presents numerous risks. To be valuable as business advisers and independent assurance providers, accounting professionals first must understand the underlying technology of e-business, and then must develop knowledge regarding the benefits, risks, and threats of doing e-business. Business advisory and assurance-service opportunities for accounting professionals who understand e-business are numberless. In this chapter, we defined e-business, illustrated its benefits, discussed the accountant's role along the information value chain, and outlined the purpose of this book.

 For more information, please visit the Companion Website at www.prenhall.com/glover.

Review Questions

1-1   What protocol catapulted the Internet into everyday living? *http*

1-2   E-business reduces the per-transaction costs of a business. In what ways do you think those cost savings are achieved? *electronic payments no mail or checks faster requires less man power*

1-3   How does e-business facilitate lower inventory levels? *streamline with JIT*

1-4   Where on the information value chain can accountants and auditors best add value to e-business?

Discussion Questions

1-5   Tina Crane, a sole practitioner CPA, has been amazed by the number of her clients that have asked about pursuing growth through e-business. Tina has decided to prepare a two-column outline to share with her clients that will enumerate the opportunities and the associated risks of e-business. After some reflection, she decides to add a third column to her outline. This third column will outline services that she would offer to clients to combat the risks. Using a format like the one displayed below, prepare the outline.

Opportunities	Risks	Services

1-6   Identify two companies in your area that have become heavy users of e-business within the last few years. Has the Internet been a "disruptive" or a "sustaining" technology for the companies you identified? Please explain your answers.

Research Case

1-7   Visit the CPA Vision home page (www.cpavision.org). Outline the profession's thoughts with regard to professional services in the e-business arena.

Notes

1. Nanette Byrnes and Paul C. Judge, "Internet Anxiety," *BusinessWeek*, June 28, 1999.
2. According to GE's 2001 Annual Report, available from www.ge.com.
3. United States Department of Commerce, "E-Stats," www.census.gov/estats, March 18, 2002.
4. Ibid. Also see Mike Koller, "Study: Online Shopping Still Growing," *InternetWeek*, www.internetweek.com, September 21, 2001.
5. Source: Gartner Group.
6. It is uncommon to refer to automobiles as "horseless carriages" because in our modern society we are relatively unfamiliar with horse-drawn carriages. Likewise, we believe that in the future e-business will be so pervasive that the "e" will lose its distinguishing characteristic.
7. This corresponds well with U.S. B2C retail trade. Just over 1 percent of total retail trade in the United States is done through the Web (see Chapter 3).
8. See Amy Borrus, "A Hotel That Clicks with Guests," *BusinessWeek*, September 18, 2000.
9. Interestingly, long-distance data traffic is predicted to surpass voice traffic in the year 2002 (source: Geopartners Research/AT&T).
10. See www.x-men-the-movie.com and Ronald Grover, "Lights, Camera, Web Site," *BusinessWeek*, September 18, 2000.

11. See the Lands' End Web site at www.landsend.com. Incidentally, in an effort to beef up apparel sales, Sears, Roebuck and Co. has recently agreed to buy the very successful Lands' End.

12. Source: Datamonitor PLC.

13. According to The Industry Standard (www.thestandard.com) in the first quarter of 2000, customer acquisition costs (sales & marketing costs divided by net new accounts) ranged from $179 to $282 per customer for five of the top online brokerage firms. In 1999, acquisition costs at these firms ranged from less than $100 to more than $800. DLJDirect spent $821 per customer in the fourth quarter of 1999. This reflects the dot-com boom of 1999 with its exorbitant and wasteful marketing expenditures, followed by a more realistic approach in 2000 as companies and vendors took a deep breath and realized they must produce long-term, sustainable results.

14. E-billing also promises to provide marketing advantages. Traditional bills contain promotions that consumers routinely throw away, but the same offerings on e-bills could be purchased with a click of the mouse, significantly reducing the effort required to accomplish the transaction.

15. See Faith Keenan, "Friendly Spies On the Net," *BusinessWeek*, July 9, 2001.

16. An *intranet* is a private network that uses publicly available Internet and Web technology but in a secure, private setting. Typically intranet access is restricted by username and password. For example, at Brigham Young University our intranet, called Route Y, gives us access to class rolls, e-mail, course-specific news groups, an incident tracking system, and many other features (see the "scenic tour" at ry.byu.edu). Route Y is supported by standard Web technologies, but the Web server uses secure encryption (see Appendix C) and requires that users authenticate before using the system. Different levels of access are granted to different users. Students do not have access to class rolls, for example. Some intranets use even tighter restrictions, such as only granting access to machines that have a specific authorized IP address (see Appendix A).

17. See Cora Daniels, "To Hire a Lumber Expert, Click Here," *Fortune*, April 2000.

18. See Larry Armstrong, "Buy.com: Anything You Sell, I Can Sell Cheaper," *BusinessWeek*, December 3, 1998.

19. See Don Steinberg, "The Smart Business 50: W.W. Grainger," *Smart Business*, September 1, 2001; and Melanie Warner, "10 Companies that Get It," *Fortune*, November 1999.

20. See Robert Hof, "Don't Cut Back Now," *BusinessWeek*, October 1, 2001.

21. See "CPA Vision," www.cpavision.org. The full CPA Vision report can also be accessed at this Web site.

22. See the editorial, "Time to Cut the Accounting Shenanigans," *BusinessWeek*, May 14, 2001.

23. See www.aicpa.org for the full report of the Elliott Committee.

traditional bookseller may need to achieve around 30 percent. This fundamental shift in the market and competition help explain why a seemingly quirky start-up company like Amazon.com, with a few hundred employees and backrooms filled with computers, quickly became a household name. The typical characteristics of a disruptive technology are also present when you compare the process of buying books at Amazon.com with the process of visiting a local bookstore. At Amazon.com, you will not be greeted by a manager who knows her customers personally, though the Web server will recognize return visitors and serve up customized content. You cannot smell the books or sit in a comfortable reading room with a cup of espresso at Amazon's Web site, though you can make your own beverage and place your computer in a comfortable home study. When you decide to purchase a book from Amazon, you do not walk out of the store with your books in hand; instead, you must wait for delivery. In many ways, Amazon takes away from the book-buying experience. However, Amazon also provides significant and innovative enhancements that compensate for what is lost (see Chapter 3).

While the Internet has disrupted some industries, for most industries the Internet and e-business affected discrete parts of the value chain, but other parts remained essentially the same. Businesses have learned that there is no inconsistency between having a physical store and an online ordering system. The Internet didn't invalidate the importance of the product, brand, distribution system, or even physical locations (stores, warehouses).

While the Internet is primarily a sustaining technology, nevertheless it has incredible power to change business. Consider the Internet marketplace. In the industrialized world, it is available largely to anyone, anywhere, anytime, for little or no additional cost. The spread and thus the impact of previous communication and transportation technologies depended on the construction of an infrastructure. The Internet and the World Wide Web erupted upon the business scene in the mid-1990s with a pre-built foundational infrastructure of worldwide network connections, computer power, and extensive databases loaded with information, all of which had evolved separately and then suddenly became united and connected. The over-hyped rhetoric that surrounded the Internet frenzy in the late 1990's and early 2000's will actually continue to pay e-business dividends for years to come. The dramatic rise and reach of early dot-coms struck such fear in brick-and-mortar businesses that they scrambled to upgrade and install systems, networks, communications infrastructure, and software. Industry analysts estimate that within a period of about three years, the U.S. achieved roughly a decade's worth of technology and connectivity investment and development. The next generation of e-business will reap the benefits.

Early Reaction to the Internet

Early business uses of the Internet involved primarily the publishing of information (e.g., general company and contract information) slowly companies began considering the Internet as a possible alternative sales channel. Many traditional businesses viewed the early hype surrounding the Internet as merely a fad. In fact, in a well-documented series of decisions, even one of the world's foremost technology companies, Microsoft, seriously underestimated the impact of the Internet. In the spring of 1994, just as the Internet hype was heating up, Microsoft discounted the Internet and announced it would focus its

Chapter 2: How the "E" Is Changing Business

To effectively address the e-business needs of companies, accountants must have a working knowledge of (1) the underlying technologies enabling e-business and (2) the potential implications of those technologies on business in general. This chapter begins with a discussion of the impact the Internet is having on business and then reviews the history, development, and technological building blocks of electronic data interchange (EDI) and the Internet. While accounting professionals do not need to be experts in Extensible Business Reporting Language (XBRL) or information technology, they do need a good conceptual understanding of the enabling technologies.

Disruptive or Sustaining Technology

A **disruptive technology** is one that can displace an entrenched technology not because it performs better, but rather because it provides an overall better value.[1] In contrast, a **sustaining technology** directly and incrementally improves upon an established technology. For some industries the Internet has been very disruptive, for most industries it is proving to be a sustaining technology. Disruptive technologies are the result of innovations that create new business models and alter the basis of competition. Examples of past disruptive technologies include steam engines, railroad, radio, television, interstate highways, telephone networks, jet travel, and micro-

Steam-Powered Locomotives Were Disruptive
Copyright © 2000 Corbis. Used by permission.

processors, to name just a few. When these technologies were developed, they challenged existing businesses to adapt to expanding markets and new delivery modes for goods and information at increasing rates of speed and decreasing costs. For instance, transportation technologies of railroad and then the automobile enabled the innovation of department stores in the retail industry. Better transportation infrastructures provided the means (1) to transport people to a central location and (2) to aggregate goods from all over the country and the world. Even though department stores underperformed local stores in customer service, they outperformed local stores in pricing and product selection. As department stores gained acceptance, many traditional local stores were forced to close.

As an illustration of a competitive disruption, consider the impact of the Internet on book sales. In the traditional bookselling business, a brick-and-mortar company wants to operate stores at full capacity and must maintain high gross margins to remain profitable. However, an Internet bookseller has virtually unlimited capacity, so high margins are not as critical. Rather, the Internet bookseller might focus on the total revenue divided by the capital investment. In order to match the return on investment capital of brick-and-mortar companies, Internet booksellers may need only a 15 percent gross margin, where a full attention on software for personal computers and their new Windows operating system, later called Windows 95. While the world's largest software company slumbered, Mark Andreessen took ideas he developed as an Illinois college student and teamed up with Jim Clark to found Netscape Communications Corporation in April 1994. By the fall of 1994, Netscape had made its Internet browser, Navigator, freely available for noncommercial use (see Text Box 2.2 for a discussion of the "network effect"). By the spring of 1995, over six million copies of Navigator had been downloaded. As the Internet took off in 1995, so did Netscape and its Navigator product. Revenues for the first full year of operation, ending on December 31, 1995, hit $81 million, representing a faster rise from the starting gates than any other software company in history. Netscape distributed 50 million copies of Navigator in two years, making it the number-two software product in the world, right behind Microsoft's Windows. Netscape's August 1995 initial stock offering set off an investor frenzy, turning a company with just $20 million in sales (at the point of the initial offering) and no profit into a Wall Street wonder with a $5 billion market capitalization after one year.

By the winter of 1995, it was obvious to Bill Gates and Microsoft that they had made a big mistake in ignoring the Internet. Microsoft immediately reversed its stand and announced a major restructuring of operations to focus on the Internet. "The Internet is the most important thing going on for us. It's driving everything at Microsoft," declared Gates. The new vision was to overhaul all of Microsoft's products to make sure they worked seamlessly with the Internet. Although they were behind in the Internet race when Netscape launched its browser, Microsoft threw its energy and considerable resources into its Internet initiatives. Much of the company's $2.1 billion research and development budget was poured into Internet products. Microsoft did not take long in acquiring and developing the means to compete with Netscape and introduced its Internet Explorer as a competitor to Netscape's browser. In 1997 and 1998, the "Browser Wars" were in full swing and Netscape-Microsoft competition was fierce, but by 1999 Internet Explorer had opened up an overwhelming lead in browser market share and today is the undisputed leader. Ironically, this catch-up game would later provide substantial evidence in the government's antitrust case against Microsoft that found Microsoft guilty of engaging in monopolistic practices.

Text Box 2.2 The Network Effect

Interestingly, the motivation behind Netscape's decision to give away its Navigator browser relates to the incentives that led Microsoft to engage in monopolistic practices—the desire to exploit the so-called network effect. A product exhibits a **network effect** if the product becomes more valuable as more people use it. A familiar example is telephone service, which has little value if there is only one customer, but increases in value as more people acquire telephones. A product that produces a network effect gives its owner an advantage over competitors, especially when that product becomes an industry standard. Thus, Microsoft's operating system monopoly has more value as application developers create more products for Microsoft Windows. The more people use Windows, the more applications are developed for Windows, which causes exponential growth as more users and designers are drawn to the operating system. As this network effect grows, Windows becomes more valuable to Microsoft. Netscape gave away its product to establish market share, with the expectation that they could sell linked services later on. Another example of an e-business company taking advantage of the network effect is RealNetworks. RealNetworks invested heavily in its streaming media players, distributed them free on the Internet, and created an industry standard now valued at hundreds of millions of dollars.

E-Business Strategies

Infomediaries and Customization

Businesses new and old are refining comprehensive e-business strategies. The evolution of the Internet as a pervasive phenomenon means that the traditional factors of production—capital and skilled labor—are no longer the primary determinants of the power of an economy. Now, economic potential is increasingly linked to the ability to control and manipulate information. Intermediaries, such as insurance or travel agents, previously were used by the seller (such as an insurance company or airline) as a distribution channel, and helped customers navigate through a sea of complex options. Now the information available on the Internet has put the customer in charge. Until the Internet, potential buyers faced difficult challenges if they wanted to find the best service or product at the lowest price. Research was time-consuming, and manufacturers and retailers closely guarded information. Customer ignorance was an important means to maintain high profit margins. Now buyers can find a wealth of information on just about any product or service, and they can find many sellers at the click of a mouse button.

Consider car sales: most consumers now visit sites like GM.com or Edmunds.com to find product and pricing information before going to visit an automobile dealer. This allows consumers to become very well educated on vehicle features, prices, and purchasing strategies. Car dealers are undergoing radical changes in response to vastly increased consumer knowledge. The vast amount of available information across the Internet can make it difficult for consumers to navigate. The glut of information has created the need for "infomediaries" to aggregate information and to bring buyers and sellers together. Infomediaries may also capture customer information and develop detailed profiles for use by selected third-party vendors. The main difference between these new infomediaries and the previously used intermediaries is that an infomediary adds value to exchanges between producers and consumers by managing *information* as opposed to *inventory*. Infomediaries on the Web are called **content aggregators** and **portals** (see Chapter 3).

In addition to improvements in information availability and price, it is expected that across a wide variety of markets customers will soon be able to describe what they want and suppliers will be able to deliver the desired product or service without compromise or delay. This customization strategy is already in use. Customers can configure or personalize their own computers, golf clubs, greeting cards, jewelry, and countless other kinds of products at numerous Web sites. This trend toward customization is another example of marketplace disruption. Until recently, most companies have been in the business of creating fixed product lines that represent best guesses about what buyers will want; and buyers have had to choose from what was offered. With e-business, the role of the customer sometimes shifts from passive purchaser to active designer.

Cannibalize or Enhance Your Traditional Business

In the face of rapidly changing and perhaps disruptive business practices, existing businesses have to determine if they need to create an e-business entity to compete against their traditional business or if their current business model can be adapted to take advantage of the changes invoked by e-business. In his best-selling book, *The Innovator's Dilemma*, Harvard Business School Professor Clayton M. Christensen examines past technological disruptions and finds recurring patterns. He finds that when industry-leading companies are faced with a big technological leap that transforms their markets, their choices are generally poor because the habits and decision processes that led to the success of top companies (i.e., actively developing sustaining technologies) are not the habits and decision processes needed to deal with disruptive technologies. Indeed, traditional management practices are purposefully designed to suppress revolutionary change, instead favoring incremental evolution. Established companies scoff, "Why give up profitable mainframes for smaller, cheaper, weaker personal computers or why invest in low-quality wireless communication when we have a successful and high-quality wire-based communication system? Especially since our best customers are telling us they don't want those lower-quality products!"

Successful established companies are usually very good at listening to what their best customers want and then delivering it. The problem is that disruptive technology changes the customer base and often the best customers are the last to embrace the new technology. A clear example, says Christensen, is how online trading of securities created an enormous disruption to the full-service brokerage firms. Full-service firms initially ignored their online competition because the online offerings did not provide the service and performance that their best customers demanded and expected. While many full-service brokerage firms kept their head in the sand, a market disruption took place—the percentage of securities trades occurring online grew enormously, which forced even firms like Merrill Lynch & Co., Inc., to take notice.

When the Internet or e-business represents a disruptive technology to a company, Christensen advocates that traditional firms "cannibalize" themselves. That is, they should establish a completely independent start-up organization that will not be burdened with existing norms and cost structure. The independent start-up would then be charged to compete with other start-ups and to directly attack the parent as well. Hewlett-Packard and General Electric have successfully transformed themselves by creating new business units that have grown to be substantial and then selling off or phasing out old units. For Charles Schwab & Co., trying to take the Internet head-on was an extremely painful, yet ultimately rewarding process (see Chapter 3 profile of Charles Schwab, p. 59). Over 80 percent of Schwab's trades are now done online, which is great for Schwab since processing online trades costs 80 percent less than offline ones. The savings go further for Schwab, because with customers doing their own trades and research, branch employees are freer to promote higher-margin services. Merrill Lynch on the other hand, was slow to adopt e-business. Unfortunately for Merrill Lynch, while they debated their Internet strategy, competitors like Charles Schwab firmly established themselves as online leaders. While Merrill Lynch does now offer lower-cost online trading in response to market pressure, they have the challenge of covering the high cost structure of the established full-service brokerage company with expensive fees as well as the enormous costs associated with setting up online trading.

When the Internet is not disruptive to an existing business model, typically a company can address the powerful changes caused by e-business and the Internet within their main businesses. In the case of mail-order catalog businesses, like Lands' End, the effects of e-business can be managed effectively within a current business model.

Barnes & Noble Inc. established barnesandnoble.com to compete with Amazon. Unfortunately for Barnes & Noble, by the time it decided to establish an online presence, Amazon had already built a loyal following. And with little to differentiate its books from Amazon's, barnesandnoble.com was forced to compete on price. This meant that Barnes & Noble sold books online for less than those on its store shelves. Barnes & Noble has struggled with the best strategy to adopt. There are several million more customers walking through the physical stores than visiting the Web site. The struggle is this—does Barnes & Noble promote the Web site in its stores and risk driving existing customers willing to pay full price to the discount online location? By 2001, barnesandnoble.com finally got its online and offline channels to work together on transactions, including returns. Sales rose 65 percent to $320 million and while it still had a long way to go to compete against category-killer Amazon.com, it is one of the most trafficked Web sites for a brick-and-mortar retailer.

History of E-Business: The Internet and EDI

While "e-business" and "Internet" are hot buzzwords today, the Internet has existed for decades in a government and higher-education context. And businesses have actually been conducting a form of e-business for over 25 years using **electronic data interchange** (**EDI**). EDI, the electronic exchange of business data between companies, was the first enabler of business-to-business e-commerce. In the sections that follow, we discuss the historical development of technologies that enabled the current e-business boom.

Development of the Internet

The **Internet** is a vast global *inter*connected *net*work of computers—literally a network of networks—owned by no single entity and accessible to anyone with a means to connect. The Internet, sometimes called the **Net**, was originally developed for national defense reasons through a collaboration of the United States government and several universities in the late 1960s. The military was interested in a communications network that would continue to function even if major sections were destroyed. The government decided it needed to develop a means of communication that was not centrally controlled, but instead would be resilient to multiple point failures, as might occur in an invasion or a nuclear attack. To accomplish this objective, researchers conceived of ways that information transferred across a network of multiple redundant communication paths could be split up into small packets, travel separately using different paths across the network, and then be reassembled at a destination computer or terminal. Thus, the Defense Advanced Research Projects Agency (DARPA) was commissioned to build a network based on packet-routing technology. The Internet was launched in 1969 as a joint project between DARPA and four universities. While the Internet met its national defense objectives, it soon became obvious that its most common actual usage related to research collaboration and personal messaging (e-mail).[2]

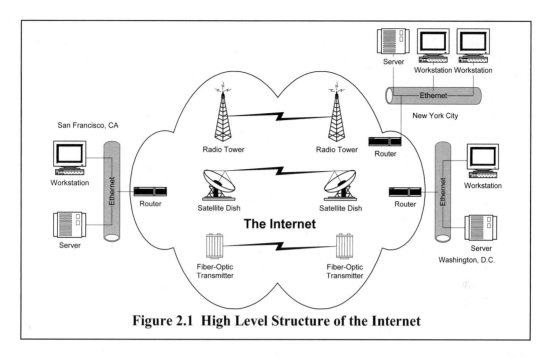

Figure 2.1 High Level Structure of the Internet

As shown in Figure 2.1, servers and workstations in **local-area networks (LANs)** are connected to communications infrastructure that uses fiber-optic or copper telecommunications lines, satellite, and even radio transmissions to communicate.[3]   Computers in a local-area network sit in close physical proximity, and are most commonly connected together using the **Ethernet protocol**.[4]   Each computer connected to the Internet is assigned a unique **Internet protocol (IP)** address (see Text Box 2.4, p. 31).   Data can be sent to a specific computer by specifying its IP address.   LANs are interconnected using **routers** that decide where to send each packet based on its destination IP address.   To connect LANs separated by great distances, the Internet uses a very-high-speed **backbone**.   Figure 2.2 (p. 30) shows a portion of the Internet backbone used by some supercomputer centers and educational institutions; thicker connection lines indicate faster connections.[5]   The Internet backbone is like a system of blood vessels: there are a few large arteries that carry heavy data flows; successively smaller veins and capillaries deliver correspondingly smaller flows to specific locations.

Internet-attached computers are all equally capable of originating, passing, and receiving electronic messages.   The messages themselves are divided into small units called **packets**, and each packet is separately addressed.   A packet begins at a source computer and travels individually to a specified destination.   The particular route of any given packet is not important; in the event of failures or network congestion, packets may travel over many distinct paths, allowing packets to be delivered even if some of the network is unavailable.   When packets arrive at their destination, they are reassembled into the original message.   If some packets are missing, the destination computer may request retransmission of the missing data.   The protocols for controlling packet transmissions are called **Transmission Control Protocol (TCP)** and **Internet Protocol (IP)**.   Today, **TCP/IP** is

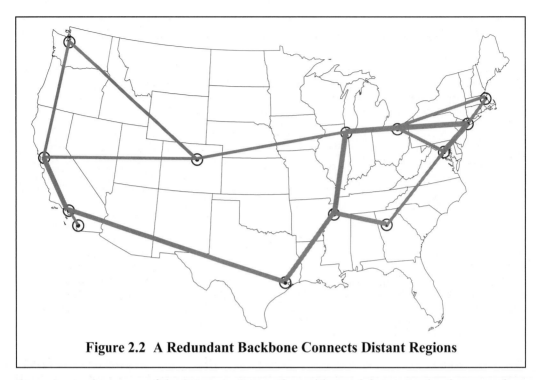

Figure 2.2 A Redundant Backbone Connects Distant Regions

the common language of the Internet. Interacting with special-purpose hardware such as routers and switches, TCP/IP coordinates packet communications over the Internet. (See the technology toolbox in Appendix A for more details about Internet technology.)

The World Wide Web

Electronic mail service was added to the Internet in 1972. By the mid-1970s, it was apparent that the Net was a very effective method to collaborate on research projects and to share news and messages of a personal nature. Because the TCP/IP protocol was freely available, it was relatively easy for a new computer to link to the network. Through the 1970s the network grew largely on the backs of government and educational institutions. Business began investigating the commercial potential of the Internet in the 1980s, but it was the introduction of the World Wide Web in the 1990s, with its point-and-click links, and the subsequent opening of the Net to commercial use that catapulted the Internet into everyday living and made e-business a viable medium for the masses.

The **World Wide Web** (**WWW** or the **Web**) was first demonstrated in 1990. The Web is a collection of **hypertext** documents (written in **HTML**) that contain cross-references or links pointing from one document to another. Users follow links by clicking on words or images in Web documents. Just as TCP/IP is the controlling language of the Internet, the **Hypertext Transfer Protocol** (**HTTP**) is the set of rules by which Web pages are requested and sent. Web servers and browsers must understand how to "speak the language" of HTTP, which is layered on top of the TCP/IP protocol.

Text Box 2.4　Internet Domains and Domain Name Service

Each Internet-attached computer has its own unique address. This is a numeric Internet Protocol (IP) address of the form 1.2.3.4. Each of the four numbers must fall in the range 0–255, so there are about 4 billion (256^4) possible IP addresses. To better manage these addresses, computers can also be given hierarchically organized names such as ebiz.byu.edu or www.prenticehall.com. Using the Domain Name Service (DNS) protocol, a computer can look up an IP address for any host name registered with DNS.

Because there are so many different computers on the Internet, it is divided into different high-level "domains" such as .edu (educational institutions), .gov (U.S. government), .com (commercial organizations), and .org (other organizations). Each country also has its own domain. Within these high-level domains are subdomains (e.g., byu.edu). Each domain or subdomain has its own "name servers" that respond to name lookup requests for names within its domain or subdomain. Each name server also has designated partners to query if it cannot resolve a name request on its own.

To look up the IP address for ebiz.byu.edu, a name server first looks in its own cache of previously requested names to see if it already knows the address. If the name is unknown, the server forwards the request to its parent. This process continues until either the parent knows the address, or it reaches a top-level name server responsible for the .edu domain. The top-level .edu server in turn knows how to find name servers for all subdomains within .edu, so it finds the byu.edu name server and forwards the lookup request. Finally, the byu.edu name server returns the actual IP address of ebiz.byu.edu. Name servers save the results of recent lookups, so the next time we request the address of ebiz.byu.edu, the DNS server will return the IP address immediately.

The Web was a vast improvement over previous systems of Internet-based document sharing. One technology that has been subsumed by the Web is **File Transfer Protocol (FTP)**.[6] FTP supports the copying of files from one Internet-attached computer to another. In its first implementation, retrieving files via FTP involved logging on to an FTP server with a user name and password,[7] then typing a command like "GET FILE-NAME.TXT." Then, to view the retrieved document, one would have to type yet another command. Even with a graphical interface to FTP, the process still involves the separate operations of logging on, downloading a file, and then opening the retrieved file. The Web provides a vastly superior way to display documents, supporting a simple one-step point-and-click platform for displaying multimedia documents that are linked in a giant web of cross-references. FTP still exists, but now it is much more common to access FTP archives via a Web browser.

It is important to distinguish the Web from the Internet; even though many people treat them as synonyms, they are distinct. The Net is the actual network that allows computers around the world to communicate with each other. The World Wide Web is a collection of services and documents that layer on top of the Internet. (See the technology toolboxes of Appendices A and B for a more complete discussion of Internet and Web technologies, respectively.) The Internet exists independently of the Web, but *not* vice versa. E-mail and FTP, for example, operate just the same whether the Web is present or not.

However, because it gives easy access to huge quantities of information, the Web is a major contributing factor stimulating the current explosive growth of the Internet. A second major factor is commercial access to the Internet. Since the Net was originally a government-sponsored project, its use had been generally restricted to government, military, educational, and not-for-profit uses. But in 1991, coinciding with rising popularity of the Web in research and government circles, the Internet was finally opened for commercial use. The .com domain soon became prime real estate in cyberspace; this has also fueled the Internet growth engine.

Stages of E-Business Using the Internet

Early forays into using the Internet for business purposes involved companies publishing pertinent information (e.g., company background, product and contact information) on their Web sites. This initial stage of Internet usage has been followed by a mad dash to use the Internet as an additional sales channel. Many companies have not taken time to develop a comprehensive e-business strategy that will help the company achieve its overall business goals. Rather, they focus on stopgap measures to begin doing "e-biz" because everybody is doing it. Though we are seeing leaders emerge, many companies are still in this immature stage of Internet usage. The next stage of e-business recognizes that to take full advantage of the enormous opportunities presented by the online economy, business processes must be re-engineered and e-business systems must be integrated with other organizational systems such as accounting and operational systems. E-business will force many organizations to rethink their overall mission and competitive advantages, especially as e-business requires tighter integration with external partners. E-business will also intensify the need to understand customer needs, delivery methods and timing, as well as overall industry risks, threats, and potential opportunities.

Having examined a brief history of the Internet, we now turn to the other major e-business technology: EDI.

Electronic Data Interchange

Simply put, EDI is the electronic transmission of business information between organizations using an agreed-upon computer-readable format. EDI lets companies interact electronically to exchange business information related to purchasing, billing, shipping, inventory, payment, account status, or notices of various kinds, just to name a few categories. Text Box 2.5 (p. 35) describes in more detail the use of EDI in a financial setting.

Figure 2.3 illustrates how an automobile manufacturer can automatically send an electronic purchase order document to a parts supplier when a particular part inventory falls below a specified level. After receiving and processing the order, the supplier then confirms the order by sending an electronic order confirmation document with pricing confirmation and expected delivery timeframe.

In order for this process to work, a minimum of four important elements are required. First, each company's computers must be connected through a network. Second, there must be a protocol that is accepted for transporting messages between machines at two companies. Third, the two computers must agree on a document format for exchanging data (think of this as an electronic envelope that both machines know how to send and receive). Fourth, the interacting computer systems need to agree on the application semantics, that is, the kinds of messages that will be processed (think of this as the kind

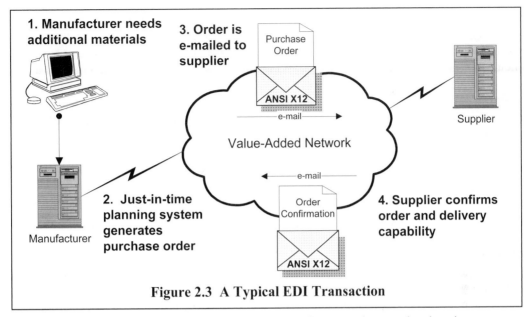

Figure 2.3 A Typical EDI Transaction

of document contained within the envelope; it may be a purchase order, invoice, or some other document). These four layers of EDI are shown in Table 2.1.

Hardware

At the lowest level, the hardware layer comprises the servers, telecommunications lines, modems, routers, and other equipment used to interconnect computers at different organizations. In the early days of EDI, before the Internet was a ubiquitous standard, it was necessary to build new telecommunications networks to connect organizations. It did not take long for the concept of the **value-added network** (**VAN**) to be developed to reduce the cost of building proprietary networks and to provide EDI software support. VAN providers built large-scale telecommunications networks and then leased connections to clients, typically charging based on usage (quantity of data transmitted or received).[8] Although it is common for trading partners to outsource to the same VAN, it is not necessary—one VAN can readily pass electronic data to another VAN. An important function of a VAN provider is to ensure that data are delivered in the right format; thus, EDI partners may actually use different standards and still successfully exchange EDI documents.

Table 2.1 Layers of EDI

Layer	Purpose
Application	Application-specific fields (e.g., date, customer ID, part no.)
Document Format	Language for presenting EDI data (ANSI X12, EDIFACT)
Message Transport	Method for transporting messages (e-mail, FTP, HTTP)
Hardware	Computer network equipment (servers, routers, cables, etc.)

The "value" component that a VAN "adds" consists of reliability, security, timely message delivery, and systems development support for EDI software. To increase this value, since the Internet was opened to commercial use in 1991, businesses have begun to leverage this public network.[9] By encrypting and authenticating communications, parties can establish a **virtual private network** (**VPN**) that keeps out unauthorized users but uses the Internet in place of private hardware. VPNs are considerably less expensive than VANs since they layer on top of existing Internet infrastructure and thus do not require the construction of redundant private networks. Even though they use the public Internet, VPNs are still secure because they encrypt all packets, effectively locking them so that even if a third party intercepts the packets, it will be inordinately difficult to decode them. Many VANs now provide both traditional private networks and newer VPN services so EDI customers can choose which networking method (and corresponding cost structure) they prefer.

Message Transport

The message transport capability is built on top of the hardware layer. Internet users send messages using numerous protocols, the most common being e-mail, file transfer (FTP), and Web requests (HTTP). EDI documents are typically sent using one of these standard protocols. However, EDI documents must conform to a standard format so that the receiving computer can understand the information sent in the document. The two major standards that have been used for years are **ASC X12** and **EDIFACT**. ASC X12 is the set of EDI standards generally accepted in North America, while EDIFACT is the collection of internationally accepted EDI standards. Work is ongoing to coordinate the two. More recently, Extensible Markup Language (XML) has emerged as a likely EDI document framework as e-commerce moves to the Internet and the World Wide Web. It is likely that ASC X12 and EDIFACT will incorporate XML support in the near future. (See Text Box 2.6, p. 37.)

Regardless of the actual document framework used (ASC X12, EDIFACT, XML), the principles of EDI remain the same. Participants agree on an interchange format, typically using a standard framework, and link their systems over a physical network using standard communication protocols.[10]

Typical Uses of EDI

EDI is a subset of e-business that is used between established trading partners, for example, a manufacturer and a supplier. If trading partners can efficiently and effectively engage in EDI, they enjoy a number of advantages including improved inventory management, reduced transaction time, and reduced cost. For instance, Wal-Mart and major supplier Procter & Gamble (P&G) have linked their information systems using EDI. P&G developed a very sophisticated software system to handle Wal-Mart's supply needs. Because of the integrated EDI systems, when a Wal-Mart store sells a P&G product, P&G immediately knows it and can coordinate production and delivery.

EDI not only involves transactions like purchase requests, but also information requests such as a current price list or current inventory levels, which can greatly improve plan-

---

Text Box 2.5 Financial E-Business

It quickly became apparent that EDI could be adapted to transfer not just documents, but also money. A large number of business-to-business payments are made using paper checks drawn on bank accounts. Due to the work involved in processing checks, there is considerable "float" associated with check payments. In other words, several days may elapse between the time a check is issued and the time when the corresponding funds are transferred to the payee's account. Also, processing checks involves labor and transportation costs that could be avoided in an automated, e-business style of payment.

In response to this opportunity, banks developed two approaches to transferring funds electronically: Electronic Funds Transfer (EFT), and Automated Clearing House (ACH) transfers. EFT allows for the rapid transfer of credit from a payer's bank to a payee's bank. In the United States, interbank EFT is usually accomplished using the Federal Reserve's Fedwire system (see www.frbservices.org). Each day Fedwire processes several hundred thousand transfers with an average value of several million dollars each. The Clearing House Interbank Payments System (CHIPS, see www.chips.org) manages most international EFTs, with similar volumes to the Fedwire transfers.

Whereas EFT is designed for rapid transfer of low volumes of high-value transactions, ACH handles high volumes of small-value transactions. Each day tens of millions of ACH transactions are processed, with an average value of several thousand dollars each; volume growth is currently in the low double digits. EFT is nearly immediate and irrevocable, but ACH transfers take one or two business days to complete and may be revoked if the payer has insufficient funds to cover the transfer. ACH transfers may be credit transfers (initiated by the payer), or debit transfers (initiated by the payee). ACH is suitable to handle electronic payments that otherwise might be made with a standard check. ACH also enables automated periodic payments such as monthly loan payments or payroll direct deposit.

An interesting feature of the ACH message format is that it provides for the embedding of financial EDI documents within an ACH transfer. When a customer makes a payment to a vendor, there are two separate EDI documents to handle: 1) the electronic payment itself, transferring funds from the buyer's bank account to the vendor's, and 2) remittance advice informing the vendor that payment has been made and the buyer's account should be properly credited within the vendor's accounting system. The ACH standard allows documents such as remittance advices to travel directly with the electronic payment, simplifying the message routing, guaranteeing that one document does not arrive without the other, and making it easier to identify the purpose of a particular ACH transfer.

---

ning and decision making. When fully implemented, EDI can allow computers at the purchasing and selling companies to perform the sorts of activities listed in Table 2.2.

EDI allows trading partners to link even if there are differences in electronic data or information systems. Once linked, trading partners enjoy benefits such as reduced processing costs, fewer errors relative to manual equivalents, and reduced ordering, delivery, and payment times. The main idea behind EDI is rather simple to understand, but it can be difficult and very costly to implement because the details are quite complex. Due to the high cost, EDI has typically been used only by large businesses with enough volume to justify the high costs. However, small suppliers are sometimes forced to use EDI by larger trading partners, as has happened in the automobile manufacturing industry. Fortunately for small companies (and larger trading partners wanting to engage in EDI with small companies), the Internet provides the capabilities of traditional EDI at a much-reduced cost. We give specific examples in Chapter 3 in the section on "extranets."

Table 2.2 Illustrative Uses of EDI

Purchasing Company	Selling Company
• Determine when inventory should be re-ordered based on a predetermined levels • Determine inventory supplier and availability of desired product • Place orders • Receive electronic invoices • Agree to terms and amounts • Transfer payment	• Receive purchase order • Send notice to warehouse to ship the goods • Send an electronic invoice • Receive notice that funds were deposited • Notify the customer that payment has been received and properly credited

Summary

This chapter examined the Internet and EDI from a historical perspective. E-business is being powered by one of the most disruptive technologies the world has yet known—the Internet. The Internet has had a more rapid and far-reaching impact on the world than previous disruptive technologies because the Internet was able to utilize the existing global communication networks, computer systems, and databases. The Internet thus created a ready-made market open to almost anyone, anywhere, anytime at little cost. The Internet changes many of the rules of the game. The information readily available on the Internet has put the customer in charge as never before. To take advantage of the e-business opportunities traditional firms must leverage the Internet. In many cases, the power of the Internet will serve as a "supertool" for applying tried-and-true business practices. E-businesses that can solve difficult distribution problems or have unique business models that are specifically targeted to the power of the online economy will be well positioned. In order to be valued business advisers and assurance providers, accountants must understand the fundamental issues involved in e-business, including its potentially disruptive nature. Accountants must also be willing to view e-business hype with an eye of professional skepticism. Glitzy Web sites and passionate claims of "new frictionless virtual markets" are not enough to make a profitable business.

 For more information, please visit the Companion Website at www.prenhall.com/glover.

Text Box 2.6 XML: An eXtensible Markup Language

Extensible Markup Language or XML, is similar in nature to HTML (Hypertext Markup Language). HTML defines a set of tags that indicate how text is displayed in a Web browser. For example, <TITLE>Skiing Conditions</TITLE> causes "Skiing Conditions" to appear in the title bar of the Web browser. <TD>1.6 m</TD> displays "1.6 m" within a cell in a table. One of the limitations of HTML is that all tags are predefined, and there is only limited meaning associated with tags. We see that "Skiing Conditions" is the title of the Web page, but what does "1.6 m" represent? HTML displays data effectively, but does not make it easy for data to be accessed by another business application.

XML enables applications to share data easily (e.g., between a vendor and manufacturer). With XML we can mark data within a document according to its type, in sufficient detail so a computer program can read and understand the XML document. XML allows user-defined tags to be created, so we could replace 1.6 m with <SNOW-DEPTH>1.6m</SNOW-DEPTH>, indicating that "1.6 m" represents the current snow depth. Further, we could specify the unit of measurement by defining a "unit" attribute: <SNOW-DEPTH UNIT="meter">1.6</SNOW DEPTH>. If all ski resorts agreed to use a common set of XML tags, we could program a search engine to look for snow condition reports and extract the data into a database. Then skiers could use our search engine to look up conditions around the world (e.g., Which ski resorts have at least 20 cm of new snow on a base of at least 1 m?)

XML is already starting to replace HTML in some Web pages. But regardless of whether HTML falls into disuse, it is clear that XML will become increasingly popular as organizations see the benefits of tagging data within their documents (see Text Box 2.7, p. 38). XML has a variety of potential uses, from storing data on personal computers (word processing and spreadsheet files), to presenting more structured data on Web pages (like snow condition reports and financial statements), to exchanging business information through EDI (purchase orders and shipping notices).

In order to use XML for information exchange, parties must agree on definitions for a common set of tags. For example, mathematicians have defined MathML to represent mathematical equations in XML. MusicML is a standard for encoding musical scores. J.P. Morgan & Co. and PricewaterhouseCoopers developed the specifications for a new protocol for Internet-based electronic dealing and information sharing of financial derivatives such as interest-rate and foreign-exchange products. The specification, FpML (Financial products Markup Language), is freely licensed and is expected to set the standard within this industry that is rapidly moving into e-business. FpML enables Internet-based integration of a range of services, from electronic trading and confirmations to portfolio specification for risk analysis.

Industry leaders in accounting, financial reporting, and accounting software are working with firms such as Microsoft and IBM to develop a common XML standard for financial reporting. This major initiative, called Extensible Business Reporting Language, or XBRL, is an XML-based financial reporting language that supports the transmission of financial reports in a format that can be processed automatically by computers. This could transform the way audits are conducted because data can be more easily transferred between computers, implying easier access to client data. For more information on XBRL, visit www.xbrl.org.

XML may play a large role in future EDI transactions. In the case of an electronic purchase order, one would expect to find fields such as customer number, purchase order number, date, billing information, shipping information, part numbers, quantities, and prices. A simplified example might look like this:

```
<PURCHASE ORDER NO="1001" CUSTOMER="1234567" DATE="20-10-2001">
   <SHIP TO>
         <ATTN>Mary Robinson</ATTN> <LINE1>123 Elm Street</LINE1>
         <LINE2>Yourtown, USA</LINE2> <ZIP CODE>12345-6666</ZIP CODE>
         <PHONE><AREA>800</AREA>555-1212</PHONE>
   </SHIP TO>
   <LINE ITEM PART="123-4567-8" QUANTITY="5" />
   <LINE ITEM PART="123-4567-9" QUANTITY="10" />
</PURCHASE ORDER>
```

Text Box 2.7 XML at Fidelity and Humana

Fidelity Investments recently underwent an enormous project to retrofit its corporate data to an XML format. The motivation for Fidelity was a need to simplify communications between consumer Web applications and back-end systems. Over the last decade, the financial services giant had installed numerous proprietary messaging formats, remote procedure calls, interfaces, and commercial middleware applications. By using XML as its core communications connection to translate data between its Web site and back-office mainframes and its Unix and Windows NT servers, Fidelity was able to eliminate a glut of translation protocols and message buffers and 75 to 85 mid-tier servers. By using a common, language programmers can now work on more important business functions than inventing new interfaces between systems.

On the other hand, while XML may be ideal for the transfer of real-time transactional information, Humana, a regional insurance company, avoids using XML-based products for transmission of large batches of data because they find it brings their systems to a crawl. It is common for doctors and hospitals to electronically transmit all their insurance claims in one batch at the end of the day. Humana has found that the flexibility of using XML—the ability to add information quickly and in real time—is lost in these batches of large data files. So even though Humana does use XML for some tasks, some of their processes are still better done with more traditional EDI techniques.

Sources: Lucas Mearin, "Fidelity Makes Big XML Conversion Investment," *Computerworld*, September 28, 2001; "Fidelity Investments Puts Faith in XML for All Corporate Info," lighthouse-partners.com/xml, October 3, 2001; and Sandeep Junnarkar, "Technology: A Beast Untamed," *CNET News.com*, www.news.com, September 26, 2001.

Review Questions

2-1　E-business began in the business-to-business arena many years ago. What was this early form of e-business called and how did it work?

2-2　What are some characteristics of a disruptive technology?

2-3　Distinguish between a proprietary network, value-added network (VAN), and a virtual private network (VPN).

2-4　What are "infomediaries" and what created the demand for their services?

2-5　What is XML and why should accountants know about it?

Discussion Cases

2-6　Pony Manufacturing purchases significant quantities of both roller bearings and light-duty control cables from Western Star Supply. Pony initiates about 5 reorder transactions a week, with about 21 products per order and an average transaction value of $8,400. Pony initiates a reorder transaction when it determines, based on projected manufacturing that it will run low on a component within 3 days. Pony's management wishes to investigate the possibility of engaging in EDI with Western Star. Pony believes that it can save money by using this technology to reduce its inventory carrying cost by requiring Western Star to monitor inventory levels and replenish supplies more frequently. Pony also believes that even though the number of transactions with Western Star will increase, the overall cost of transaction processing will fall. Evaluate Pony management's rationale for engaging in e-business with Western Star. Are there other issues that Pony is ignoring?

2-7 The "network effect" can simultaneously help and hinder a company's product sales by changing both the *overall* product-category acceptance and the *within* product-category acceptance. Identify situations in which a company or an industry has adopted a sales strategy that is based on taking advantage of the network effect.

Research Case

2-8 There are several different models an entrepreneur might follow in order to get a business online. He or she might outsource the whole online endeavor, allowing a service provider to design, build, and maintain the Web presence. Under this model, the entrepreneur would receive only reports of goods to ship and payments collected. Alternatively, the entrepreneur may choose to have a site hosted by a service provider that provides only the Web space and transaction processing capabilities. The entrepreneur would be responsible to design and maintain the content of the site in addition to receiving reports of goods to ship and payments collected. Finally, the entrepreneur might choose to build his or her own site, leasing a high-speed connection and purchasing the necessary computer equipment and Web transaction processing software. Investigate each of these possibilities and find vendors to support the entrepreneur's wishes. Determine the relative costs of operating a Web presence in each environment. Appendix E, Getting a Small Business Online, is a good starting point; however, full-credit solutions will not reference the vendors included in that appendix.

Notes

1. See Clayton M. Christensen, *The Innovator's Dilemma: When New Technologies Cause Great Firms to Fail* (Cambridge, MA: Harvard Business School Press, 1997). Christensen distinguishes his concepts of "disruptive" or "sustaining" technologies from the more widespread notion of "incremental-versus-radical" technologies. That is, the fact that a technology is radical does not imply that it is also disruptive. A disruptive technology exhibits worse performance, at least for the short term. Dr. Christensen writes of disruptive technologies, "But they have other features that a few fringe (and generally new) customers value. Products based on disruptive technologies are typically cheaper, simpler, smaller, and, frequently, more convenient to use." Products progress along technology trajectories. Sustaining technologies advance a product along its same trajectory (this is what customers tell you they want). Disruptive technologies create a new, competing product that follows a new trajectory. Eventually a disruptive technology's trajectory will progress to the point that it satisfies the market need. At this point, consumers see that the new technology satisfies their need and does so more economically. So the disruptive product then begins to displace the previous technology.

2. For an interesting look at Internet history, visit the Internet Society's history page on the Web at www.isoc.org/internet/history or see Robert H'obbes' Zakon, "Hobbes' Internet Timeline v5.0," www.isoc.org/guest/zakon/Internet/History/HIT.html.

3. There are numerous ways to transmit a physical signal from one point to another. Other notable media include microwave, infrared light, and laser pulses. It is likely that many more possibilities will be developed in the future. For now, the Internet uses the same physical infrastructure as the phone network, mostly relying on copper and fiber-optic cables. But wireless technology is widely recognized as the logical next step for the expansion of the Internet.

4. In the sense of information technology, a "protocol" is a set of rules that defines how systems behave and interface. To interact with an Internet service, one must follow the necessary protocol. For example, the e-mail protocol specifies the message format that a mail server expects to see. To initiate the process of sending an e-mail, an e-mail client program first opens a connection with an e-mail server. The server sends the message "220" followed by the server's identifying information. The client then sends the message "HELO" (this is not a typo; to programmers, efficiency sometimes overrules spelling) along with the client's identifying information. The server then responds with a message of "250" if there are no errors. As this "conversation" continues, the client follows the rules of the e-mail protocol to give the destination address and then the body of the message.

5. See www.vbns.net for full details of the vBNS+ network services that connect participating supercomputer centers, research organizations, and academic institutions. Figure 2.3 diagrams only a portion of the vBNS+ backbone. The commercial Internet uses a high-speed backbone with a similar structure to connect major metropolitan areas.

6. Gopher is another technology that has been almost entirely displaced by the Web. Gopher servers stored hierarchically organized collections of ordinary text documents (with no embedded graphics or sounds). Gopher servers could also provide cross-links in their document directory trees, but not within the text documents themselves. You can still find some active gopher servers (the URL starts with gopher:// instead of http://), but these are becoming increasingly rare. Most Web browsers still support the Gopher protocol. The Penn State Gopher server was still active at the URL gopher://gopher.cac.psu.edu/ as of summer 2000.

7. Many FTP servers support anonymous logins, which means you enter the user name "anonymous" and then your e-mail address as the password. Servers usually do not check e-mail addresses, so most anonymous FTP users enter some other string of letters for the password.

8. In the same way that many companies currently outsource major portions of their payroll functions to payroll specialists because of the economies involved, many companies also now outsource their EDI functions to specialists.

9. The Internet is a public network in the sense that any two computers attached to the Net can generally communicate, and data sent over the Internet cannot usually be assumed to be private. It is relatively easy to set up a "packet sniffer" that will capture all packets being sent through the local segment of the Internet. If you type your password while using a protocol that does not encrypt packets, a sniffer could easily capture your password. Protocols like FTP, TELNET, and HTTP do not encrypt packets. See the technology toolbox in Appendix C for more information on encryption.

10. For more information on EDI, see the Data Interchange Standards Association home page (www.disa.org), the ASC X12 home page (www.x12.org), and the EDIFACT home page (www.unece.org/trade/untdid). For an example of industry-specific EDI guidelines, the U.S. Department of Commerce publishes conventions used in the federal procurement systems (is2.antd.nist.gov/dartg/edi). Yahoo.com also lists many companies involved with EDI under "Business and Economy > Electronic Commerce > Electronic Data Interchange (EDI)."

Chapter 3: E-Business Models

In this chapter, we discuss how e-business is accomplished today. We also classify and describe several major e-business patterns or models. A **business model** is a pattern or method of doing business, typically emphasizing the underlying strategy and revenue model. We can classify **e-business models** along many dimensions. Tapscott et al. differentiate general types of e-business models according to degree of economic control and level of value integration (see Figure 3.1).[1] In their typology of business webs (b-webs), they define five categories:

- An **agora** is a marketplace like e-Bay where buyers and sellers come together to execute transactions.[2] The main theme of agoras is *dynamic pricing*.
- An **aggregation** is an e-business like Amazon.com, where the main value is *selection and convenience*. Amazon aggregates the products of many suppliers in a single convenient online store.
- An **alliance** is a creative, collaborative enterprise involving consumers who are also producers (so-called **prosumers**). Alliance members work together to achieve a common goal. A good example is the freely-available Linux operating system: users not only consume, but also freely contribute to the development of the software.
- A **value chain** is characterized by vertically integrated processes that add significant value to raw-material inputs. For example, Dell Computer turns components such as CPU's, disk drives, and power supplies into complete PC's that are far more useful to most customers than are the isolated parts.
- A **distributive network** performs the role of allocating and distributing rather than producing or consuming goods, services, and information. Distributive networks, such as WorldCom or United Parcel Service, provide infrastructure that enables other forms of e-business.

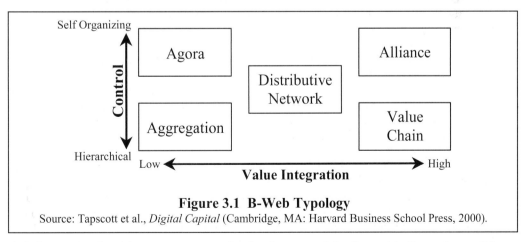

Figure 3.1 B-Web Typology

Source: Tapscott et al., *Digital Capital* (Cambridge, MA: Harvard Business School Press, 2000).

Another researcher chooses to categorize business models along the dimensions of functional integration (from single function to multiple integrated functions) and degree of innovation.[3] This functional integration dimension is similar, but not identical, to Tapscott's value integration dimension. Other researchers have created business model taxonomies that focus on more narrow revenue models. One summary of numerous e-business models divides them into the categories of brokerage, advertising, infomediary, merchant, manufacturer, affiliate, community, subscription, and utility.[4] The popular press tends to categorize e-business models according the to latest technology fad.[5]

Because innovation is occurring so rapidly and so much hybridization occurs, we have chosen to categorize e-business models along the simple dimension of who participates in transactions: businesses or consumers. In general, there are two main categories of e-business transactions: business-to-consumer (B2C) and business-to-business (B2B) trans-actions.[6] Naturally there are many variations on these themes; the variety of e-business models is limited only by entrepreneurial vision.[7] Companies are constantly innovating to compete in the marketplace. Thus, we expect to see continual refinement of the business models presented here, and we are confident that new important models will emerge over time, while others now prevalent will fade away.

For most people, the term *e-business* evokes an image of online shopping—using a Web browser to find convenient bargains on the Internet. But B2C only accounts for a small part of total e-business transactions. B2B generates much greater revenue volumes. The U.S. Census Bureau estimates that in 2000 B2B revenue accounted for 94 percent of all e-commerce.[8] On the other hand, B2C generates far more Web traffic than B2B. This makes sense because with B2C many consumers interact and generate smaller transactions, while in B2B fewer participants generate larger transactions.

Yet there is no clear line between B2B and B2C. A model that works well in the B2C space might apply equally well to B2B. In this chapter, we examine both B2C and B2B models. Along the way, we use many real-world examples and draw insights into what makes e-business work. It is important for students and practitioners in accounting to understand e-business models in order to serve effectively as auditors, assurance providers, and business consultants. The material in this chapter will help you become conversant in the major issues driving different e-businesses.

Comparing B2C and B2B

A major difference between B2C and B2B is the corresponding market structure and how companies must be organized for growth. In the B2C space, a successful vendor achieves large scale in the size of its customer base. A B2C player must be able to attract and retain a sufficient number of individual consumers. In B2C, one must balance customer acquisition and retention costs against the long-term profit returned by a single consumer. In contrast, a successful B2B company attracts customers who themselves are large and thus purchase substantial quantities of products and services. Ideally, B2B customers are also plentiful, but a B2B player must be prepared to scale and optimize its operations to produce large volume from a comparatively smaller number of customers.

Business-to-Consumer Models

In the short lifetime of the digital economy, the following four major categories of business-to-consumer models have developed:

- Online Stores, Marketplaces, and Services
- Content Providers
- Content Aggregators and Portals
- Infrastructure Providers

Within each of these categories there are many different business models, and there is an enormous amount of hybridization and innovation taking place. In this chapter we will examine Dell Computer Corp., Amazon.com, eBay, and Charles Schwab & Co. as examples of online stores, marketplaces, and services in the B2C arena. We will also briefly review the other three categories of B2C companies. For more information on some B2C revenue opportunities, see Text Box 3.1 (p. 44).

There is also cross-pollination between B2C and B2B variations of these models, because much of what works for B2C also applies to B2B. For example, W.W. Grainger, a B2B catalog company, uses the Web as a vastly more efficient delivery vehicle for its cavernous catalog business. Dell is equally comfortable building personal computers (PCs) and servers to order for large businesses as well as individual consumers (in fact, we expect Dell prefers building the more-profitable servers). Internet-based electronics and semiconductor distributors include such companies as Marshall Industries, Ingram Micro, NECX, and Tech Data. VerticalNet hosts B2B portals, storefronts, and marketplaces for numerous industry segments, including electronics engineering, wireless networks, meat and poultry, paint and coatings, dentistry, and many more. Our point is that many B2C models, with some modification, work well in the B2B space, and indeed many companies that started in B2C are now also targeting B2B for obvious reasons.[9]

Business-to-Business Models

Besides the significant shift in customer profile (B2B customers are fewer and larger), B2B customers are also more likely to be involved in trade, not just purchase. B2B companies make money not just by selling products and services, but also by becoming more efficient in their interactions with partners. At the core of B2B e-business models is the competitive advantage provided by using electronic means to transfer information. Electronic information and processes flow at lower costs and increased speeds compared to traditional information and process flow (see Chapters 1 and 2).

Consider the information flow when a company purchases products from suppliers. Traditionally, some employee of the purchasing company would generate a printed purchase order, route it through internal approval processes, mail it to the supplier, wait for delivery, and then process the shipment. Personnel are required to create the purchase order, select appropriate vendors, track the purchase order through various levels of management approval, mail purchase orders to vendors, and follow up on orders that have not been fully delivered on time. In the e-business version of this process, computer-based systems do the following (compare with Table 2.2 in Chapter 2):

1. Create an electronic purchase order (PO), perhaps automatically.
2. Route PO to the appropriate manager(s) for approval (some purchases may be automatically approved according to rules defined in the system).

Text Box 3.1 Additional Sources of E-Business Revenue

Besides deriving revenue from the online sale of products or services, there are numerous ways today's e-businesses generate revenues.

Advertising and Marketing: The display of ad banners is a common revenue model, though industry observers have continually questioned whether advertising revenue alone can fund a long-term e-business success. The "click-through" rate of ad banners (the number of times a user clicks on an ad) currently hovers around 5 per 1000 impressions, but this number is expected to fall to perhaps 1 per 1,000. It is increasingly common to see paid advertising supplemented or supplanted by joint marketing arrangements where strategic partners provide an agreed-upon level of advertising for partners. The IRS recently ruled that such arrangements constitute barter that is not generally subject to taxation. The value of advertising increases with site traffic, so an advertising revenue model works best for more popular sites such as portals. In addition to straight pay-per-impression advertising, many firms enter into strategic marketing partnerships. For example, a site may choose a particular preferred credit card, and sales made using this card would be subject to lower transaction rates. By splitting the difference with consumers, overall purchase prices are lowered, while margin on such sales is increased. In another approach, firms A and B set up a partnership where A makes an equity investment in B and provides endorsements, links, or even integrates B's site directly with A's. In exchange, B also pays a hefty marketing fee.

Your Information for Sale: In the course of interacting with consumers, companies collect a large quantity of personal information and transaction patterns that are valuable for marketing. Sale of marketing data is a significant source of revenue for some companies. There are privacy issues to work out, but any site that has user registration and long-term relationships with customers has a potential marketing gold mine. Depending on the kinds of customers and the nature of a company's relationship with them, it may or may not be practical to sell such information. For some customer groups, such a sale will alienate them and result in lost business. An e-business should not sell marketing data when it jeopardizes long-term customer relationships.

Reel Them In Slowly: Many different kinds of "hooks" are used to pull in customers gradually. One heavily used strategy on the Web is to provide a basic product or service for free, but to charge for a version of the product with more advanced features. Historically, the Internet is a sharing community and users have come to expect free information, goods, and services on the Web. Some very high quality products are available using this model.[10]

Pay You Now, Pay Me Later: Another hook used to pull in customers is to offer a cash rebate in exchange for a long-term service contract. CompuServe (www.compuserve.com) began offering a $400 rebate on the retail purchase of a new computer regardless of brand or price. In exchange for an up-front rebate, CompuServe received a 3-year, $21.95/month subscription with a new customer. Other companies have imitated the CompuServe strategy with varying levels of success. When firms believed rapid growth was paramount, this type of strategy made more sense than in the current profit-oriented atmosphere.

Custom Electronic Coupons: Online coupons are an excellent way to generate new sales revenue. Coupons can be used to attract new customers or encourage inactive customers who have not purchased for a while to return to a Web store. For repeat customers who generate good volume, coupons or other incentives (like frequent-flyer miles) can be a valuable way to nurture the ongoing relationship. Some e-businesses offer cash rewards for using their services (iWon.com, Bizrate.com) or for referring new customers (DVDExpress, PayPal.com). But coupons can also be used successfully in lieu of cash as a reward for referring a new customer or achieving a specific transaction volume.

A Piece of the Action: A common technique for attracting additional customers or generating new sales is to offer referral fees to Web sites that link to yours. Known as "affiliates" or "associates" programs, these linking arrangements pay a third party a percentage (typically 5–25 percent) of each transaction consummated as a result of following third-party links. It is possible for consumers to pay less by recapturing some of these referral rewards. Bizrate is a purchasing portal that rebates referral rewards to consumers, minus a small check-processing fee. Bizrate also sells aggregated marketing research based on its members' activities.

3. Select the appropriate vendor after investigating inventory and vendor price information (intelligently selecting vendors based on price, timeliness of delivery, or other criteria).

4. E-mail the approved electronic purchase order to the appropriate supplier. The electronic PO is sent to and received by the vendor immediately, whether the vendor is next door or on the other side of the globe.

Thus, the e-business version of purchasing can do a better job in much less time than the traditional paper-based approach. Some of B2B's e-business leverage points include reduced costs (such as labor, transportation, and supplies), faster process cycles (and hence faster time to market), increased accuracy and reliability (thus increased product quality and decreased rework), collective purchasing power, and an overall ability to handle larger quantities of information. E-business results in greater competition and new economies of scale. We now illustrate B2B advantages in more detail.

Timeliness Value of Information

Systems that never sleep are valuable because information has a timeliness value. For example, information on the direction and quantity of change in the Dow-Jones Industrial Average would be of much greater value *before* the fact. After a change occurs, the value of knowing about that change rapidly diminishes. Each kind of information exhibits its own timeliness value curve. When the timeliness of information is critical, it naturally follows that electronic delivery systems that reduce delivery time can return significant value. Even when the timeliness value of each individual transaction is small, electronic delivery of large quantities of information can produce large cumulative values.

Increased Reliability at a Decreased Cost

Electronic systems can also increase reliability of delivery while simultaneously decreasing the cost to deliver. The United States Postal Service and other couriers provide excellent service, but there are many potential failure points in a paper-based delivery mechanism, from internal purchase-approval routing processes (e.g., purchase order is lost or routed to the wrong person), to physical delivery (e.g., delivered by mistake to the wrong address), to routing within the vendor's order fulfillment system. While e-business replaces physical failure points with virtual failure points, the likelihood of failure is smaller with an electronic system. Computers are best at performing repetitive information-processing tasks humans find tedious, and machines do not get bored or make mistakes in the traditional sense (though computer programmers and operators do make many mistakes). Periodic hardware failures do occur, but proper preventive maintenance can catch many impending problems ahead of time. Failures in a computer system are highly correlated with infrequent events like initial installation and periodic "upgrades."[11] Once an e-business system is in place and working, it tends to continue working given appropriate periodic maintenance. On the other hand, e-business opens up new kinds of risk, which we describe in Chapter 4.

Greater Scalability from Automation

The incremental cost to transmit an individual message electronically is typically minuscule because most of the system cost is usually fixed (hardware, software, maintenance), so there is little variable cost to sending an electronic message. In contrast, there is a relatively high variable cost for each piece of traditional mail sent (packaging material, packaging labor, postage). It is costly to have people involved in business processes because human labor is relatively expensive in comparison to computer processing. Thus, a significant factor in the B2B e-business equation is the elimination or minimization of human intervention in business processes. The history of computers has been a study in replacing humans with machines to handle repetitive, mundane tasks. Some may feel threatened by this trend, but most people would rather be involved in creative processes, not mundane tasks. B2B e-business explicitly focuses on ways to continue this trend.

Competitive Advantage from Cost and Time Savings

Cost and time savings provided by the electronic transmission of information can lead to increased product quality, increased production capacity, or decreased unit cost. Combined with labor savings and the convenience of using networked, integrated systems, these factors add up to comparative advantage over competitors who are not engaging in e-business.

Opportunities for B2B e-business savings abound in all industries, from construction and manufacturing to insurance and health care. The U.S. construction industry spends $650 billion annually, of which about $200 billion goes to correct mistakes or pay for delays.[12] In response, construction companies are deploying Web sites that allow all project participants (clients, architects, subcontractors, etc.) to communicate better. An added advantage of this approach is that project documentation is created and recorded in a single permanent repository. As these companies become more experienced with Web-based construction project management, further opportunities for savings will develop such as:

- Lessons learned from multiple well-documented projects can help improve future construction techniques.
- E-business procurement systems can be integrated to reduce cost and manage just-in-time (JIT) inventory.
- Clients educated in how to use the system will have better information or knowledge, and thus be able to make better decisions about project modifications (e.g., what will be the true cost of a particular change, both in money and time, based on available inventory, personnel, and other factors).

Similar opportunities to increase efficiency through e-business technology exist in virtually all industries. Thus, it is not surprising that long before "e-" and ".com" started showing up in company names, B2B e-business was already taking place on an aggressive scale, mostly in the form of electronic data interchange (EDI), as seen in Chapter 2.

Models for B2B E-Business

The cost savings from replacing manual processes with computer-supported automatic processing was so dramatic that even expensive private networks were cost-justified in the original EDI models. Many companies still perform traditional EDI over private networks, but the Internet is revolutionizing EDI along with almost every other business practice. Now virtual private networks (VPNs) are squeezing the costs out of traditional private networks, allowing EDI to be performed over a securely encrypted connection using the public Internet. The Web's XML technology is also making EDI feasible on a larger scale than before. We expect to see various forms of EDI continue to grow along with other types of B2B e-business. Besides EDI, the other major aspect of B2B e-business is in the area of supply-chain management, where extranets and online marketplaces are changing the way companies buy and sell goods and services with each other.

Chapter Roadmap

We now explore the general aspects of the different categories of business models within our framework. We start with the online stores, marketplaces, and services, because this category is the most visible of the e-business models. We explore four cases of leading B2C and B2B e-business firms (Dell Computer, Amazon, eBay, and Charles Schwab & Co.) in some detail. Next we examine B2B models, showing how extranets, B2B marketplaces, and supply-chain management work to make companies more efficient. We finish the chapter by briefly exploring the remaining three categories in our framework: content providers, content aggregators and portals, and infrastructure providers. In one chapter, we can examine only the major models in place today, and thus this chapter is not intended to be the complete and final word on e-business models. Additional models will be developed and variations on these themes will appear in the future.

Online Stores, Marketplaces, and Services

Direct sale of product through an online store is what most people think of when they hear the term *e-business* or *e-commerce*. Online stores come in many shapes and sizes, from inexpensive replicas of mail-order catalogs to highly sophisticated build-to-order systems. You can find almost anything for sale on the Web.[13] Products range from services to durable goods, which may be new, used, or refurbished. Anything sold in the physical world is a candidate for sale in cyberspace. Part of the beauty of an online store is that it is available all the time to people around the world. The extensive potential customer base is a huge attraction to companies large and small. Thus, sellers—of both commodities and niche goods—are literally flocking to the Web. The U.S. Census Bureau estimates that retail e-commerce trade sales at U.S. Web sites (excluding most service industries) in 1999 totaled $20 billion, or 0.5 percent of retail sales in the United States. In 2000 these numbers jumped to $29 billion and 0.9 percent respectively. By 2001 it was $32.5 billion and just over 1 percent respectively.[14] We list major B2C retail merchandise categories in Table 3.1.

Table 3.1 Selected Categories of B2C Online Retail Sales, in Millions[14]

Merchandise Line	2000	1999
Computer hardware	$6,077	$4,224
Books and magazines	2,083	1,604
Apparel and footwear	1,960	828
Office equipment and supplies	1,432	610
Music and videos	1,282	809
Computer software	1,115	768
Electronics and appliances	1,071	464
Furniture and home furnishings	849	288
Toys, hobby goods, and games	795	398
Drugs, health and beauty aids	671	232
Food, beer, and wine	568	233

Small Businesses and Niche Providers Have a Home in Cyberspace

Indeed, many unusual niche goods and services are available through the Web. Are you an aficionado of hot sauces? Visit www.hothothot.com to buy gourmet hot sauces from a wide variety of selections. HotHotHot has a retail store, and they were an early adopter of Web storefront technology. Without abandoning the retail store, HotHotHot has done (dare we say it?) *hot* business on the Web for years now. Are you tired of that standard stick-shift knob in your vehicle? Come to www.rocknob.com and buy a unique replacement knob made from a fine Utah rock. Rocknob started not as a retail store, but as a hobby on the Web. However, Rocknob did not grow just by creating a Web site. Without traditional offline techniques to grow the business, it would have remained a hobby, but the initial testing of the concept happened online. Without a platform like the Web, companies like HotHotHot would likely have remained retail stores with limited reach, while companies like Rocknob might never have been launched in the first place. With the extensive reach of the Internet, even small ventures can be worthwhile.

Advantages of Online Stores

Besides enabling a wider variety of commerce by drawing more kinds of companies to the Web, online stores have other advantages. Customers can make more informed decisions because of the company and product information available on the Web. An online store can automatically tell customers whether particular items are in stock. Online stores can dramatically reduce costs. Though inventory shrinkage still occurs, shoplifting losses *per se* do not exist.[15] Large, expensive storefronts are replaced by Web sites that essentially have zero incremental cost for displaying an additional item.[16] Phone costs (inbound 800-number calls, for example) can be replaced by online information systems that let customers answer their own questions and place their own orders. The cost of printing and distributing catalogs, product fliers, and promotions to customers can be replaced with inexpensive e-mail and Web delivery mechanisms. Properly constructed, online stores for many kinds of products can generate large cost savings over traditional stores.

Lessons to Be Learned

In the earliest days of Web-based commerce, it was common for a company to put its catalog in HTML format, post it on a Web site, and call it an online store. Customers would typically order by phone or e-mail. If a site was sophisticated, it supported a graphical interface for entering orders using a Web browser. The state of the art has advanced quite a bit in the past decade. Online retail stores even have their own buzzword: they are **e-tailers**. Below, we profile four companies that have done well with Web sales, each using different, sophisticated strategies. Custom manufacturer Dell Computer Corporation has built its business by listening to the customer, and now plays a strong hand in both B2C and B2B sales. Classic e-tailer Amazon.com is an example of an early mover that has established an enormous Web presence by continually innovating. Online auction leader eBay shows how to bring together supply and demand to create a virtual marketplace where before there was none. And forward-looking brokerage firm Charles Schwab & Company demonstrates how a firm can survive the transition to a new, disruptive technology.

Dell's Build-to-Order Model: A Lesson in Effective Communication

Dell Computer Corporation of Round Rock, Texas, was founded in 1984 by Michael Dell on the simple premise that by selling computers directly to the customer (with no retailers or resellers in the loop), he could deliver more effective solutions at a lower price.[17] In its two-decade history, Dell has achieved truly remarkable growth, and Dell's leadership, especially with respect to e-business, has revolutionized the PC industry. Dell has leveraged the direct-to-customer principle to its considerable advantage and has pioneered the concept of building products according to the customer's specifications. Auto manufacturers envy Dell's flexible build-to-order model, and want to do the same thing for cars that Dell has done for computers (see Text Box 3.2 on p. 50).

In a keynote speech at Dell's DirectConnect conference, CEO Michael Dell told his customers there are three keys to successfully harnessing the Internet. These include increasing a company's velocity (i.e., shrinking time and distance), being more efficient in operations execution, and providing a superior online experience compared to the physical-world experience a customer could have.[18] In all these areas, Dell has set an excellent example.

Dell's key competencies are (1) it has highly efficient procurement, manufacturing, and distribution processes; (2) it provides excellent product customization; (3) it understands the customer very well and manages the relationship accordingly; (4) reliability, service, and support are among the best in the industry; and (5) the company continues to leverage its existing position to provide e-business leadership within the industry. Future goals for the company include moving more sales and technical support online and continuing to better understand customer needs so Dell can tailor product offerings to match those needs.

Text Box 3.2 The Dell of Automobile Manufacturing

Both Ford and GM have announced their desire to enter the build-to-order business and be the Dell of automobile manufacturing. In a recent *Wall Street Journal* article, GM executive Harold Kutner described how his firm would have to change its entire operations, from automobile design to plant structure to shipping, in order to be successful. GM's goal is to be able to deliver a custom-built car in 4–11 days, down from the current 3–8 weeks. GM hopes to do this by 2003.[6] Dell has set a good example of how to effectively employ e-business and how to listen and respond to customers. Unfortunately, e-progress is slow for the big three auto manufacturers. We suspect it will be a while before you will be able to custom order your car online with the same ease as your PC. There are social problems with the online car sales model too. Most customers want to "kick the tires" or at least test drive a vehicle before ordering, so auto dealers who stock sample vehicles will not go away in any practical car-sales model. Indeed, state laws protect many U.S. auto dealers from online competition, ensuring that auto dealers will not be "disintermediated" in the near term. However, if Internet tax issues could be worked out, perhaps more states would be willing to allow more extensive online automobile sales experiments. It turns out that automobile dealers, who were first suspicious of e-business, are discovering that they have much to gain by embracing the Web and its efficiencies. Good Web sites give potential customers enough information that the customers are more comfortable going to the dealer's store to "kick the tires."

Dell is currently the leading manufacturer of PCs in both the United States and the global market. The value of Dell stock since its initial public offering (IPO) in 1988 has increased about 300 times. Dell's growth has consistently outpaced the growth rate of the PC industry as a whole. For fiscal year 2002, Dell revenue totaled more than $31 billion annually.[19]

Dell's products include PCs (desktops, workstations, notebooks), servers, storage devices, services (technical support, on-site service), and PC software and peripherals. Dell dominates in the low-margin category of desktop and laptop PC sales, and it is the fastest-growing company in server sales, which have relatively high margins. Dell sells through several channels, including in-person sales calls (mostly to corporate and institutional customers), telephone orders, and orders placed over the Web.

Dell first established a Web presence in 1994, and soon deployed an order-tracking application for customers to use in lieu of calling a Dell representative. Currently, Dell handles about 75 percent of order-status inquiries using its Web interface, which cost $3 to $10 to handle by phone as opposed to virtually no incremental cost via the Web. About half of Dell's technical support transactions take place over the Internet. In 1996, Dell first added online ordering to its Web site. Figure 3.1 shows a screen shot of a portion of Dell's Web ordering interface; this page allows a user to customize a particular computer configuration according to a set of preselected options such as central processing unit speed, memory size, monitor size, and so forth. Currently, approximately half of all sales are Web-enabled.

Dell segments its customers into large business, small business, government, educational institutions, and individual consumers. Two thirds of its sales come from corporate and institutional accounts (B2B sales). Part of Dell's strategy is to better segment its customer base over time as the firm learns more about the specific needs of each kind of customer. Managing "hypergrowth" and providing top-quality customer service are key issues for most e-businesses, and the segmentation strategy helps in both these areas.

Select options, update price and add to your shopping cart below.

Dimension L Series (Required)   ❓ Learn More

DELL DIMENSION L

The Dell Dimension L Series offers a combination of hardware and services that can grow with your needs while keeping your budget in mind

| NEW Dimension® L500r, Pentium® III Processor at 500E MHz | ▼ |

Memory   ❓ Learn More

| 64MB SDRAM | ▼ |

Hard Drive   ❓ Learn More

For hard drives, GB means 1 billion bytes; total accessible capacity varies depending on operating environment.

| 4.3GB Ultra ATA Hard Drive | ▼ |

Figure 3.1 Dell's PC Configurator, January 2000

Dell's e-business infrastructure is continually evolving to match its customer segments, and their Web system is designed to offer the level of interaction best suited to each segment. For example, a B2B customer has Web access to Dell's "Premier Page," which provides several value-added features, such as a catalog of preselected computer configurations arranged by the customer's purchasing department, access to Dell's data warehouse of sales and order tracking data (just the data for the specific customer), access to customer-specific support pages, and other features. This kind of segmentation takes considerable effort to maintain, but information technology can help. In 2000, more than 50,000 businesses used this service, and each customer had to be set up and maintained by a Dell sales representative. If a customer wanted a change, the salesperson had to manually revise the page. By allowing customers to make changes themselves, Dell's Web-supported customer segmentation and sales support is now easier to maintain.[20]

Communication with suppliers is as important as listening to customers. Like other e-business leaders, Dell has established an **extranet** to link its suppliers into Dell's information systems (we discuss extranets in more detail later in this chapter). Using the extranet, suppliers can read their "scorecard" (Dell's assessment of the supplier with respect to various metrics) and they can compare their own scorecard with other suppliers in their same category. Dell also provides inventory information through the extranet, so suppliers can tune their output to Dell's specific needs. In the "old days" of PC manufacturing, companies might have had 60 days' inventory. Dell has consistently pushed the just-in-time inventory envelope, and currently Dell turns its inventory an amazing 91 times a year (every 4 days). Vice Chairman Kevin B. Rollins compares PC components to vegetables: "As you look at the value of lettuce, the longer you have it away from the store or away from the field, you notice that it starts to decrease in value... PC components are similar."[21] Dell is able to ship a fresh product that uses the latest technology at a good price, all because of its advanced e-business–style inventory management processes.

A major lesson learned from Dell's experience is that using e-business to more effectively listen to the customer can pay big dividends. Because of the direct-to-customer model, Dell has been able to respond to customers better and more cost-effectively than have competitors with indirect channels. Equally important, being an e-business is not something that happened overnight; Dell moved online carefully and built up its competencies over time. Since the company was nimble and responsive, Dell has been able to successfully reinvent itself as an e-business when the Internet opportunity arose. By focusing on the customer relationship, and what e-business can do to enhance that relationship, Dell has built a highly successful business in both the B2C and B2B arenas.

Amazon.com: Bookstore or E-Store? Staking a Claim in Cyberspace

Amazon.com wants to be the company to sell you anything you would like to buy over the Web.[22] Amazon is perhaps the most successful of the current e-tailers. However, Amazon has yet to show it can sustain a profit. At the same time, it seems that every competitor wishes it could be like Amazon (Text Box 3.3, p. 54, describes a few of these companies). Why all the excitement?

Jeff Bezos founded Amazon.com in Seattle, Washington, in 1994. After flirting with the oddball name "Cadabra," Bezos decided to name his company after the river that carries more water than any other river on earth. Amazon was opened for online business in July 1995. The original idea was that a company could sell books on the Web with very little inventory and considerable value added compared to a traditional bookstore. *Selection* and *convenience* were the goals of this online venture.

In a dynamic online store, it is easy to recommend related products. If a consumer looks at the Web page for a book about roses, she might also be interested in titles on gardening, so each Amazon page contains links to other recommended books. Tracking the purchasing habits of many customers can lead to more accurate targeting of recommendations. Another helpful element of the Amazon experience is that you can see the book's current ranking on Amazon's best-seller list. Popularity is also used in determining which books to include in lists of recommended books. And readers can write their own reviews to post on Amazon's Web site. If you want to screen a particular book, start by looking carefully at the readers' comments (summarized neatly into an overall rank on a 5-star scale). Then, if you decide you have something useful to say about a book, you can submit your review to the site. Online reviews help customers build a sense of community as they communicate and share ideas—a virtual version of a physical bookstore lounge or café. Amazon also adds value over traditional bookstores by sending book reviews by e-mail when new books are available in your areas of interest. More recently, Amazon added a "special occasions" notification service, so you can receive a reminder about birthdays, anniversaries, or other special dates you have registered. With the event notification, Amazon can recommend appropriate gifts, all of which are (of course!) conveniently available through the Amazon Web site.

Amazon's ambitions did not stop at books. Realizing the strategic advantage of being an early mover in cyberspace, in the late 1990s Amazon added music, DVDs, videos, electronics, software, toys, video games, and home improvement categories to its product line (see Figure 3.2). For its first several years, Amazon focused on growth. Amazon's customer base expanded steadily from 1.5 million in 1997 to 14 million in 1999, and 25 million in 2001. Then after the dot-com bubble burst, Amazon focused on cost-cutting, as it

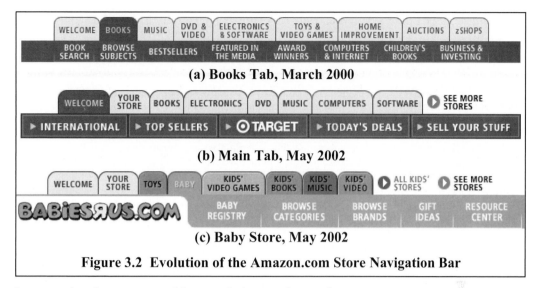

(a) Books Tab, March 2000

(b) Main Tab, May 2002

(c) Baby Store, May 2002

Figure 3.2 Evolution of the Amazon.com Store Navigation Bar

became clear investors would not wait forever for profits. Amazon management soon realized they could leverage their high traffic, accumulated customer base, and e-tail operations expertise to sign strategic agreements with other dot-coms, renting high-profile Amazon Web space and providing world-class technology services to its partners. For example, online pharmacy drugstore.com is paying $105 million over three years for a tab on Amazon's main navigation bar (shown in Figure 3.2). Living.com agreed to pay $145 million over five years to be Amazon's preferred Web store for furniture. Amazon typically takes an equity stake in the other dot-coms as part of the strategic partnerships.[23] However, these arrangements come with significant risk. Living.com died in August 2000 before paying much of the $145 million. Other current partnerships include Toys "R" Us, Target, Circuit City, and Borders. By virtue of its position as the biggest e-tailer, Amazon has significant potential to realize revenue from strategic partnerships.

Seeing the great success of auction site eBay (profiled later), Amazon has also added online auctions to its Web site. Many merchants use auctions much like an online store, listing multiple products for sale at a minimum bid price that usually ends up being the final product price when the auction closes. To make this kind of transaction more efficient, Amazon invented a new concept called "zShop," a place for online merchants to list products for sale within Amazon's Web site. The concept is similar to an auction, except prices are fixed and customers can buy at any time, rather than waiting for an auction to close. Customers can pay zShop owners directly or they can pay through Amazon using a credit card. To build customer trust, Amazon provides a guarantee of up to $1,000 against seller fraud in both zShops and auctions. Through its own online catalogs, auctions, zShops, and strategic partnerships with other dot-coms, Amazon is able to offer its customers access to literally millions of different products. The company hopes to leverage this position to become a portal for *all* your Internet shopping. In Amazon's ideal world, you would come to Amazon to ask about any product, and they would refer you to either their own listing or a partner's or, if necessary, point you to a third party.

Text Box 3.3 E-Tales Don't Always End Happily Ever After

In *Field of Dreams*, a farmer received inspiration in the form of a whisper, "If you build it, he will come." Taking a huge risk, he plowed up a cornfield and built a baseball diamond. It sounded crazy, but ultimately the gamble paid off. However, e-tail success is not guaranteed by the existence of an online store.

Do We Know What We're Building? One year after Levi Strauss & Co. first announced plans to sell directly online, the firm withdrew that strategy and decided to sell only through Web sites of existing retailers. Although Web traffic was healthy, Levi.com had failed to account for many hidden costs of transitioning from manufacturer to direct seller and underestimated the costs (including customer support and product fulfillment) of starting and maintaining a world-class e-commerce site. Equally significant was the issue of channel conflict: existing brick-and-mortar retailers were not excited about having to compete with an online Levi Strauss, while other e-tailers were completely locked out of online sales of Levi Strauss products. Another problem was overlooking the limitations of the target audience: a typical teenage Internet surfer with a 28.8Kbps Internet connection could easily be overwhelmed by all the bandwidth-consuming bells and whistles at Levi.com; and most teenagers lack a credit card or parental permission to purchase goods online. Other manufacturers like Reebok are following suit, moving back toward existing retailers and e-tailers with established relationships.[24] In another example, Beyond.com began as a B2C play, selling software and computer-related products directly to consumers. Over time, Beyond expanded beyond its original vision and now builds and manages Web sites for businesses and sells software-related goods in the government, corporate, and consumer markets. Beyond soon announced a restructuring plan, laying off 20 percent of the workforce and seeking a new CEO to better focus on the B2B market. But even that did not save the company, which filed for bankruptcy in early 2002. Focus on core competencies is still a prized jewel. Bottom line: "We built it, they came, but we didn't like what we had built."

Can We Build It before They Come? Boo.com is a fashion boutique that has made a few mistakes implementing its online strategy. First, the Web site launched almost six months behind schedule, while its $25 million marketing campaign launched on time. The result: $25 million wasted on drawing people to a Web site that effectively said, "We're still building it, but please come back." When the Web site finally did go online, there were the normal start-up glitches, but more seriously Boo.com recommended that visitors have at least a 56Kbps connection. As in the Levi.com experience, there were many bells and whistles slowing down site navigation.[25] Ultimately, Boo.com succumbed to its woes, went into receivership, and its technology assets were sold for a mere £250,000.[26]

Can We Build Only in Cyberspace? Avoiding channel conflicts suffered by Levi Strauss and Reebok, Gap fully integrates its 2,600 existing retail outlets with its Web site in a highly successful "clicks-and-mortar" model. Complete integration lets Gap market its retail outlets and its Web site together, rather than separately. References to Gap.com are found at each cash register and window display. Sales associates are trained to refer shoppers to the Web site when customers do not find the exact product they want. Gap has even installed "Web lounges" at its high-traffic stores. The goal is for customers to feel that Gap.com is just the online version of a retail outlet. Early-mover status is no guarantee, and Gap needs to be careful. Gap.com was up and running a full year before any product was offered for sale. Internet time means shorter cycles, and Gap must move fast to stay ahead of the competition. A successful strategy is in place, but Gap must keep a watchful eye on competitors like Wal-Mart and Abercrombie & Fitch.[27]

Will They Ever Come Back Again? Many e-tailers are discovering that customers expect a high level of service. Customer acquisition is expensive (up to hundreds of dollars per customer), and it often takes a long-term relationship for a customer to become profitable. E-tailers can't live with the tag line, "We built it, they came, but we haven't seen them since." Customers must be treated as a long-term asset.

Lessons: After the dot-com implosion we can cite many more examples of e-tail woe. A lot of e-tailers failed quickly because they didn't have sustainable business models. Instead, they were living on venture capital rather than revenue generated by company operations; and when it became clear that the market was in a classic speculative bubble, new funding dried up quickly. Some brick-and-mortar firms have learned that e-tailing is a lot harder in practice than it is on paper and have pulled back temporarily from their initial experiments. But e-business makes fundamental sense, and over time it will continue to grow.

Given this vast online storefront, what happened to the original concept of keeping a lean inventory that can be turned 150 times a year? In the early days, Amazon limited its inventory to best-sellers and then ordered other books from distributors as needed. But when you rely on third parties for fulfillment, service may suffer because quality control is difficult. This is especially true given the diversification of Amazon's product line. Many things can go wrong in order fulfillment: an order may be broken into multiple shipments more often (these are harder for the customer to return and more expensive for Amazon to ship); credit cards might be billed before items have actually shipped (customers dislike this practice); more steps involved in fulfillment implies greater opportunity for miscommunication or shipping errors. In 1999, Amazon began building state-of-the-art warehouses designed specifically for e-business. This warehouse system cost hundreds of millions of dollars, and product inventory is similarly expensive. But now when you purchase items online from Amazon, a system of conveyor belts and automated bins collects your merchandise in a holding bin without human intervention. Once all the items are in your holding bin, a light comes on and a human worker comes over to pack your shipment. The result is that Amazon can fulfill your order more efficiently than most other e-tailers, and they are able to deliver a higher level of service to customers because of the capital investment. Amazon managed only 12 inventory turns in 2000, but improved to 16 in 2001.[28]

Another creative way Amazon has built its business is by setting up a network of "associates." You can provide links to Amazon from your own Web site, and if customers purchase through your links, Amazon gives you a referral fee of 5 percent to 15 percent. This not only makes sense for a high-traffic general interest site, but also for someone with expertise in a specialty area. For example, an amateur astronomer with an excellent tutorial site might list a collection of must-have books for **newbies** (beginners). By linking these books to Amazon's site, the astronomer can receive 15 percent on sales generated by clicking on the links.

Amazon aggressively uses patents to protect its innovations. Amazon and Barnesandnoble.com were locked in patent litigation over the "one-click checkout" process for more than two years before finally settling the lawsuit out of court.[29] Amazon also obtained a patent on its affiliate program, and despite sometimes loud protests, Amazon continues to build its patent portfolio. Business methods could not be patented until 1998, and it takes 2 to 3 years for a patent application to be approved, so we expect to see many more e-business–related patents in the near future. Historically patents have not had much impact on e-business, but that is starting to change. There will be much discussion about what is truly new, useful, and not obvious (elements required for a patent). Regardless of whether most patents are upheld, it is clear that dot-coms need to pay attention to the issue. Patent protection can be a potent weapon for maintaining an advantage.

For the fourth quarter of 1999, Amazon's net sales reached $676 million but, due to its high growth strategy, Amazon reported a net loss of $323 million. However, Amazon claimed that its book division actually achieved profitability for the first time. In 2000 Amazon reported net sales of $2.8 billion but a net loss of $1.4 billion. In 2001 the loss was $567 million on sales of $3.1 billion. But in a move that boosted investor confidence, Amazon finally recorded a company-wide pro forma profit of $35 million in the fourth quarter of 2001. Because the firm is saddled with over $2 billion in debt and there are significant ongoing risks such as strong competition, some analysts predict Amazon will not survive. Others believe Amazon's future lies in transforming itself into an e-tail technology and fulfillment services provider. $225 million of Amazon's 2001 revenues came from operating highly profitable Web stores for its partners. Gross margin on services was 56 percent, more than twice the rate for books and DVD's.[30]

As illustrated by the Amazon.com case, Web territory can be extremely valuable, especially for early movers. High-traffic sites sell more product and command more advertising revenue. However, early-mover advantage is not sufficient (see Chapter 2). Customer service is also extremely important, especially because it is easy for a customer to switch to a competitor who offers better service. Interestingly, service is more important to customer loyalty than price, though price is a factor. Amazon recently added *lowering prices* as the third pillar of its customer experience (as we mentioned, *selection* and *convenience* are the other two). Another important factor in maintaining a leading position in e-tailing is continual innovation. A short list of Amazon innovations includes one-click checkout, warehouses designed specifically for Web shopping, and a product search capability extending beyond Amazon's own offerings. Such innovations must continue for Amazon to remain a leader in the industry.

eBay: Immediate Profit in Creating a Virtual Marketplace for Consumers

We now turn to an e-business that is equally innovative, but has demonstrated a consistent record of profitability. The premier Internet auction site in the United States is eBay (www.ebay.com), launched in 1995 by Pierre Omidyar. He developed the idea after his wife, who collects Pez candy dispensers, told him what a nice thing it would be if she could interact with other collectors on the Internet. There are newsgroups, chat rooms, and Web sites for people with shared niche interests, but these fall far short of the infrastructure provided by eBay that allows individuals to buy and sell items in a **consumer-to-consumer** (**C2C**) marketplace with some assurance that transactions will be safe and satisfactory (see Figure 3.3). eBay participants may also be businesses, and so there are aspects of B2C and B2B within the eBay model. We consider C2C to be a subset of the B2C category, though there are special C2C issues (see Text Box 3.4).

In March 2002, eBay received over 29 million unique visitors, and the company claims over 42 million registered users.[31] In 2001, more than 423 million items, with an ap-

Featured Auctions in Musical Instruments

Current   = Gallery   = Picture   = Hot!   = New!

Status	Item	Price	Bids	Ends PST
	Cherry Wood Horsehair Cello Bow	$24.99	-	04/11 19:55
	VINTAGE R JONES ~GUITAR~ Excel. Cond. NO RES	$210.00	5	04/10 17:49
	Antique Stradivarius Violin -- MUST SEE	$350.00	8	04/09 21:00

Figure 3.3 eBay Gives a Quick Overview of Auction Status by Product Category
(Items listed here are fictitious.)

Text Box 3.4 Safe C2C Transactions

In the C2C transaction world, how can you avoid fraud? First, eBay rates each member of its auction community. As transactions occur, partners have an opportunity to rate each other. Someone with a high rating over time is generally a safer partner than an unrated new eBay member. Also, eBay provides insurance for each transaction (up to $200, with a $25 deductible) in case you don't receive an item or it was less than promised.

But how about securing the actual exchange of money and goods? For large transactions, eBay uses an escrow partner, i-Escrow, as a trusted intermediary for both payments and refunds. For smaller transactions, one way is to ship COD (incurring another handling fee). Or the buyer can send a check in the mail. For money orders or cashier's checks, the seller can ship immediately, but for personal checks—especially for large dollar amounts—the seller usually waits for the check to clear before shipping. Both of these methods are less convenient than buying goods online from a merchant using a credit card.

PayPal.com was created to address a distinct opportunity: safe and convenient person-to-person payments. When both parties have a PayPal account, the buyer can transfer money immediately to the seller, and PayPal will send an e-mail when the seller's account has been credited. For eBay users, this means payment can be made almost instantaneously, even if the seller does not have a credit card merchant account. There are three options for PayPal account holders to use their money: (1) leave it in the account for future PayPal purchases, (2) transfer funds electronically to your bank account, or (3) have PayPal mail a check. PayPal is also useful for such transactions as splitting a lunch or party bill. Rather than charge transaction fees, PayPal makes money by investing current account balances in liquid instruments.

Amazon directly brokers credit card payments for its zShops and auctions. eBay also entered the market with its Billpoint service, a joint venture with Wells Fargo Bank. eBay expected consumers would pay transaction fees for the convenience of electronic payments. But two years later, eBay finally succumbed to the popularity of the PayPal service, and eBay agreed to acquire PayPal, Inc. for about $1.5 billion.

---

proximate aggregate value of $9.3 billion were listed on eBay.com. Given the scale of these numbers, it is not hard to see that from modest transaction fees eBay can generate significant revenues. In the past two years, net income has exploded from $9.6 million in 1999 to $48.3 million in 2000 and $90.4 million in 2001. Overall, from a variety of fees, eBay's take was about 8 percent of the $9.3 billion in gross sales through its Web site.

Leveraging technology to assist bidders, eBay lets you set up a virtual agent to bid on your behalf: by entering a "proxy bid," the computer automatically increases your bid each time someone else out-bids you, up to a confidential maximum amount you specify. E-mail is used to notify interested parties when various events occur (e.g., you have been out-bid, or your bid won an auction).

Auctions on eBay are primarily B2C and C2C. C2C auctions are the equivalent of an Internet-based yard sale on a much larger scale than is possible in the physical world. B2C auctions offer interesting new possibilities for both traditional and Web-based firms. Suppose you are a music retailer with no online storefront, and you have excess inventory of a particular CD. Rather than continue to lose shelf space to a stagnant product, you can widen your audience considerably by listing the CDs on eBay. Thus, eBay can be an intermediary to better inventory management. In order to access an additional channel, many businesses with a Web storefront also regularly list their products in eBay auctions.

We observed in the first edition of this book that eBay could do a better job of accommodating B2C transactions by implementing a concept similar to the Amazon.com zShop,

---

Text Box 3.5 A European Auction Twist

German online auction venture Ricardo.de began by selling new, not used, products (mostly discontinued or overstocked items, but still a somewhat upscale image compared to some eBay products). Combining commerce with entertainment, Ricardo increases its "stickiness" by periodically hosting real-time, live auctions, with a human moderator to interact with bidders. In a bid to battle eBay more effectively in Europe, QXL.com and Ricardo.de announced their merger in May 2000. We expect to see continuing innovation as competitors slug it out in the marketplace.

---

and indeed, in September 2001 eBay launched its eBay Stores merchant mini-shop concept. The venture has had its share of birthing pains, but eBay Stores adds a third fixed-price purchasing element to the eBay portfolio. Earlier in 2001, eBay rolled out a "Buy It Now" feature that allows buyers to purchase an auction item immediately for a fixed price. Once serious bidding starts, the "Buy It Now" price is no longer available. In 2000 eBay also bought Half.com, a Web site that sells used items at fixed prices. eBay continues to operate Half.com as a separate Web site (half.ebay.com).

eBay could also expand its services into the lucrative B2B auction space. In 2002, eBay has more than $1 billion in cash and investments. Many of those investments are in other e-business auction firms. For example, eBay invested $22 million in B2B auction start-up Tradeout.com. As part of the deal, Meg Whitman, eBay CEO, serves on Tradeout.com's board of directors. She has asserted that eBay is not planning to move into the B2B space, but Whitman wants to keep an eye on B2B auctions because "it's a very adjacent space." On the other hand, Whitman says eBay is expanding into international mid-tier auction markets and regional auctions for hard-to-ship goods such as automobiles.[32] Managing growth and continuing innovation will be ongoing challenges.

Currently, Amazon.com and Yahoo! are the main direct online competitors to eBay, but there are literally hundreds of auction sites on the Web. And as eBay increasingly moves

---

Text Box 3.6 Reverse Auctions and Demand Collection

An interesting alternative to eBay's auctions is Priceline.com's so-called "demand collection system." (While priceline.com claims its model is the same as a reverse auction, the distinction is nuanced.) At Priceline, consumers indicate a price at which they are willing to purchase a particular product such as airline tickets, hotel rooms, or telephone services (long distance and wireless). Consumers guarantee payment through a credit card, and must hold their offers open for a specified period of time. Furthermore, consumers must be flexible with respect to brands and product features. Priceline matches customer bids with a database of offers from sellers, and locks in those bids that are sufficiently high. Even if the price paid is well below retail, a seller turns a profit as long as the buyer's bid covers the variable costs associated with providing the service, if there is excess capacity. Companies can use Priceline to dispose of excess or distressed inventory without impacting their retail operations, because Priceline does not disclose the seller until after the transaction has been approved. Priceline's growth has been sporadic. The dot-com implosion of 2000 was very difficult on Priceline, which has since had to focus sharply on its core products. Despite sometimes impressive growth, Priceline has yet to earn a profit, though losses are diminishing ($1 billion in 1999, $327 million in 2000, and $16 million in 2001).

In early 2002, Priceline began a fascinating experiment, announcing a deal to begin offering airline tickets through a partnership with eBay. Cleary there is a consumer segment that does not want to "name [its] own price" because of the associated uncertainty (the customer has to be flexible with respect to the brand and actual product delivered). It will be interesting to see how consumers respond to airline tickets available for auction or at "Buy It Now" fixed prices.

into the fixed-price purchasing arena, it will tend to compete with the rest of the retail and discount sales community. However, as an early mover in consumer-oriented online auctions, eBay holds a commanding lead in Web auction traffic.[33] Even more impressive, in stark contrast to many e-businesses, eBay has been profitable since its inception.

Eat or Be Eaten? Charles Schwab & Co. Does Both

What happens when you cross Salvador Dalí with Lee Iacocca?[34] Well, you get something that looks odd but has plenty of business sense, like what happened when Charles Schwab & Co., Inc., addressed their digital future. As discussed in Chapter 2, it is relatively uncommon for industry leaders to survive disruptive technology transitions, but Schwab made some painful choices and currently has an excellent position among retail brokerages with respect to the Internet and e-business. In 1996, faced with an opportunity for online trades over the Internet, David Pottruck, Co-CEO of Charles Schwab, determined to establish an online unit, e.Schwab (later renamed Schwab.com).

e.Schwab was given its own staff and offices, and was charged to aggressively develop online investing services. As one would expect, e.Schwab was to compete with other online brokers, but in a stunning move, Pottruck also let e.Schwab compete with its parent for customers. After e.Schwab's $29.95 trades made serious inroads on Schwab's traditional trades that averaged $65, Pottruck decided it was time to swallow the bitter medicine of moving all trades to the flat $29.95 model. This would cost $125 million in revenues, reduce short-term profits, and certainly pummel Schwab's share price. Indeed, as the new pricing took effect in January 1998, Schwab's share price fell about 30 percent. Since taking the plunge, Schwab has more than doubled its accounts from 3 million to over 7.9 million (including 4.3 million active online accounts), it has added billions of dollars in new customer assets, its share price has increased significantly, and growth continues apace. As of May 2002, Schwab customer assets totaled $858 billion, of which $342 billion were held by active online investors.[35]

So did e.Schwab cannibalize its traditional parent company? The answer appears to be "only partially." In fact, soon Schwab realized that the market would bear higher transaction fees for broker-assisted trades. After trying a $39 commission for a while, in April 2002 Schwab raised the minimum fee for a broker-assisted trade to $54.95.[36] Increased commissions and fees are the result of the extended downturn in the stock market, and the consequent drop of enthusiasm for all forms of stock trading, including online.

To be more effective, Schwab realized it had to drive additional costs out of the supply chain. It needed to improve the efficiency of corporate procurement using a Web-based methodology to optimize the brokerage's purchasing of high-volume, low dollar-value commodities and services. The firm also needed to link supply chain partners via the Web and build an infrastructure that takes into account expected changes in Schwab's business as well as continued growth. In October 1999, Schwab implemented a highly complex commerce portal, driven by Ariba software, to automate Schwab's commerce chain. Schwab has improved the way staff purchase commodities. Purchasing volume has increased, no additional staff were required, and processing costs were reduced.

Schwab's main competitors in the online investment world include E*TRADE, Ameritrade (which recently bought Datek), TD Waterhouse, and Fidelity Investments. Schwab's fees are higher than most competitors, but its value returned is likewise higher. The company's substantial growth and recent pricing moves show that customers perceive this value and are willing to pay for it. In February 2000, Schwab acquired day-trading firm CyBerCorp, and other online brokerages soon looked to make similar deals. More recently E*TRADE acquired closely-held Tradescape, a firm specializing in professional trading. Price competition for active traders is fierce: Schwab lowered trade commissions to $14.95 per trade for customers who exceed 60 qualifying trades in a quarter; E*TRADE's base rate is $9.99 for customers who trade at least 75 times per quarter (less active traders typically pay $14.99 or $19.99 per trade). Some observers are highly critical of the recent Ameritrade/Datek merger, which gave Ameritrade access to 837,000 new accounts but at a high price of $1,500 per account.[37] Even though Datek accounts are more active than the industry average, one wonders whether the investment will pay off. The anticipated online brokerage shakeout is in full swing, and we expect to see continued consolidation and transformation in the online brokerage industry.[38]

Even though pricing often takes the spotlight, competition on features and innovations is also significant. For example, E*TRADE offers customers and potential customers the opportunity to play the "E*TRADE Game." Players are given $100,000 of virtual money to manage a hypothetical portfolio. The game provides an opportunity for individuals to experiment and learn about investing techniques in a hands-on environment. Cash prizes are awarded to the best performers each month, and players can learn from one another by examining other players' portfolios. Education is a major part of being a financial services firm, and E*TRADE makes the learning process enjoyable. Schwab also provides a significant education opportunity through its "Learning Center," where you can enroll in online courses on various investment-related topics.

E*TRADE started out as a **pure Internet play**, but Schwab has long been a **clicks-and-mortar** business. Schwab marries a strong online presence with a widespread physical presence to provide a multi-channel solution for both online and offline investors. Originally making its name as a discount brokerage, Schwab now wants to be known as a full-service investing firm that empowers its customers by giving them easy access to information and investing services. Customers interact with Schwab in three ways: in-person at more than 400 branch offices, over the telephone day or night, and using the Internet. As Schwab continues to develop its online offering, it slowly attacks the customer base of traditional full-service brokerages like Merrill Lynch, who have been comparatively slow to enter cyberspace.

Schwab's strategy for long-term growth is to leverage its competitive advantages, which include strong national brands, a wide range of products and services (Schwab is known for excellent research and analysis), multiple channels (Web, phone, physical branches), and continued investment in technology.[39] Merrill Lynch and E*TRADE are fighting back of course, imitating Schwab's multi-channel model. E*TRADE is taking an Amazon-style approach. Through acquisitions, E*TRADE has moved toward its goal of becoming a one-stop financial services shop, encompassing commercial and investment banking, loans and mortgages, credit card services, and any other financial product. Like Amazon, E*TRADE learned that it needed bricks. E*TRADE is now a leader in the ATM network space, and the firm is looking for partners than can add more physical infrastructure. The firm is opening "E*TRADE Zones" in several dozen Target stores and is partnering with Ernst & Young to provide advice services to customers with $100,000 or more in their accounts.[40] This diversity has buoyed E*TRADE in the market downturn of the past couple of years—E*TRADE would not have survived as a pure play. In response, Schwab realizes it needs to continue to add banking and other financial services.

The Schwab case demonstrates a couple of important lessons. First, the firm has done an excellent job leveraging its physical-world brand into a clicks-and-mortar Internet hybrid business model. Retail traders know and trust the brand, so Schwab commands higher trading commissions than its competitors. Also, in the event of technology glitches, multiple access channels (physical branches, phone operators) provide alternate routes to perform transactions. Second, Schwab is a successful example of how self-cannibalization by an early mover can turn a traditional firm into an e-business ready for the New Economy. Schwab gave its Internet division the autonomy it needed to truly innovate, and then pulled the division back into the parent at the right time to give a unified front to its customers. Schwab currently has a substantial lead, which it will clearly need in order to fight off Merrill Lynch's slower advance onto the Internet.[41]

B2B: Supply-Chain Management

EDI fostered a revolution in supply-chain management and procurement processes, and the push to e-business has increased the pace and scale of this revolution. While EDI enabled such practices as just-in-time inventory management, the massive scale of Internet technology penetration has lowered barriers to setting up so-called extranets, enabling even better supply-chain management. In this section, we describe extranets, B2B auctions, and the online marketplaces that are beginning to revolutionize B2B e-business.

Extranets

An **extranet** is a private network built on Internet technology, available to a company's business partners and customers, and protected from unauthorized use by multiple layers of security technology such as passwords, encryption, and firewalls (see Chapter 4 and the technology toolbox in Appendix C). The purpose of an extranet is to let business partners conduct business securely, using relatively inexpensive Internet technology. Dell Computer Corporation, for example, uses an extranet to link suppliers to Dell's inventory database. Customers can access the extranet to order products and receive information needed to plan future purchases. Besides enabling interactive collaboration with business partners, an extranet also increases a company's reach to include smaller and more geographically distant partners who otherwise would not be logical to include as partners.

EDI is excellent for highly structured documents like purchase orders, invoices, or planning schedules. Such documents have rigid formats defined, and these must be carefully programmed into the interacting systems. EDI is not as well suited for processes that have less structure or are ad hoc in nature, such as the processes that occur when business partners collaborate interactively (e.g., searching for a less expensive alternative in a product design, or submitting product specifications for custom manufacture). Extranets, however, are very well suited to such ad hoc collaborations. Open Internet protocols allow for the easy interchange of multimedia documents such as HTML pages containing embedded graphics and even sound.

As EDI and extranets increase in popularity, companies are using them to share sales data and planning information so suppliers can be prepared to meet company needs. As a company's production needs grow or shrink, that information is communicated to suppliers quickly and efficiently. Using extranets, suppliers can compete with each other for a company's business, either by competitively bidding for contracts or by scoring better on performance measures established by a company and published to members of the extranet. Extranets allow companies to more efficiently communicate information such as product changes, promotions, and future plans.

B2B Auctions

E-business is also making supply chains more efficient through the use of business-to-business auctions. This is not a new idea—many companies manage B2B auctions—but B2B auctions hosted on the Internet are a more recent phenomenon. The Internet allows market efficiencies to be realized more readily, pulling in a larger pool of both sellers and buyers, large and small, near and far. Growth of B2B auctions is projected to be significant as online B2B auctions draw in companies that do not participate in offline auctions. As more companies see how easy it is to tap an additional sales channel through online auctions, there will be a greater level of overall market efficiency.

There are many styles of auctions.[42] An auction can use the bid-up principle, wherein the price keeps ascending as potential buyers compete (**English** and **Yankee auctions**), or it can use the bid-down principle (**Dutch auctions**), wherein the seller continues to drop the price until a buyer steps forward to purchase. There are **sealed-bid auctions** in which the item is awarded to the highest bidder (**first-price auctions**). There are also sealed-bid auctions in which it is the second-highest bidder who wins (**second-price auctions**); the purpose is to help assure buyers that they will not pay significantly more than true market value. **Silent auctions** let all bidders know what the current highest bid is, but they do not know who the other bidders are. **Commodity auctions** are much like the process at the Chicago Board of Trade—buyers and sellers continually update bids and offers in a commodities-style, frenetic rush; at any time, sellers can accept a buy offer or buyers can accept a sell offer that suits them.

The two major business models for conducting auctions are independent and private auctions. **Independent auctions** are hosted by an independent third-party specialist, such as FreeMarkets. According to the company's Web site (www.freemarkets.com), FreeMarkets conducts "online auctions for industrial parts, raw materials, commodities and services. In these auctions, suppliers compete in real time for the purchase orders of large buying organizations by lowering their prices until the auction is closed." Independent auctioneers receive a percentage of the sale and may levy various participation fees.

A **private auction** is hosted by a company offering its own goods for sale. Companies often use private auctions as a way to salvage a better return from excess inventory. By eliminating intermediaries, the seller receives a higher price and the purchaser pays less. A private auction does not involve transaction fees to a third party, but there is a significant investment in the infrastructure needed to support an online auction. Whether a private auction or an independent auction is more cost-effective for a company depends on the scale and frequency of the company's auction needs and information technology (IT) competency. An organization with an existing extranet might already have an IT infrastructure to leverage.

Automobile Industry Supply-Chain Management

In November 1999, automobile manufacturers Ford and GM announced similar initiatives to build online marketplaces to integrate suppliers in a system beyond simple EDI. Ford's AutoXchange and GM's TradeXchange were extranets designed not only to link Ford and GM with suppliers, but also to link suppliers with each other. Participants would conduct online transactions in three ways: online catalog, online bid/quote process, and B2B auction. Interestingly, these marketplaces would also be open to competitors. For a few months, GM and Ford raced each other, mostly producing competing press releases arguing who was winning, but also making real progress. In February 2000, GM and Ford announced that they would merge their efforts and bring DaimlerChrysler into the venture, creating a massive online marketplace for the whole industry. Annual volume of the combined trade exchange site, called Covisint (www.covisint.com), was expected to be enormous, approaching half a trillion dollars. According to one report, "the combined exchange is expected to handle $240 billion in annual spending world-wide by the three car companies. In addition, a substantial portion of the $500 billion that each auto maker's suppliers spend each year is expected to flow through the system."[43]

Why the move from competition in online marketplaces to cooperation? For one thing, as Ford and GM dueled, parts suppliers made it clear they were unhappy with the prospect of having to integrate into at least two separate systems (and perhaps more as other automakers launched their own additional sites). One of the difficult challenges facing automotive industry suppliers is managing the sheer quantity of different usernames and passwords required to sign on to dozens or hundreds of different customer or partner portals.[44] Integrating two systems is challenging, but integrating dozens is far more difficult. Also, a combined site more easily attracts additional parties to the marketplace, driving volumes up and costs down. A greater number of participants means that competition will increase, and as weaker suppliers are squeezed out, the overall market becomes stronger and more efficient.

The automotive marketplace will initially lower the cost of purchasing by streamlining the purchasing process itself (e.g., online auctions mean participants do not have to travel to attend a traditional, in-person auction, so the online version saves employee time and travel expenses). Also, the extended extranet will allow manufacturers and suppliers to exchange parts blueprints and specifications more easily, thus reducing product design time. Eventually, it will also help lower costs for all members of the supply chain (i.e., multi-layer inventory management can reduce the total cost of inventory throughout the supply chain), so the actual cost of goods purchased should eventually decline. By allowing competitors to use their extranets, the big three automobile manufacturers can benefit from greater economies of scale. Furthermore, by reducing a supplier's costs of selling to multiple manufacturers (e.g., by reducing redundant incompatible systems within the supplier's business processes), Ford, GM, and DaimlerChrysler indirectly reduce their own cost of materials and parts.

Another important strategic benefit of using extranets in this manner is that they help integrate automobile manufacturers with the Web and they enable faster time to market—the supply chain is more nimble online. Currently, the major manufacturers are not prepared for a Dell-style build-to-order Web system for cars. But with an online marketplace integrated into their own extranets, the big three come a little closer to the well-managed supply chain and business processes needed to support such an initiative.[45]

So how successful has Covisint actually been? 2001 was its first full year of operations, and while full details of the closely-held firm are not available, Kevin W. English, Chairman, CEO, and President reported that in 2001 Covisint brokered more than $50 billion in online auction bids and more than $100 billion in future program awards through the Quote Manager product.[46] The early months and years of Covisint have been a bumpy road (as one would expect), marked by considerable infrastructure development, reorganization, FTC scrutiny, and pummeled by a generally weak economy. There has been infighting among the partners, and it could readily be characterized as a shaky start.[47] Nevertheless, Ford already claims to have recouped its investment in Covisint, saving as much as $350 million in 2001; and GM alone was willing to handle $100 billion of its procurement contracts through Covisint in 2001.[48] It seems the exchange has a future. Covisint management expects the company to be profitable by the end of 2002.[49]

On a smaller scale, Chemdex (www.chemdex.com), E-Steel (www.esteel.com), Direct-Ag.com (www.directag.com), and many others have already proven the online marketplace concept in other industries. We expect most industries will eventually use online marketplaces in one form or another to streamline their supply chains. A current trend among B2B auction and marketplace sites is consolidation of separate sites around industries. GM/Ford/DaimlerChrysler is just one example. After observing GM and Ford's earlier attempts at separate Web sites, the aerospace industry decided to launch a unified Web site for e-business transactions, MyAirplane.com. Recently, there have been a number of similar announcements of group initiatives in other industries. 2001 saw a lot of shake-out in the B2B exchange market, but this is another area where e-business makes fundamental sense, and eventually industries will find the right combinations that work well.

Content Providers

The earliest e-business model was to provide better information to consumers through a new communication channel. Companies who publish information via the Web are called **content providers**. The first companies on the Web did not start by selling product. Instead, they established information sources to deliver company information, product information, technical support, and marketing materials. The contents of a typical

---

Text Box 3.7 Company Information on the Web

Vecna Home Page, May 2002

Copyright © 2002, Vecna Technologies, Inc. Used by permission.

Many firms provide access to a variety of information and services on the Web. Vecna Technologies (www.vecna.com) is a privately held consulting firm that distinguishes itself by providing, among other things, access to project tracking information via a secure intranet. With Vecna's Web system, customers know exactly where their projects stand.

Notice that the Vecna home page is clean and simple, giving links to essential company information and Vecna's intranet. (Public companies typically also include an "investor relations" link that gives access to information like annual reports and public financial data.) An effective Web site does not have to be elaborate, and it does not always include an online storefront. This home page, like many others, uses clean, attractive colors and uncomplicated, pleasant designs to convey basic company information.

---

company Web site might include a mission statement and other materials describing the company, contact information, product listings and descriptions, press releases, links to related resources, and files to download (see Text Box 3.7).

Even without attempting to sell products and conduct direct commerce over the Web, the advantages of providing information on the Web are significant (also see Chapter 1):

- **Reduced transaction costs.** Dell Computer saves money every time a customer uses Dell's Web site to check order status instead of calling a human sales representative. Software companies like Microsoft save money by letting customers look up technical support information on the Web. Most manufacturers of PC peripherals (e.g., graphics cards, modems) supply "device driver" updates via the Web; before the high-speed Internet was ubiquitous, consumers usually had to wait for such updates to be mailed on diskette or CD-ROM. The e-business approach is dramatically more efficient for both companies and consumers. Software firms now routinely notify registered users of available upgrades by e-mail; these upgrades can often be downloaded directly from the Internet.

- **Improved services.** Microsoft introduced a feature in Windows 98 called "Critical Update Notification." When a Windows user is connected to the Internet, this feature can periodically check the Microsoft Web site to see if there are important Windows updates available for download. Consumers using this feature can be sure that they will receive, for example, important security updates for Microsoft's Internet Explorer browser in a timely fashion. This service adds real value to the Microsoft product offering by providing improved customer service.
- **Reduced marketing costs.** Many companies use e-mail newsletters to communicate with their customers. These newsletters can contain information such as news releases, case studies, or general educational material related to a company's mission. Newsletters and special offers can be tailored to customer circumstances. For example, suppose you have downloaded an evaluation version of a software product. The manufacturer could send you a case study showing how similar consumers have used the product effectively. If you do not purchase the product during the trial period, the company could send you a special discount offer to try to pique your interest. Direct e-mail campaigns can efficiently supplement traditional marketing techniques at a low incremental cost.
- **Availability of new advertising and endorsement revenues.** A high-traffic site like Amazon.com can offer space on its Web pages to advertisers. Ads and endorsements come in several forms, from small icons (e.g., a Visa logo on the site, saying Visa is Amazon's preferred credit card), to relatively large ad banners. Even at fractions of a penny per image displayed, a site with millions of "hits" per month can collect substantial advertising fees. Note, however, that advertising as the sole source of revenue rarely works. A comprehensive business model uses ad revenues as just one supplemental component.

Publishers and Media on the Web

For companies in the information publishing business (book publishers, magazines, newspapers, encyclopedias), there are additional benefits to providing content online:

- Some consumers will pay for certain kinds of valuable content such as research reports or professional reviews. Edmunds (www.edmunds.com) provides a great deal of online information about car prices and buying strategies. Consumer Reports, on the other hand, charges $12 for a new car price report that is functionally similar, but contains proprietary recommendations and advice. When contemplating a relatively large and infrequent purchase, $12 is a small price to pay for high-quality, well-packaged, pertinent information. Many magazines and newspapers with sterling brands, such as the *Wall Street Journal* (wsj.com) and *Consumer Reports* (www.consumerreports.org), restrict most online access to paid subscribers only. If you plan to charge for access, very high quality content is critical in the Internet environment where consumers have an expectation of receiving most information and software at no charge.
- An online publication can be far more dynamic than a printed page. A news organization can send e-mail alerts of breaking stories of interest to subscribers. A publication's home page can make new articles available in "real time" as they

are written. Such dynamism makes it more likely for subscribers to return to the site frequently. In contrast with printed media, online materials are easily searched. Online archives of past publications can also be searched with the same mechanism. Since the incremental cost of content storage is small, extensive archives are relatively inexpensive to maintain. And unlike static printed pages, Web sites can incorporate multimedia content (audio, video, animations) and link to related Web pages. And Web pages can be programmed with dynamic scripts that include fill-in forms, buttons, and other graphical user-interface features. Online publication also allows for improved dialog between authors and readers, or among readers themselves. Like many others, Ziff-Davis (www.zdnet.com), publisher of technology news, lets readers post responses to articles and participate in instant polls.

For traditional information publishers, the Web revolution is a classic example of disruptive technology. As the Web has exploded, traditional publishers have become very nervous. How can a newspaper compete with e-mail abstracts and Web news sites? Does a Web site providing the content of a periodical at no cost undermine the subscription base for the printed magazine? Indicative of the mood among Old Economy veterans, Ted Turner told *Fortune* magazine, "I wouldn't want to be in the newspaper business. I think the Internet is going to eat them first."[50] We note, however, that traditional media is still alive and well.

Some publishers have responded to the Web revolution by creating barriers to online use of their materials. Others have given in to what they see as the inevitable transition to free online digital content. In contrast to the *Wall Street Journal*, mentioned earlier, the *New York Times* (www.nytimes.com) provides free access to content, supported by ad revenue, marketing partnerships, and the sale of marketing information (users must register to access certain portions of the Web site such as searching archives). Some customers would rather pay money for high-quality content that is relatively free of advertisements. Others would rather endure longer download times and ad-covered Web pages in order to get free access to content. However, even subscription-supported publications also use ads to increase revenues, so it is relatively uncommon to find commercial Web sites devoid of ad banners.

Will consumers pirate digital copies of copyright-protected content, thus eroding the market for subscriptions or purchases? The music industry has been particularly aggressive at protecting its copyrights (and the royalty stream generated by those copyrights), but as the popularity of the MP3 digital music format has shown, online music is definitely here to stay. With ever-increasing Internet bandwidth, filmmakers are now worried that the same thing that happened to music with the peer-to-peer file sharing services like Napster will also happen to movies. Bootleg copies of recent blockbuster films like *Spider-Man* and *Star Wars Episode II: Attack of the Clones* have appeared online even before the movies were released in theaters. There are many court battles yet to be fought, and copy-protection schemes will continue to be debated. But ultimately society will have to find a way to deal with the convergence that digitalization is forcing. The bottom line is that we see the media industries undergoing evolutionary changes as they develop

---

Text Box 3.8 Healtheon/WebMD: A Vertical Portal for Health Care

Healtheon/WebMD is a combination of two giants in online health care. The company's goal is to facilitate improved health care around the world by connecting consumers and providers more efficiently using Healtheon/WebMD's Internet technology infrastructure. One of the ways it does this is by providing separate portals for consumers, professionals (one for physicians and another for nurses), employers, and educators. Consumers get health news, physician directories, chat rooms, a place to store their own health records, and a wealth of health-related information. Professionals receive access to continuing medical education courses, medical libraries and databases, a career center, claims and referral processing, and a host of other features.

Healtheon/WebMD ultimately wants to make money by charging per-transaction fees for doctors to access patient records, file claims, check lab work, and so on. The conglomerate is currently in the midst of a number of strategic acquisitions as it tries to build the critical mass of physicians and consumers needed to make the business model work.

---

e-business strategies that really work. Perhaps one day the Internet will support pay-per-view digital movies; but this will certainly not happen overnight.

Online Communities

An important source of information published on the Web is consumers themselves. A natural effect of the Web is that people with similar interests are able to interact with one another conveniently. An ideal outcome is the sharing of product reviews. Screen It (www.screenit.com) is an ad-revenue–supported site for movie reviews.[51] Parents concerned about what their children might be exposed to can find very detailed reviews of movie content at the Screen It site. Amazon.com allows authors, editors, and readers to submit reviews online. Amazon summarizes reviews into an overall book rating (up to five stars) displayed on the book's main page. CNET (www.cnet.com) provides product reviews and links to purchase products online. Like Amazon, CNET allows users to submit opinions and product rankings, but CNET also provides reviews written by its own staffers; certain products are also labeled editor's choice. Thus, not only can consumers learn about products from manufacturers and professional reviewers/editors, but people can also tap the large online community of fellow consumers to learn about their personal experiences with particular products. The increase in consumer awareness benefits manufacturers, giving them another channel for feedback and product suggestions. This in turn benefits consumers as manufacturers produce better products that are targeted more accurately to real consumer wishes, with improved post sale product support.

Even when online sales are a minor part of a company's business model, a Web site is still a vital tool in the e-business arsenal. It can help drive customers to brick-and-mortar stores, and it can help bring in new partners, investors, and employees. Web sites play a crucial role in consumer education and product branding, and the kind of information published via a Web site should be a key element of most e-business models.[52]

Content Aggregators and Portals

As Web growth began to skyrocket, it quickly became apparent that there would be demand for mechanisms to find information on the Web. Anyone who has tried to do re-

Text Box 3.9 Britannica.com: From Publisher to Portal

In 1999, publishers of the *Encyclopædia Britannica* found themselves at a digital crossroads. In the face of declining sales of their traditional printed encyclopedia combined with the dramatic rise in popularity of the Web as a place to do research, Britannica decided to become a dot-com. It determined to publish its encyclopedia online at no direct cost to end users. Britannica would generate revenue from ads, sales in its online stores, sales of its CD-based encyclopedia, and strategic partnerships. Rather than seeking barriers to protect its intellectual property, Britannica leveraged its own valuable content and established relationships with many partners to become not just a content provider, but also a portal, Web directory, and content aggregator. In a clear attempt to establish a sense of community, Britannica.com called itself a "free knowledge and learning center for people who seek thoughtful and engaging context to today's affairs" (www.britannica.com). To support this goal, Britannica emphasized the value added by its editorial staff in organizing and presenting relevant information. The following features were included in the first version of Britannica.com:

- *Encyclopædia Britannica* content
- News articles from major magazines and newspapers
- A directory of Web sites, each ranked on a 5-star scale
- Related-books search (linked to online ordering through barnesandnoble.com)
- Weather, stock, and sports information
- Web search service
- An online store
- Free e-mail

The user community greeted Britannica's announcement with great enthusiasm. Like so many new Web sites, Britannica found it was unprepared for the swarm of visitors who swamped the site on its opening day. It took some time for Britannica.com to scale up its systems, but now it can handle large loads.

Britannica also discovered that its free model did not work so well. With the post-bubble economy came significantly reduced Web advertising revenues. In July 2001, Britannica introduced a premium service and reduced the amount of free content on its Web site (for example a free user might see a short paragraph on the B-1 bomber, while a premium subscriber can access a complete article with more details and photos). Originally a monthly subscription cost $5, but in 2002 the monthly fee had increased to $9.95. Britannica continues to innovate in order to attract consumers to the premium service. For example, premium subscribers have access to a pop-up dictionary that quickly looks up a word in the Merriam-Webster dictionary and thesaurus just by double-clicking the word in the online article.

search on the Web knows how difficult it can be to find the right information. The World Wide Web—the largest database ever compiled—is incomprehensibly large and there is no end in sight to its continued rapid growth. Early attempts to create management tools for locating information centered on two approaches: search engines and directories. More recently, portals and meta-search engines have also become popular. These business models revolve around the concept of **infomediary** described in Chapter 2.

A **search engine** lets a user enter key words, and then returns a list of pages that contain many occurrences of those words. A **directory**, on the other hand, is a site that compiles a list of links to sites of interest, organized by subject (much like a traditional library's subject index) and often annotated with editorial commentary. Instead of searching for key words, directory users browse a hierarchical listing of subjects. Later attempts at helping users tame the Web generated the idea of **meta-search engines** that submit a query to several regular search engines and then return the results after eliminating duplicate pages. Some companies make information more accessible using a **content aggre-**

gation approach. Rather than just linking to other sites, they can actually pull content from multiple sites into a single location, where users interested in a particular subject (such as comparing CD prices) can assemble to access the content.

Content aggregators and search services naturally morphed into **portals**, which are points of entry, or gateways, to the Web. A portal gives easy access to Web sites and content selected by editors for their relatively high quality and relevance to portal customers. Some portals are designed for general audiences, while others are organized around the specific interests of a particular community (e.g., a company's employees or customers). Portals often let users specify a profile to tailor content to the user's main interests. Some Web sites track user **click trails** as a basis for customizing the content displayed to particular individuals.[53] Other common portal features include access to e-mail accounts, news groups, chat rooms, online calendars, shopping facilities, and more. See Text Box 3.8 (p. 68) and Text Box 3.9 (p. 69) for descriptions of two different kinds of portals.

In the earliest days, there was a clear distinction between the different kinds of search services and content aggregators. For example, the Yahoo! Web directory was created by human experts who scoured the Web and judged sites, while the AltaVista search service used automated **spiders** to crawl the Web looking for pages to index. More recently, hybrid models have appeared, providing all three services (keyword-based search, human-generated directory, content aggregation) in a single portal.

A portal company's goal is to be the home page from which users access all other Web content. Keys to portal success include attracting a high volume of traffic and getting visitors to return often (increasing the portal's **stickiness**). By engaging users in e-mail, calendars, and other customized features, portals not only entice customers to return often, but they also raise the cost (measured in time and aggravation) for a user to switch to a competitor. A sticky portal can generate significant advertising revenues. Yahoo! is the current "gold standard" for Internet portals, though competition in the portal arena has been heating up. Most of the top Web sites, measured by the number of unique visitors to those sites each month, happen to be portals.

There is clearly a role for infomediaries in the New Economy. Because of the vital role portals have begun to play in Web usage, most e-business models can benefit by incorporating elements of the portal concept.

Infrastructure Providers

Supporting the massive e-business infrastructure are many technology and service providers that help make the Internet go. There are telecommunications firms such as WorldCom, Sprint, AT&T, and Qwest that provide the big pipes, or "backbone," through which Internet traffic is routed. Hardware manufacturers like Sun Microsystems, Dell Computer, and Compaq make the servers and workstations connected to the Net, while network hardware companies such as Cisco Systems and 3Com build the routers, switches, and hubs needed to connect those computers. Internet service providers like AOL, EarthLink, MSN, and PSINet connect end users (both companies and individual consumers) directly with the Internet. Many other professional services are needed to make e-business operate smoothly, including advertising and metrics, business and management consulting, Web hosting, and logistics. At still another level, software developers provide prepackaged e-business solutions ranging from operating systems and Web browsers to databases and Web storefronts or even B2B marketplace software.

These infrastructure providers are a critical component of the New Economy, but except for the Internet service providers and PC vendors, they are largely hidden from the view of consumers, and typically operate more in the B2B space than they do in B2C. Without trying to be comprehensive, Table 3.1 lists some of the major e-business infrastructure firms. Included in this list are hardware manufacturers, telecommunications firms, software developers, and service companies. Unlike many Web start-ups, most of these companies are well established and are making money now on their products.

These infrastructure companies make money like any other business would, except they are often attuned to the special opportunities of e-business. Dell (profiled earlier) is an excellent example; Dell is now beginning to leverage its position as a manufacturer of server computers to move into e-business consulting and Web hosting services. Software developers as a whole have done a good job at leveraging the Web. Starting with Web-based technical support, software developers have rapidly moved to a model of downloadable products. Just a few years ago, it was common to receive a large printed manual with a newly purchased software product. Then manufacturers began to put their documentation on CDs, and printed manuals became smaller and less common. Now you do not even need a CD—just download the product and its documentation from the Web (after paying an appropriate licensing fee, of course).

The good news for consulting firms is that e-business requires a fair amount of professional services at the infrastructure level. For example, PricewaterhouseCoopers is considered to be a leader in privacy services, and its Privacy Risk Management group audits

Table 3.1 Examples of E-Business Infrastructure Providers

Category	Example Companies
Computer hardware	Intel, Dell, HP/Compaq, IBM, Sun Microsystems, Apple
Internet backbone	WorldCom, AT&T, Sprint, Qwest
Networking hardware	Cisco Systems, 3Com, Lucent, Nortel, Motorola
B2B software	Ariba, CommerceOne, i2 Technologies, Manugistics
E-commerce software	BroadVision, Divine, Inktomi
Support software	Sun Microsystems, Microsoft, Netscape/AOL, Oracle, RSA Security
Advertising & metrics	DoubleClick, Jupiter Media Metrix, Nielsen Netratings
Consulting services	Andersen Consulting, PricewaterhouseCoopers, Ernst & Young, IBM
Hosting & Web services	Exodus Communications, Sprint, UUNet, Digex, Akamai
Shipping & logistics	UPS, FedEx, U.S. Postal Service

the privacy practices of many Web sites. Ernst & Young is strong in customer relations, supply-chain management, and designing or building sites. Andersen Consulting partners with companies large and small to develop custom e-business systems. Professional services are likely to experience sizeable growth for the foreseeable future (see Chapter 5).

Summary

An accounting professional who wishes to serve as an effective e-business adviser must have a basic understanding of e-business models. There are two major categories of e-business—business-to-consumer (B2C) and business-to-business (B2B). Both B2B and B2C are growing rapidly because of the compelling value and efficiency advantages outlined in Chapters 1 and 2. The B2B market is much larger than B2C, but both segments are important in the New Economy.

We have categorized B2C businesses into four general groups: online stores and marketplaces; content providers; content aggregators and portals; and infrastructure providers. B2C models also generally apply in the B2B space, and indeed numerous B2C firms also have B2B operations. Many of the B2C players are start-ups that are currently losing money as they attempt to grow into a dominant market position. There are pure play Internet companies and firms that marry brick-and-mortar with an online presence in a clicks-and-mortar model. The latter tend to be more successful, and we expect to see fewer pure-play e-businesses in the future. Revenues come in the form of sales of goods and services, ongoing subscription fees, advertising fees, referral fees, resale of marketing information, and strategic partnerships.

B2B e-business is built on the foundation of EDI, extended in the Internet age into public networks. The concept of an extranet, where outside business partners are integrated into a company's internal information systems, is extremely valuable for cutting costs by augmenting traditional EDI with increasingly intelligent, automated systems. B2B elevates the importance of partners by including them directly into a company's business processes. By doing so, firms improve supply-chain management, communication and collaboration, and overall operational efficiency. Of interest to accountants is the fact that the need for these interdependent partnerships results in increasing demand for assurance regarding the reliability of partners' systems (see Chapters 4 and 5). Finally, many players in B2B are infrastructure providers, generating the technology, software, and services needed for e-business.

There is currently a lot of excitement about e-business, but not all companies succeed. We expect to see ongoing "churn" in the e-business landscape, both in terms of the leading companies and the most successful e-business models. One of the determinants of which companies will succeed and which will fail is a company's level of effectiveness in focusing on a business model that provides real value to customers, then identifying and managing the risks inherent in e-business. This is the topic of the next chapter.

For more information, please visit the Companion Website at www.prenhall.com/glover.

Review Questions

3-1 List and describe the categories into which most B2C e-businesses fall.

3-2 The dot-com crash has dampened enthusiasm for e-business in many firms. If you were a manager, how would you build a successful case for rolling out a new e-business initiative? Describe the types of revenue models that are available and which you think will bring long-term success. Are there other ways besides securing direct revenue to cost-justify e-business initiatives?

3-3 What do we learn from Amazon's e-tailing experience? Can an e-tailer grow to an industry powerhouse without investing in physical assets? Do you think Amazon.com will ultimately survive or fail? Explain.

3-4 Many companies, such as LifeFitness, an exercise equipment manufacturer, establish a Web presence but do not offer goods or services for sale from their Web sites. What benefits would justify a company's creation of a Web presence if the company does not offer products or services for sale over the Web?

3-5 What are the most common causes of failure among e-businesses? What can we learn from these failures?

3-6 How did Dell Computer use e-business to enhance its operations? Is Dell's success due to its use of e-business or is that success due to other factors? Explain.

3-7 Is Charles Schwab & Co.'s success due to e-business or other factors? Explain.

Discussion Cases

3-8 Without all of the fanfare that B2C e-commerce has generated, B2B accounts for the largest dollar volume of e-business. Discuss why media coverage historically focused so much on B2C. What implications does this have for you when you wish to get the most up-to-date B2B information?

3-9 Melody and Robert became acquainted in college as they took a few courses together. They found that they both shared a passion for curling and decided that they wanted to create the best unofficial curling Web site in order to promote the sport, profile the best players, cover tournaments, and offer opinions on the sport, players, and tournaments. After they created the site and published it, they submitted it to all of the search engines to promote it. In a short period of time, it became quite popular, with thousands of visitors a day. Seeing their success and noting the amount of continuing effort required to maintain the content of the site, they decided that they would like to generate some income from the site. Discuss how they might generate a revenue flow from their successful Web site.

Research Case

3-10 As noted in the text, many B2C concepts apply in the B2B world. Consider online auctions. The B2C (perhaps C2C) auctions such as eBay and Yahoo! auctions are fairly well known. Can you find some B2B marketplaces that include auctions on the Web? Are the B2B marketplaces consolidated at a couple of principal sites or are they distributed across the Web? Are there any organizational characteristics that are unique to B2B marketplaces?

Notes

1. Don Tapscott, David Ticoll, and Alex Lowy, *Digital Capital: Harvesting the Power of Business Webs* (Boston, MA: Harvard Business School Press, 2000).
2. *Agora*, which comes from the Greek, means "a gathering place; especially: the marketplace in ancient Greece." See Merriam-Webster's *Collegiate Dictionary*, www.m-w.com.
3. Paul Timmers, *Electronic Commerce: Strategies and Models for Business-To-Business Trading* (Chichester, England: John Wiley & Sons Ltd, 1999).
4. Michael Rappa, "Business Models on the Web," digitalenterprise.org/models/models.html, May 9, 2002.
5. Does anyone remember the "push" technologies that would stream information automatically to your desktop? This was one of the earliest press-darling fads.
6. Some analysts also propose C2C and C2B models. A marketplace like eBay is the archetypal C2C model, but C2B is a bit more esoteric. Others add even more categories like "business-to-government" or "business-to-employee." We prefer to consider only B2C and B2B categories because an individual supplying a product or service acts like a business.
7. "Opportuneurial" vision also generated many (failed) creative e-business models as well. See "What's So New About the New Economy? Glad You Asked...," *Business 2.0*, August 2001.
8. United States Department of Commerce, "E-Stats," www.census.gov/estats, March 18, 2002.
9. As the dot-com bubble burst, many companies reinvented themselves as B2B plays. Then it became clear that B2B had also been over-hyped, and many in the B2B space had to reinvent themselves yet again, or die.
10. For example, Sun Microsystems Inc. (www.sun.com) announced that Solaris 8, Sun's flagship Unix operating system, would be available at no charge for use on systems with fewer than 8 processors. Sun makes money from Solaris when a company uses it on a large system or purchases related products and services (such as 24×7 server monitoring to ensure that a critical server remains in operation at all times). This free end-user license to Solaris 8 is not a lightweight product giveaway—it covers the full release of Solaris 8. Another quality tool, JBuilder, used for Java development, is available at no charge from Borland Software Corp. (www.borland.com). Editions of the product with more bundled features can be purchased, but the free edition of JBuilder is powerful. There are many more such examples of software and services available at no charge on the Web.
11. We put the term "upgrades" in quotes because as often as not, IT upgrades lead to short-term difficulties for end-users, even when there are clear long-term benefits. Initial releases of software are especially notorious for causing trouble. Many IT specialists recommend waiting 6 months to a year before installing a new software release. This gives the vendor time to discover the inevitable problems and develop "patches" to fix them.
12. "Construction and the Internet: New Wiring," *Economist*, vol. 354, no. 8153 (January 15, 2000): 68.
13. Seriously, folks. eBay has to keep constant watch over the products listed by its multitude of creative and sometimes uninhibited sellers.
14. United States Department of Commerce, "E-Stats," March 18, 2002, www.census.gov/estats.
15. Merchants still have credit-card fraud risks and shrinkage due to theft.

16. This doesn't mean you *should* always add that extra item. E-tailers such as Ashford.com have discovered that you can easily overwhelm a customer with choices.
17. Many of the facts in this section are drawn from Michael Dell with Catherine Fredman, *Direct from Dell* (New York, NY: HarperCollins, 1999); and the Dell Web site, www.dell.com.
18. See "Michael Dell Speech Archive," *DirectConnect*, www.dell.com, August 25, 1999.
19. As of June 2000; see www.dell.com.
20. David Rocks, "Streamlining: Dell Computer," *BusinessWeek*, September 18, 2000.
21. Kevin B. Rollins, "Leadership in Business Technology," published by the Marriott School at Brigham Young University, *Exchange*, (Fall 1999): 4–13.
22. Facts in this section come from Amazon.com's Web site, numerous articles on the company as widely reported in the press, and personal experience.
23. It is virtually certain that Amazon's navigation bar will have changed by the time you read this. We invite you to visit www.amazon.com to see what new strategic partnerships Amazon has made, and how those relationships have affected the navigation bar.
24. See Cindy Waxer, "501 Blues," *Business 2.0*, January 2000; Bernhard Warner, "Reebok Stumbles," *The Industry Standard*, January 31, 2000.
25. Bernhard Warner, "Boohoohoo.com," *The Industry Standard*, January 28, 2000.
26. See Erik Portanger and Stephanie Gruner, "Boo.com's Shareholders Pull Plug; Firm Fails to Gain More Funding," *Wall Street Journal*, May 18, 2000; and related news reports in the May 19, 2000, edition. The £250,000 sale price was reported on May 28, 2000, by *Bloomberg News*; see news.cnet.com/news/0-1007-200-1973048.html.
27. Louise Lee, "Clicks and Mortar at Gap.com," *BusinessWeek,* October 13, 1999.
28. See Amazon.com's 2001 Annual Report, available on their Web site, www.amazon.com.
29. See Troy Wolverton, "Amazon, Barnes&Noble Settle Patent Suit," *CNET News.com*, www.news.com, March 6, 2002. The "one-click order process" is a means of speeding up the order process so it can be finalized with a single mouse click. As a customer shops, items are added to an electronic "shopping basket," and to finalize the purchase, the customer clicks on the one-click checkout button. To do this, the Web site must be able to identify a repeat customer (this is done by storing a "cookie" on the customer's computer), and the Web site needs to store shipping and billing data entered previously by the customer (this data is stored in a database on the company's computer). When a customer returns to the Web site, the server first retrieves the customer's cookie and then locates the corresponding customer data in its database. See Appendix B for a discussion of cookies.
30. Gross margins on technology services are nearly 60 percent. See the Amazon 2001 Annual Report and Jane Black, "The Shape of a Profitable Amazon," *BusinessWeek*, November 20, 2001.
31. Source: Jupiter Media Metrix, May 2002. Other facts in this section are derived from the eBay Web site, eBay's 2001 Annual Report, numerous articles in the press, and personal experience.
32. See eBay's 2001 Annual Report; "Internet Intuition," *Computerworld*, vol. 34, no. 2, January 10, 2000, pp. 48–50.
33. First-mover advantage can be very important in determining market dominance. Yahoo! achieved dominance in the Japanese auction market because it was the first major player to deploy online auctions in Japan. eBay sees much of its future growth coming from international expansion. But because so much of eBay's success derives from aspects of community, eBay will need to work extra hard to manage the often-difficult cultural distinctions as it cultivates international auction communities.

34. Salvador Dalí (1904–1989) was a controversial Spanish painter and printmaker of the Surrealist genre. His bizarre paintings often depict subconscious imagery. See the article on Dalí in the *Encyclopædia Britannica* at www.britannica.com.

35. Source: Charles Schwab's "About" page, www.aboutschwab.com, May 22, 2000.

36. See Gaston F. Ceron, "Charles Schwab to Raise Some Trade Commissions, Fees," *Wall Street Journal*, April 30, 2002.

37. See Paul Kedrosky, "Ameritrade Parties Like It's 1999," *Wall Street Journal*, April 11, 2002.

38. See Olga Kharif, "How Valuable is E*TRADE's Crown?", *BusinessWeek*, May 10, 2002.

39. See Charles Schwab's 2001 Annual Report, available from www.aboutschwab.com.

40. Eric Wahlgren, "E*TRADE Is No One-Trick Dot-Com," *BusinessWeek*, January 28, 2002.

41. Also see Jerry Useem, "Internet Defense Strategy: Cannibalize Yourself," *Fortune*, September 6, 1999, pp. 121–134.

42. For a review, see Louise Fickel, "Bid Business," *CIO Web Business*, vol. 12, no. 16, June 1, 1999, pp. 46–54.

43. Robert L. Simison, Fara Warner, and Gregory L. White, "GM, Ford, DaimlerChrysler to Create a Single Firm to Supply Auto Parts," *Wall Street Journal*, February 28, 2000.

44. AMR states that "Understanding why a unified portal strategy is necessary is as easy as opening the top drawer of any Automotive Information Technology executive's desk. At the top of the pile in every desk drawer, just above the latest AMR Research Report … is a spreadsheet that contains anywhere from 20 to 300 usernames and passwords for customer and partner portals. One supplier executive displayed a list of more than a hundred names and passwords that he uses just to comply with one Original Equipment Manufacturer customer." See "Automotive and Heavy Equipment Outlook: Portal Proliferation Drives Supplier Compliance Costs," *The AMR Alert*, AMR Research, www.amrresearch.com, January 17, 2002.

45. See Robert L. Simison, Fara Warner, and Gregory L. White, "Big Three Car Makers Plan Net Exchange," *Wall Street Journal*, February 28, 2000.

46. See Kevin W. English, "Remarks Before the Automotive News World Congress," January 16, 2002, available online in the speeches section of www.covisint.com.

47. For example, there have been complaints of fundamental unfairness in some auction procedures. See Ralph Kisiel, "Information Technology: Supplier Group Forms Reverse-Auction Rules," *Automotive News*, www.autonews.com, May 13, 2002.

48. See Steve Konicki, "Great Sites: Covisint," *InformationWeek*, August 27, 2001.

49. See Jeff Bennett, "Measure of the Auto Industry: Covisint Refines Online Ways to Connect Buyers with Suppliers," *Auto.com*, Detroit Free Press, www.auto.com, February 19, 2002.

50. Marc Gunther and Irene Gashurov, "Publish or Perish?" *Fortune*, January 10, 2000.

51. Given the downturn in Web advertising, ScreenIt is studying whether to offer a premium subscription service instead of or in addition to its current service.

52. According to eMarketer, in 1998, the top five reasons for establishing a business Web site included: (1) enhanced customer service; (2) saving money (efficiencies); (3) stimulating presale, purchase interest, leads; (4) conducting sales (e-commerce); and (5) branding.

53. A "click trail" is the path of links a user followed during a visit to a Web site. For example, one trail might be: home page, investor relations, annual report, home page, products and services. By examining click trails and looking for common patterns, companies can refine their Web site to be easier to use. It may also be that different users can be classified according to their click trails (e.g., Does this visitor act more like a prospective customer, a returning customer, or an investor?). If so, the Web server can identify early in a user's visit what kind of information it should display to a particular visitor.

Chapter 4: Identifying and Managing the Risks of E-Business

There is much more illegal and unauthorized activity going on in cyber-space than corporations admit to their clients, stockholders and business partners or report to law enforcement. Incidents are widespread, costly and commonplace. Post-9/11, there seems to be a greater appreciation for how much information security means not only to each individual enterprise but also to the economy itself and to society as a whole.[1]

On February 6, 2000 Yahoo! Inc., one of the most visited Web sites on the Internet, was hit by an onslaught of illegitimate requests for information from its Web server. The company's giant search engine was soon disabled, unable to handle the pressure created by the "cyberassault." The following day, Buy.com, eBay, and Amazon.com, all major e-business sites, were also brought down in a similar fashion. The next 24 hours saw a virtual "jamming" of other Web sites as well, including E*TRADE and Ziff-Davis.[2]

The fact that these were only "virtual" attacks—buildings or equipment were not destroyed—might lead some to discount the seriousness of such occurrences. But for Web-based companies like Yahoo!, such attacks bring enormous financial consequences. The dollars lost for Yahoo! and other e-businesses are every bit as real as when physical assets are destroyed. The FBI estimates that computer losses in the United States total $10 billion a year. The Bureau also estimates that only about 10 percent of all computer crimes are reported to law enforcement officials. For obvious reasons, companies hesitate to tell their customers and competitors that crucial computer systems have been compromised.[3]

In its first annual report, the Internet Fraud Complaint Center (IFCC) reported 49,711 complaints from January 1, 2001 to December 31, 2001. This total includes many different types of complaints, from criminal computer intrusions to spam (unsolicited or junk e-mail). The IFCC referred 16,775 complaints of fraud, the majority of which were committed over the Internet. The total dollar loss from all referred cases of fraud was $17.8 million, with a median dollar loss of $435 per complaint. Internet auction fraud was the most commonly reported crime, comprising 42.8 percent of complaints.[4]

Ernst & Young LLP, in its Global Security Report for 2002, says only 40 percent of organizations are confident that they would be able to detect a covert systems attack, and that 40 percent of organizations do not even investigate information security incidents. However, the survey also indicates that, in light of the events of September 11, 2001, (9/11) many companies have wisely sharpened their focus on protecting critical infrastructure resources.[5]

Successful attacks on top Web sites highlight the fact that success in e-business is greatly dependent on the ability to handle threats associated with interconnecting information systems and operating online. To effectively manage these threats, enterprises must first understand them. For accountants to be valued business advisers and assurance providers in an e-business environment, they also need an understanding of these risks and threats.

Risk

What Is Risk?

Risk can be defined as the likelihood that an unwanted or injurious event will occur. We all deal with risk in one form or another on a daily basis. We often have to take chances as part of our efforts to accomplish our goals. From a capital investor's standpoint, risk is usually associated with a reward, called a **risk premium**. As the risk of an investment increases, the risk premium or potential for favorable returns on the investment also increases. As we indicated in Chapter 1, the mirror image of opportunity is risk. This principle points out that while not all risk is to be avoided, *uncompensated* risk should be mitigated and controlled to the greatest extent possible.

The risk-reward relationship and the management of risk play an important role in the success of a business. Many business failures can be attributed to lack of awareness of significant risks or lack of effective risk management. Many of the risks that e-business enterprises face are common to all businesses that rely heavily on information technology (IT). While e-business mitigates some risks, it heightens others and even introduces new ones. This chapter illustrates why risk identification and management are vital for companies wanting to succeed in cyberspace, for accountants seeking to be valued business advisers to e-business enterprises, and for auditors seeking to evaluate internal controls and express an opinion on the fairness of an e-business enterprise's financial statements.

Risk in E-Business

Business risk is a term used to describe the risk inherent in a firm's operations. When a firm engages in e-business to expand its potential opportunities, its business risk typically changes in nature and increases. This increase is due to the nature of e-business, including increased reliance on technology and the fact that this technology changes rapidly. For example, enhanced connectivity and easy access to information is both a great advantage of e-business and also a source of increased risk. Business managers and assurance providers should understand that the entire enterprise is affected when e-business becomes a part of a company's strategy.

Risks of e-business stem primarily from an organization's information systems and the way these systems interact with external parties, who in turn operate their own information systems and interact with other e-business entities. Many of the risks taking center stage in e-business environments are similar to existing risks common to all business enterprises. In some instances, e-business can actually reduce or remove some traditional business risks by establishing new controls and procedures and eliminating manually introduced errors. However, while some traditional risks are mitigated in e-business environments, many are greatly amplified.

While many e-business risks stem directly from reliance on information technology, the heightened risks associated with e-business do not all relate directly to the underlying computer hardware and software. For example, companies wanting to engage in e-business must be cognizant of **Internet time**—the concept that business cycles and the emergence of competitive threats are greatly accelerated. Traditional firms taking a slow and deliberate approach to e-business may lose market share to other companies who achieve a **first-mover advantage** (being the first to enter a market and thus capture most or all of the early market). However, first-mover advantage does not ensure success. In the rapidly evolving world of e-business, companies must be aware of market changes and react quickly. It is unlikely that a company's current e-business strategy will remain an effective long-term strategy. To be successful in e-business, companies must be innovative, adaptable, and nimble. A firm's management team must never assume they own or will continue to own a marketplace. The profiles of e-business failures discussed in previous chapters highlight the risks associated with poor e-business strategies, such as costly expenditures on ineffective marketing or damaged supplier relationships.

Deloitte and Touche LLP, a global leader in risk management consulting, has identified common risk-increasing characteristics of firms engaged in e-business. Some include:[6]

1. Rapid growth
2. Mergers and acquisitions
3. Formations of new partnerships
4. Obtaining financing through debt and equity offerings/initial public offerings
5. Upgrading or installing new technology
6. Taking new products to market
7. Complex information systems
8. Changes in management
9. Regulatory compliance difficulties
10. Increasingly complex business models and processes[7]

Any firm's risk management program should be comprehensive enough to encompass the risks stemming from these characteristics.[8] However, effectively managing these risks is a matter of heightened priority for e-business firms because they currently tend to exhibit these characteristics more than other enterprises.

We reiterate that e-business is not merely the buying and selling of goods and services over the Internet. Rather, any electronic transfer of information that facilitates a company's operations can be termed e-business. Consequently, the risks of e-business are as broad as the term itself. This chapter is not intended to provide a comprehensive coverage of risks and controls common to all businesses—such coverage would fill a college textbook. Rather, we focus on the identification of risks and controls that are either more important in, or are unique to, today's e-business environment.

The categories of e-business risk discussed in this chapter are summarized in Figure 4.1. As the figure illustrates, e-business risks can be associated with an enterprise's IT infrastructure, either through inherent vulnerabilities or through internal or external attacks. Vulnerabilities in IT infrastructure can create exposure to other e-business risks, such as those associated with falsified identity, compromised privacy, and malicious code. Pervading the four risk categories are human factors and system interdependencies. Human factors often contribute to an enterprise's exposure. System interdependencies can make an e-business enterprise vulnerable even if it effectively manages the risks within its own boundaries.

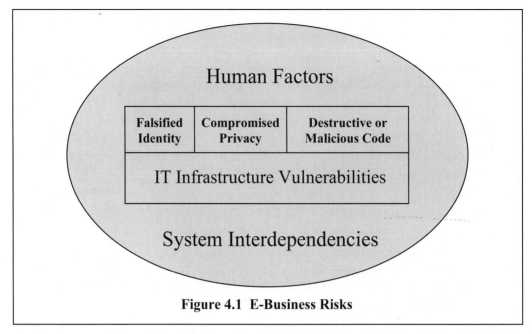

Figure 4.1 E-Business Risks

In order to create a secure information system, including relationships with partners, one needs an understanding of the risks that affect the system. The security of an information system is enhanced as the organization becomes aware of its vulnerabilities and associated exposures. The rest of this chapter focuses on the nature and control of e-business risks, and is organized in accordance with Figure 4.1. We begin our discussion of the risks of e-business with the largest, and most central, of the four categories, the organization's infrastructure.

Infrastructure Vulnerabilities: Risks and Controls

Risks Associated with IT Infrastructure Vulnerabilities

> *Critical infrastructure is a matter of corporate governance and risk management. Senior management must understand that they are responsible for securing corporate assets—including information and information systems. Corporate boards must understand that they are accountable, as part of their fiduciary duties, to provide effective oversight of the development and implementation of appropriate infrastructure security policies and best practices.*[9]

This quote from John S. Triak, Director of the government-sponsored Critical Infrastructure Assurance Office, illustrates that one of the primary sources of risk facing e-business enterprises stems from vulnerabilities in the organization's IT infrastructure—the hardware, software, and processes and people that allow day-to-day operations to be carried out (see Text Box 4.1). For any enterprise that relies heavily on IT to conduct its day-to-day activities, infrastructure weaknesses can result in costly or even disastrous interruptions of vital data flow. These risks are greatly heightened in an e-business environment due to nearly complete dependence on information technology to communicate and conduct transactions.

An example can be seen in the experiences of Egghead.com, an online retailer of personal computer hardware, software, peripherals, accessories, and other consumer and business products. On December 22, 2000, Egghead acknowledged that the company's servers had

> **Text Box 4.1 A Note on Protecting Infrastructure**
>
> Protecting against infrastructure vulnerabilities starts by hiring honest people. Experts estimate that up to 60 percent of unauthorized entries into a computer system are from company insiders. Hackers may also have access to sensitive information because they work for a computer security company. One law enforcement official who caught a hacker later saw the offender with a firm that was bidding to do the Web site security software for the White House. The alleged hacker walked into the room where the law enforcement person was, and very abruptly walked back out!

been **hacked** by network intruders and that customer credit-card numbers were potentially stolen.[10] While Egghead initially had little idea of the extent of the attack or how many credit card numbers were stolen, estimates placed the losses at 3.7 million credit cards. The investigation into the loss cost Egghead not only money and publicity, but also cost credit card companies an estimated $2 to $5 per new card issued.

On January 8, 2001, Egghead announced that its internal investigation indicated that no customer data had been compromised in the attack.[11] Although customer data was apparently not compromised after all, Egghead suffered an enormous blow to its reputation of being a safe place to do business.[12] Apart from the publicity generated directly by the hacker attack, the company was widely criticized for designing its IT infrastructure in a way that made the company's credit card database Web-accessible.

According to Paul Robertson, senior developer for security service firm TruSecure Corp., Egghead was using Microsoft's Internet Information Server (IIS), a common e-business platform. IIS is known to have had several security flaws over the years, including a "remote data services" flaw and a relatively new "Unicode" flaw that can result in an attacker gaining complete control of the server. However, these holes should have been covered using easily available **patches**.[13] Says Robertson, "It really doesn't matter what Web server you are running ... if you are not keeping up with patches, you're insecure."[14]

Egghead filed for bankruptcy on August 15th, 2001. The company's assets were subsequently purchased by Amazon.com through bankruptcy court for $6.1 million in cash.

A firm's IT infrastructure includes the critically important interface that allows the business to interact with customers and suppliers. Many Internet-based companies, such as eBay and Amazon, interface with customers only through a virtual Web storefront. Any interruption in the availability of the site can be extremely costly. When an e-business company experiences an enterprise-wide IT system outage, it is unable to provide service to customers, process transactions, or otherwise carry out its normal operations—the business is essentially shut down. The following sections detail some of the other risks associated with an enterprise's infrastructure. While not all threats involve stolen credit card information or IT infrastructure shut-downs, they can all be very costly to an e-business.

Denial-of-Service Attacks

Interruptions in service can result from a variety of sources, including intentional attacks and natural disasters. **Denial-of-service (DoS)** attacks are deliberate attacks to disable a communication system such that an organization cannot provide services. A DoS attack is carried out by overloading a system with millions of illegitimate requests for information or services to a server. If successful, the attack overloads the server and legitimate requests are denied because the server does not have the resources to respond. The Computer Emergency Response Team Coordination Center (CERT/CC), formed by the United States Department of Defense in 1988, warns that *any* system linked to the Internet is subject to DoS attacks.[15]

"Technically speaking, these attacks are one step up from spray paint on the highway overpass."[16] The ease of obtaining software designed to launch DoS and other types of attacks is a major concern of security experts. Software capable of orchestrating such attacks is readily available on the Internet, free of charge. Organizations should do all they can to assess and to mitigate the risk of downtime in primary systems and should actively plan for the contingency of a denial-of-service problem. Managers need to be aware of the denial-of-service risks and ensure that these risks have been properly addressed.

DoS attacks still pose a significant threat to companies even two years after the widely publicized attacks on eBay and Yahoo!. Since then, several technologies have emerged that help users detect and respond to DoS attacks far more quickly and effectively than before. But the increasingly sophisticated attack methods and the growing range of systems targeted in DoS attacks continue to pose a challenge. During a three-week period in

---

Text Box 4.2 World Economic Forum Web Site Crashed; DoS Attack Possible

The World Economic Forum (WEF) had planned to share highlights and live session broadcasts of its annual meeting in New York City with the public through its Web site, but that site went down since the meeting opened on January 31, 2002.

"We don't know what's causing the site problems. Your guess is as good as ours," said WEF director of communications Charles McLean. High traffic is a likely cause, he said, but the WEF isn't sure whether traffic spikes are coming from reporters and the public or from protestors deliberately hitting the site in a denial-of-service (DoS) attack.

A group called the Electronic Disturbance Theater (EDT) had been trying to arrange a denial-of-service attack on the WEF site, encouraging visitors to its own Web site to download a "virtual sit-in tool" to flood the WEF site with traffic.

Based on traffic reports logging the number of unique visitors to the EDT Web site, the group estimates that about 100,000 people from around the world are participating in its protest, according to EDT co-founder Ricardo Dominguez. That number probably isn't enough to crash the WEF site, he said.

"I think that something else happened to the WEF URL or, perhaps, the WEF infrastructure is as badly built as the WEF's economic vision during the last 31 years," Dominguez said via e-mail.

More than 81,000 unique visitors hit the EDT's protest Web site yesterday, Dominguez said; about 43,000 of those visitors downloaded the program to flood the WEF site. The day before the WEF meeting opened, 39,349 unique visitors were logged at the protest site.

Adapted from: Stacy Cowley, "World Economic Forum Web site crashed; DoS attack possible," *Computerworld*, www.computerworld.com, February 1, 2002.

mid-2001, researchers from the University of California, San Diego, detected approximately 12,800 DoS attacks against more than 5,000 targets. Recent examples include attacks against the World Economic Forum's Web site in February (see Text Box 4.2), as well as those that drove British Internet service provider CloudNine Communications out of business in 2002.[17]

Degradation-of-service attacks represent a variation on a conventional DoS attack. Such assaults, which are more difficult to detect than other DoS attacks, involve short-lived bursts of spurious traffic directed at a target from multiple sources and are aimed at slowing network performance.[18]

Another specific type of denial-of-service attack is called a **distributed denial-of-service (DDoS)** attack. In this type of attack, DDoS programs are surreptitiously planted in several hundred computers, called **zombies**. At a later time, the attacker activates the zombies which, unbeknownst to their owners, then launch hundreds of thousands of packet transmissions, all aimed at a single target. Distributed attacks not only damage the victim's system, but may also damage the systems used to execute the attack. The attacks launched against Yahoo!, Buy.com, eBay, and other e-business sites discussed in the introduction to this chapter were DDoS attacks.

Other Forms of Service Interruptions

As the example at the beginning of the chapter illustrates, a denial-of-service attack can be so severe that it causes a system outage—the entire system being brought to a halt. Service disruptions can result from intentional attacks or from unintentional infrastructure vulnerabilities. CyberSource, an e-business security provider, has identified five different types of outages: physical, design, operations, environmental, and reconfiguration.[19]

Physical. Physical outages are caused by hardware failures. Worn or broken components can result in service-level downtime. In addition, lack of sufficient resources dedicated to a function and the resulting lack of service capacity can lead to unacceptable slowdowns and outages. One example of a physical outage occurred in August 1999, when a frame-relay outage at WorldCom caused the Chicago Board of Trade to lose all electronic trading capabilities. Apparently, neither WorldCom nor the Chicago Board of Trade had adequate contingency plans, causing the Chicago Board of Trade to lose valuable time and money until the network service company was able to get back online.[20] As discussed on pp. 85–86, control techniques such as the use of "hot sites" and "mirroring" can reduce the risk of an outage from hardware failures.

Design. Faulty hardware or software products can also be the cause of a service outage. According to market research firm the Standish Group, software flaws cost United States businesses $100 billion in lost productivity in 2000. In February 2000, The NASDAQ Stock Exchange, Inc. suffered an outage when a problem in a communications feed to one of its mainframe computers caused the NASDAQ Composite Index to be frozen for two-and-a-half hours. Stock prices remained unchanged until the company solved the problem, after which time the information queued in the system prevented real-time updates for an additional time period. This kind of down time is extremely expensive.

Operations. Errors or malicious acts by operations personnel are sometimes the cause of outages. A company insider with administrative access to a network can wreak havoc on an organization's information system. Outsiders can also sometimes gain access to the "inner workings" of a company's information system by "hacking" through the controls that may be in place to prevent unauthorized access.

Environmental. Natural disasters and war are examples of the environmental outage category. Natural disasters may come in the form of flood, fire, tornado, or earthquake. As discussed on pp. 85–86, the effects of these events can be mitigated through the establishment of disaster recovery plans and distributed operations in hardened facilities.

Reconfiguration. Reconfiguration activities include software upgrades, database work, hardware changes, and any other change to an information system. Reconfiguration is usually a planned activity that often requires the system to be shut down for a period of time. In traditional IT operations, it is common to schedule regular system downtime to accommodate maintenance activities. Most e-businesses try to avoid planned outages, but IBM, before selling its Internet access service to AT&T, regularly scheduled about two hours of planned downtime each week! (Clearly this practice could not last long.) Besides causing temporary planned outages, reconfiguration can also cause unintended subsequent outages. As an analogy, most household light bulbs typically fail when the power switch is turned on, because the act of turning on power generates a voltage surge that can overpower the relatively weak filament in the bulb. Just as turning on the light is a high-risk activity for a lamp, applying software, hardware, or operational-process changes is a high-risk activity for an information system. In a complex system, it is not always obvious what the precise impact of a particular change will be (for example, see Text Box 4.3). Thorough testing and contingency planning are necessary to ensure the absence or timely mitigation of unintended consequences.

Data Theft

Theft of electronic data is a concern for both businesses and consumers. IT managers and assurance providers should be aware of the critical points in an e-business infrastructure at which data can be stolen. A business running a Web site with its own server might house sensitive information relating to other businesses or customers that could be accessed by inside employees or hackers. For example, in December 1999, over 300,000 credit card numbers were stolen from CD Universe, an Internet music retailer. Some of the numbers were later posted on the Internet.[21] Customer information stored in an Internet service provider's database may also be vulnerable to theft.

Text Box 4.3 Sometimes the Cure Is Worse than the Disease

Planned technological upgrades can cause unplanned and costly downtime. Royal Doulton, a manufacturer of fine china for more than 200 years, planned to avoid potential Y2K problems by installing a new computer system. Their efforts resulted in losses of up to $19 million in sales due to shipping delays attributed to the new system. The problems occurred just as Royal Doulton was preparing for the Christmas season, typically their best sales period. In a similar event, Hershey lost candy sales around the lucrative Halloween season because a new information system could not accurately track shipments and inventory levels.

See "Y2K 'fix' cost firm $19M in sales," *USA Today*, November 11, 1999.

Sniffing

Sniffing is a term used to describe the viewing of information that passes along a network communication channel. Specialized hardware **sniffers** may be attached to a network to monitor or record all traffic passing through the network. Sniffing software is also readily available and can be used legitimately by managers to monitor message and data flow within a company's e-business infrastructure. An example of a sniffing package is the Federal Bureau of Investigation's monitoring program, DCS1000, formerly called Carnivore. This program, when attached to an ISP, allows the FBI to tag packets of suspicious information that pass through the ISP's network. Unfortunately, unauthorized parties can also use sniffing techniques to capture passwords or other sensitive information. Sniffing is effective only when the data are transferred in plain-text form or if the perpetrator has a key that enables decryption of encoded messages. Thus, **encryption** techniques such as Secure Sockets Layer (SSL) are useful in protecting information as it passes through a public network (for more information on encryption, see the brief discussion on encryption in this chapter and the toolbox in Appendix C).

Unauthorized Access to Passwords

In today's interconnected world of e-business, password protection is often the only barrier to unauthorized access. If you have ever accessed your bank account online you know that all it takes to conduct transactions on your account are your account number and password. One of the greatest security risks to an organization is poor password administration. According to Ernst & Young LLP expert Eric Schultze, recent heightened security awareness in the IT world has not been sufficient to increase password effectiveness in many company networks.[22]

Backup and test servers are often found to have weak passwords. Hence, these computers are common targets for hackers. Lax password controls frequently result in stolen information and disruption of a system's integrity. The integrity of an IT infrastructure is highly dependent on the effectiveness of the chosen password policies and controls.

The protection of an organization's e-business infrastructure should be high on the list of priorities, for obvious reasons. Some of the controls that should be in place to guard against IT infrastructure vulnerabilities are discussed in the next section.

Controlling Risks Associated with Infrastructure Vulnerabilities

Disaster Recovery Plan

Companies stand to lose millions of dollars in equipment, software, and sensitive information when a disaster strikes. Enterprises should prepare to minimize the effects of disasters by having a good **disaster recovery plan**. A disaster recovery or contingency plan delineates general responses of an organization to unusual or unanticipated events (see Text Box 4.4, p. 86). A good disaster recovery plan includes regular backups of the enterprise's data—such as customer information and accounting files. Backup storage devices should be kept separate from the primary premises.

Another important component of a good disaster recovery plan for an e-business can involve the use of "flying start," "hot," or "cold" sites. A **flying start site** is a backup facility outfitted with everything an organization needs to continue its operations on very short notice in the event the primary system fails for any reason.

> ### Text Box 4.4 KPMG Security Survey
>
> Eleven percent of the companies that report having a disaster recovery plan have never actually tested the plan. Approximately half had tested their plan in the last six months. Eighty-four percent of responding companies reported to have a plan in place in the event of a loss to the computer equipment in the company.
>
> Reported in *The Toronto Star*, June 7, 2000.

A flying start site has computer equipment and software already installed, ready to take over in an instant. These sites may actually process primary transactions in **shadow mode**, doing everything the primary system does so that if a transition is necessary, operations continue uninterrupted. Switching from a primary system to an online backup can be done automatically. A **hot site** is similar to a flying start site except that time must be allowed for critical data files to be transferred to the site so that processing can begin. A **cold site**, on the other hand, is essentially an empty alternate location that allows for an entity to set up its operations in the event the organization must leave its own facility. A complete disaster recovery plan for an e-business, including alternate back-up sites, can cost millions of dollars to put into place. Of course, an essential aspect of an effective disaster recovery plan is that the plan must be tested regularly. The need to practice, practice, and practice cannot be overemphasized (see Text Box 4.4).

Software-Based Security

Information security is clearly critical in an e-business environment (see Text Box 4.5), and software-based security packages are an essential part of controlling risks relating directly to infrastructure vulnerabilities. Several different types of software security packages exist, including firewalls, intrusion detection packages, scanners or security probes, and security suites.

Firewalls. **Firewalls** are software applications designed to block unauthorized access to files, directories, and networks. Firewalls are used extensively in the e-business community and are even available to individual users with Internet connections (even home users with always-on digital subscriber line connections should deploy firewalls, especially if they use a static IP address). As with other electronic security software programs, firewalls are secure only if they are configured properly. One study, reported by the International Computer Security Association, found that 70 percent of companies using firewalls were still vulnerable to unauthorized access.[23] These vulnerabilities are primarily due to the fact that firewalls are essentially "perimeter" controls. That is, they provide security unless a hacker finds an open door, such as a modem pool that is not password protected—once inside the "perimeter" defined by a firewall, the firewall is irrelevant.

There are many types of firewalls, each varying in purpose, complexity, and functionality. One of the most powerful is known as a proxy firewall. Packet-filtering firewalls are another type of firewall. A more technical discussion of firewalls is contained in the technology toolbox on firewalls in Appendix D.

Text Box 4.6 Microsoft Updates IIS Security Holes

Microsoft Corp. released a patch that fixes ten security holes in various versions of the Internet Informa-tion Server (IIS) component of Windows NT 4.0, Windows 2000, and Windows XP that allows an Inter-net-attached computer to publish Web pages. The most serious of the flaws could allow an attacker to take over computers running IIS, moving Microsoft to label the cumulative patch "critical" and to urge all customers hosting Web sites using the affected software to install the patch immediately.

Microsoft said it found two of the flaws itself, possibly as part of the effort to clean up its code. The software maker thanks various security vendors and experts for reporting the other vulnerabilities. Sys-tems administrators are cautioned to read the caveats section in Microsoft security bulletin MS02-018 before applying the patch. This reflects the fact that "patches" have a spotted history—mostly they work well, but on occasion a patch can make things worse. Caveat administrator.

Adapted from: Joris Evers, "Microsoft Fixes 10 Flaws with 'Critical' Patch for IIS," *Computerworld*, April 10, 2002.

---

been properly secured, so security probes can be very helpful in testing systems as they are deployed in actual operation.

Security Suites. **Security suites** offer users multiple security mechanisms in one pack-age, including such tools as firewalls, security probes, virus protection programs, and cookie detection/management abilities. Users looking for a particular security feature may evaluate the features of a certain suite to match the user's security preferences. For example, Aladdin Knowledge Systems' eSafe Protect, which covers a variety of security threats, includes a program for users to test downloaded files, thus protecting the system from being infected by a virus or other malicious code.

Encryption

One of the most effective ways to protect confidential or sensitive information from be-ing "sniffed" or stolen is through the use of encryption technology. For example, **public key encryption** allows information to be sent in an encrypted format over unsecured networks like the Internet. Public key encryption has achieved widespread use to protect data and ensure privacy in the e-business world. In a public-key arrangement, the parties who will be communicating have two keys, one that is made public and another that is held private. These keys are inversely related: if one key is used to lock a message, the other must be used to unlock it. Thus, a message locked by a public key can be read only by the party holding the private key. Similarly, a message that can be unlocked by a par-ticular public key could have originated only from the party holding the corresponding private key. Public-key encryption can thus be used both for **privacy** (by locking a mes-sage with the intended recipient's public key) and for **authenticity** (by locking a message with the originator's private key). The basic principle behind this kind of cryptography has existed for centuries, but the demand for secure e-business communications is creat-ing a demand for ever more advanced forms of cryptography. Encryption over Web con-nections is often handled by technologies such as Secure Sockets Layer (SSL) described in Appendix C (also see Text Box 4.7).

An important note about SSL and other encryption techniques is that they protect data only as it travels from point to point. Once the message has reached its destination, it is

---

Text Box 4.5 Corporate Information Systems Remain Vulnerable after 9/11

Despite heightened awareness of the need for security since the September 11 (9/11) attacks, many corrate information systems (IS) remain dangerously vulnerable to cyber attacks, according to the "14th /nual Critical Issues of Information Systems Study" by Computer Sciences Corp. (CSC), an informat technology consulting firm.

In a post-9/11 addendum to the international survey of more than 1,000 information technology exec tives, 46 percent of respondents report not having a formal information security policy in place. Additic ally, 68 percent fail to conduct security risk analyses or track security status regularly, and 59 percent not have a formal compliance program to support their IS function.

Completed one month before the terrorist attacks on the World Trade Center and Pentagon, the origin survey asked executives to select which issues were most important to their organizations. The techno ogy executives listed getting maximum value from their existing enterprise system and optimizing orga izational effectiveness, principally by partnering with senior management, as their top two prioriti respectively. Eliminating system vulnerabilities to minimize risks and to safeguard information resourc ranked only fifth. However, findings from the addendum indicate that, following 9/11, information sec rity has become a top priority for North American IS executives as well as for financial services exec tives around the world.

Adapted from: "CSC Survey Reveals Inadequate Information Security Practices among Companies Worldwide," Computer Sciences Corp. Press Release, www.csc.com, November 19, 2001.

Intrusion Detection. Intrusion detection software constantly monitors a system and components. Intrusion detection notifies users of unauthorized entrance into the syste as well as inappropriate use of system components by authorized users. In essence, intr sion detection acts as a filter to alert management to any peculiar activity relating to t system. Such activity may take many forms, such as abnormal sales prices, repeated u successful attempts to enter a secure area, or a breakdown of a security application with the system.

Not only do these detection systems have the ability to alert management of unauthorize entrance into the system, but they can also be immediately reactive. When an intrusic detection system is set up, management can program it to proactively limit access when detects an intruder or possible security violation. For example, if an intrusion detectio system detects repeated unsuccessful attempts to log on to a user account, it can immedi ately lock that user's account until cleared by the network administrator.

Scanners or Security Probes. **Security probes**, also called **scanners**, test the strength o security measures by actively probing a network for vulnerabilities. The SATAN and COPS probes, available for free on the Web, are examples of general security probes Password cracking programs such as Cracker are another form of probe. There are many known weaknesses in the major operating systems and Web servers available today, and more problems are discovered continually. Security probes use known weaknesses to attempt to break into systems. Vendors release patches to fix known problems (see Text Box 4.6, p. 88), but as with the Egghead example, companies do not always apply these patches immediately. This is not to say that users are incompetent; keep in mind that applying a patch also exposes a system to risk inherent in system reconfiguration. And there are so many software patches that it is not always clear which patches need to be applied to a particular system.[24] It is exceedingly difficult to know when systems have

---

Text Box 4.7 Amazon.com Web Site Security Description

We guarantee that every transaction you make at Amazon.com will be safe. This means you pay nothing if unauthorized charges are made to your card as a result of shopping at Amazon.com.... Why is Amazon.com so safe? Safety in Numbers: When you shop at Amazon.com, you'll be one of millions of customers who have safely shopped with us without credit card fraud.

Safe Technology: *Our Secure Sockets Layer (SSL) software is the industry standard and among the best software available today for secure online commerce transactions. It **encrypts all of your personal information**, including credit card number, name, and address, so that it cannot be read as the information travels over the Internet.*

Source: www.amazon.com, May 2002.

---

no longer encrypted. Protection of data behind a Web site must be afforded by other security mechanisms, such as firewalls. As you will see later in this chapter, encryption technology is also very important in controlling the risks associated with falsified identity and compromised privacy.

Physical Controls

Physical controls deal primarily with physical access to a company's network and e-business resources. These controls are important in any business enterprise, including e-businesses. Physical controls relate particularly to e-businesses in the sense that in addition to software-based security, the software and hardware that make up the IT infrastructure must be physically secure. For example, only authorized personnel should have access to computers and servers that store sensitive information. All routers, switches, and servers should be placed in locked and secured rooms that only network administrators can access. These rooms should not be near any high traffic areas or in areas accessible to the general public. Access to network administrative offices should be physically restricted to essential personnel only. Sometimes physical infrastructure is so sensitive and critical to e-business operations that the system is placed in a **hardened** facility that can withstand substantial physical attacks or natural disasters.

Equally important, computers are shrinking in size and becoming easier targets for thieves. Computer equipment should be physically secured. For example, multiple PCs on desks or tables can be linked together and locked down. Controls should also be in place to limit the amount of confidential information that is downloaded to laptops, which are easily—and often—stolen. When it is necessary to store confidential information on laptops or removable disks, encryption technology should be used to secure the data in case of physical theft.

Password Selection and Change

Passwords are a vital part of the security of any electronic system, but they often constitute a weak link in a system's security, because they involve people. Passwords generated randomly by the system are difficult to remember. Having too many passwords, a common situation, also make it hard to remember passwords. Thus, people often write down their passwords (even self-chosen passwords) and keep them nearby, in a desk drawer, under the keyboard, or even on sticky notes attached to the monitor. A written

---

Text Box 4.8 EBay Plugs Password Hole

Online auction powerhouse eBay Inc. closed a security hole in a password-maintenance feature on April 3, 2002 that could have allowed attackers to take over a user's account and commit fraud. The vulnerability existed in the feature that allowed registered eBay users to change the passwords they use to log-in to the site. The feature has since been fixed and put back online. The vulnerability would have allowed an attacker who knew the publicly available name used by an eBay member to change that user's password, thereby taking over the account. eBay was first notified that the attack was possible by an eBay user. Although the potential existed for attackers to access accounts, unlike Egghead, credit card information was not available to them because eBay stores that data on separate servers not accessible through the Web.

Adapted from: Sam Costello, "EBay Closes Password Security Hole," *Computerworld*, April 3, 2002.

---

password near a network access point represents a serious security problem because unauthorized users can easily find the password and gain access to the system.

At the same time, passwords created by individual users without proper guidelines can often be easily cracked. For example, many users create passwords that are easy to remember. An employee's password may be based on such easily available information as name, birth date, or job title. Unless the system requires periodic password changes, an employee's password may remain unchanged until he or she is replaced. Easily cracked passwords represent a common security weakness. Software that manages passwords must also be carefully tested to ensure it is secure (for example, see Text Box 4.8).

In view of the importance of passwords for maintaining the security of an enterprise's e-business infrastructure, the company should have a formal policy governing the creation of acceptable passwords. Employees should be instructed to avoid using passwords that contain the employee's name, birth date, or job title. The company should also use a password program that requires users of confidential data to change their passwords on a regular basis. In addition, the company should have a clearly communicated policy regarding disclosure of passwords to third parties. As will be discussed later in this chapter, intruders often get passwords simply by calling users and claiming to be a network administrator. Employees should be taught to never disclose their passwords over the telephone or in an e-mail message.

In a recent graduate-level class, we performed a small experiment. We explained how to choose a secure password (see Text Box 4.9), had the students each select a password, and then ran a freely available password-cracking program on the encrypted passwords. Despite our "end-user training," a significant number of the chosen passwords were easily cracked. Enterprises that do not employ rigorous password standards (and periodically scan for weak passwords) also suffer significant password-related weaknesses.

Falsified Identity: Risks and Controls

Risks Associated with Falsified Identity

As Figure 4.1 (p. 80) indicates, falsified identity is a major source of exposure and risk in conducting e-business. For an electronic transaction to take place, each party to the transaction needs to be confident that the claimed identity of the other party is authentic.

Text Box 4.9 Choosing a Secure Password

Modern computer systems are powerful enough to exhaustively search all possible passwords less than 7 or 8 characters long. Sophisticated password-cracking software also uses dictionaries and rules to guess passwords. Any proper name or word that would be found in a dictionary is highly vulnerable to cracking, because cracking software can search millions of possibilities very quickly. Cracking software also applies common rules like appending a single digit to a word, reversing the word, or trying variations of the user ID. We recommend choosing an 8-letter password that uses at least one digit or other nonalphabetic character, and that uses a mixture of upper- and lowercase letters. Sometimes a pronounceable nonsense phrase can be encoded, such as I83#cats. If you use a mnemonic device to create an easily memorized password, be sure it is not a simple combination of words like chosen1 or your user ID followed by a digit.

These threats are less of a concern in traditional electronic data interchange (EDI) settings because traditional EDI involves relatively limited access points, dedicated lines, and established value-added network providers as intermediaries. But authenticity is a significant concern for transactions conducted through electronic channels in an Internet-based e-business environment. It is also a major concern for individual consumers—identity theft is now the leading source of consumer fraud, with an estimated 500,000 to 700,000 victims a year![25] Hackers with even a minimal level of sophistication cloak their identity when going about their malicious activities. E-mail spoofing, IP spoofing, and false Web sites are examples of risks associated with identification and authenticity.

E-Mail Spoofing

Hackers can hide their identity by simply changing the information in an e-mail header. Unauthorized access often results when an imposter, posing as a computer support technician or network manager, convinces employees to divulge passwords and other confidential information. Kevin Mitnick, arguably the world's most notorious convicted hacker, claims he seldom had to resort to high-tech methods to penetrate computer networks. Instead, he most often simply tricked insiders into sharing passwords and other secrets that allowed easy access.[26]

E-mail spoofing can also be associated with virus transfers and "spam" mail. **Spam** is any unsolicited e-mail message, usually advertising a service or product, generally sent in bulk to many recipients. **Spammers** often operate under a falsified e-mail address. Viruses created for the purpose of corrupting a victim's system and sent through e-mail are also often sent under a false e-mail address. Text Box 4.10 (p. 92) illustrates the steps that one government is taking to fight back against the use of spam in a fraud scheme.

IP Spoofing

Some security measures, such as firewalls, may be configured to disallow access to incoming requests with certain IP addresses. By changing the IP address to one that the security system will not block, an unauthorized person can sometimes gain access to the system. One risk associated with a spoofed IP address is that legitimate e-mail may be sent to an imposter instead of the legitimate party. One of the best defenses against a spoofed address is a good firewall (see Appendix D). If configured incorrectly, however, firewalls can leave valuable information exposed to many security threats—including theft or alteration.

Text Box 4.10 Nigerian Government Fighting Back Against e-Fraud

Have you received an e-mail claiming to be from Nigerian government officials or petroleum executives trying to smuggle money out of their country? It's an old scam in a modern package.

The Nigerian government is apparently tired of it too. The African nation recently created a Web site to target the scheme, offer tips on combating fraud, and offer advice on making legitimate investments in Nigeria. The site targets the most common scam, in which the spammer says he is a government official who has a large amount of money that he wants to get out of Nigeria. In the e-mail, the spammer says he is looking for help and usually asks for a processing fee, a bank account number, or a blank sheet of corporate letterhead.

The site also describes other scams, including an appeal for Americans to coach basketball in Nigeria and asking for a $150 registration fee. Another scam offers the recipient 20 percent of millions of dollars held in a Nigerian bank account that is supposedly held by a businessman who died in a plane crash. The e-mail recipient is asked to stake a claim of being the deceased person's next of kin, and a fee is requested to process the will.

Adapted from: Brian Sullivan, "Nigeria Launches Web Site to Target E-Mail Scams," *Computerworld*, March 26, 2002.

Customer Impersonation

Like traditional businesses that accept checks or credit cards, e-businesses face the burden of verifying customer identity. If a consumer has falsified his or her identity, businesses can lose money on fraudulent requests for products or services. Viruses are frequently associated with impersonations and false identities. Companies should strive to minimize dealing unknowingly with impersonators; such associations may not only be costly, but may also taint a company's reputation.

False Web Sites

Also called **false storefronts**, **false Web sites** are set up to grab confidential information, leading to further misdeeds. For example, a false Web site might look like the site of a real bank or online retailer and have the capability to collect identification and credit card numbers from unsuspecting customers. This is a variation of the old **Trojan horse** scam, in which a hacker logs on to a shared computer system and then runs a program that looks like the main log-on screen. The next user to access the computer sees what appears to be a legitimate log-on prompt, and enters the user ID and password as usual. But instead of logging on to the system, the data is captured by the Trojan horse, which then terminates itself so that a subsequent attempt to log on will be successful, and the user can be tricked into thinking the initial failure was just a mistyped password. To combat this type of attack, Windows NT uses the Control-Alt-Delete sequence as a secure mechanism for accessing a log-on screen. To combat false Web sites, it is imperative that e-businesses use secure servers (i.e., SSL encryption) and digital certificates.

A legitimate Web site may also be altered to contain false information, as in the case when hackers broke into the Web site of Aastrom Biosciences, Inc., a biotechnology company in Ann Arbor, Michigan. The hackers indicated on the company's Web page that Aastrom would be merging with competitor Geron Corporation, of California. The news of the merger sent shares of the two companies skyrocketing on Wall Street. The

Text Box 4.11 Is It Really a $138,805 Diebenkorn?

In May 2000, an eBay participant using the alias of "golfpoorly" offered a painting he claimed he picked up at a yard sale. His wife, he said, made him store the piece in the garage, where it suffered slight damage by his child. The painting is signed "RD '52," causing some to speculate that it might be an early piece by the late abstractionist Richard Diebenkorn. The painting was sold for $138,805. Unfortunately for the buyer, the painting was not likely a Diebenkorn. Mr. "golfpoorly" turned out to be Kenneth A. Walton, an unmarried Sacramento lawyer who had previously sold 33 different paintings on eBay under a variety of aliases, and who had previously been threatened with legal action on one of the prior sales. eBay tracks sales to detect potential fraud and when this sale was posted, eBay immediately stepped in and voided the sale. Walton has been suspended from further sales on the eBay Web site.

Adapted from: "IsItAGenuineDiebenkorn.com?" *Newsweek*, May 22, 2000.

hack was later exposed, and both companies indicated they had no intentions to merge.[27] (Based on the market's reaction, perhaps subsequent merger discussions might have been a good idea!)

E-Mail or Web-Visit Hijacking

E-mail messages and Web visits can be **hijacked** because Internet host names can be subtly different. For example, computer.com and computer.org are two completely different host names that could easily be confused. If the two names are owned by different entities, one site could mimic the other and trick users into thinking they are dealing with the original. Such an attack can also fall into the false storefront category described above. E-mail can be hijacked in a similar fashion. E-mail hijacking is made easier in part because many companies run their e-mail systems and Web sites using the same address. Often the addition or omission of a single hyphen or letter is enough to send the e-mail to the wrong recipient.

E-mail hijacking has affected law firms and political campaigns as well as businesses. For example, confidential information and e-mail addresses have unintentionally been lost to outside parties. Although some may question the legality of e-mail hijacking, some "e-mail pirates" consider the receiving of someone else's e-mail as similar to answering the phone and finding that someone has called the wrong number. On the other hand, companies claim that trademark laws are being violated and that the slightly different Web site names deceive customers. Another problem with e-mail hijacking is that the sender does not know if the e-mail reached its proper destination, as no "undeliverable" message will be returned to the sender in such a case.

An important security measure to protect against e-mail and Web-visit hijacking is the practice of registering all variations of a host name, including common typographical errors. For example, ShoesForLess.com might also want to own Shoes-For-Less.com, Shoe-For-Less.com, and ShoesForLess.org (among many others), in order to keep customers from landing on a competitor's site or sending information to an illegitimate destination.

Controlling the Risks Associated with Falsified Identity

The evolution of e-business has caused a shift in the area of identity issues. Traditional EDI users usually do not have concerns about the authenticity of a party to a transaction because most exchanges take place between known partners, between whom a formal contract is usually in force. With the emergence of the Internet as the primary vehicle for e-business, the potential exists for a virtually unlimited number of parties to attempt to initiate transactions. There is clearly a need for controls that allow for authentication and identification in an e-business environment.

Digital Signatures and Certificates

Digital signatures and **certificates** are important keys in managing identification concerns in e-business. Just as a signature on a paper document serves as authorization or verification of a procedure or important information, a digital signature provides beneficiaries the reassurance that, for example, the e-mail message received or the order placed is valid. As discussed previously, encryption is used to protect data against sniffing and other forms of unauthorized access. However, encryption is also an important component in the use of digital signatures and certificates, which help verify the identity of an unseen partner. As discussed in the previous section, encryption and SSL technologies involve identity verification procedures prior to initiating transactions (also see Appendix C).

Tokens and Biometrics

Tokens are electronic devices issued to specific individuals; the most common token is a form of "smart card." Authentication is stronger when an individual both produces a token and offers a biometric measure to gain access to an information system.[28]

Biometrics is one of the most promising areas of technology and systems security, involving the use of unique features of the human body to create secure access controls. Because each human possesses unique biological characteristics (e.g., iris and retina patterns, fingerprints, voice tones, facial structures, writing styles), scientists have been able to develop specialized security devices that have the potential to be highly accurate in authenticating a party's individual identity. A biometric access control process is implemented by first obtaining a biometric reading from a user and creating a reference template by abstracting the biometric reading. For subsequent access attempts, the system takes another reading and compares it with the reference template. Access is granted or denied based on how similar the subsequent reading is to the reference template.

Biometrics still has barriers to overcome before IT managers will feel confident using the technology on a large-scale basis. For example, the false accept/reject rate of some biometrics systems is unacceptably high for use in high-security applications. A false acceptance rate refers to the number of times the biometrics program allows an unauthorized user to enter the system. A false rejection rate indicates how often the program disallows entrance to an authorized person. These are potential barriers to the wide acceptance of biometrics techniques. The rejection of authorized personnel may cause frustration, and some people simply feel uncomfortable about engaging in a retinal scan or other biometrics test. However, we expect to see a continued increase in the use of biometrics for access control because biometric approaches do not suffer from the same shortcomings as password-based systems. See Table 4.1 for a presentation of the effectiveness of various types of biometric scanning devices.

Table 4.1 Comparison of Biometric Technologies[29]

Biometric	Univer-sality	Unique-ness	Perma-nence	Collect-ability	Perfor-mance	Accept-ability	Circum-vention
Face	High	Low	Medium	High	Low	High	Low
Fingerprint	Medium	High	High	Medium	High	Medium	High
Hand Geometry	Medium	Medium	Medium	High	Medium	Medium	Medium
Iris	High	High	High	Medium	High	Low	High
Retinal scan	High	High	Medium	Low	High	Low	High
Signature	Low	Low	Low	High	Low	High	Low
Voice print	Medium	Low	Low	Medium	Low	High	Low
Keystrokes	Low	Low	Low	Medium	Low	Medium	Medium

Compromised Privacy: Risks and Controls

Risks Associated with Compromised Privacy

Figure 4.1 (p. 80) indicates that compromised privacy is another primary source of risk and exposure in e-business. Many consumers are concerned that their privacy may be violated if they engage in e-business transactions. Several recent surveys have found that the biggest concerns of shoppers who buy over the Internet are privacy and security.[30] And online shoppers have good reason to be concerned. Many of the risks associated with privacy are created by organizations with lax internal control. Other privacy risks stem from situations wherein companies collect information on consumers who visit Web sites. The issue of compromised privacy is an important consideration for e-business enterprises, because if consumers suspect that an e-business might not actively preserve and protect their privacy, they are less likely to interact with that enterprise (see Text Box 4.12). Despite the lip service many companies pay to privacy, the past several years have witnessed a string of embarrassing privacy snafus. For example, even Amazon was recently caught gathering more personal information about customers than the shoppers could possibly have known by reading the site's privacy policy. In response, outraged consumers filed a number of class action lawsuits.[31]

Consumers have reason to be wary even if a Web site has an explicit privacy policy. For example, InfoBeat, ReverseAuction, and RealNetworks have all been accused of sharing

---

Text Box 4.12 Consumers Concerned about On-Line Privacy

According to a Harris Interactive study sponsored by the American Institute of Certified Pulic Accountants (AICPA) and Ernst & Young, the misuse of customer information poses a significant risk to business. In fact, 83 percent of consumers said they would stop doing business entirely with companies if they find that a company misuses customer information. Conversely, the poll also shows that companies with good privacy practices stand to gain customer loyalty; almost 50 percent of consumers said they would buy more frequently and in greater volume from businesses that establish strong, trustworthy privacy practices.

Adapted from: *The Journal Entry,* 82, no. 4 (April 2002): 18.

information that they promised not to share. As another example, the California Health-Care Foundation recently sponsored a study of the actual privacy provided by 21 popular health-related sites. It found that most of the sites betray their visitors, sometimes even violating their own explicit privacy policies. The study concluded that advertisers on those sites may be able to obtain visitors' names and addresses, and that third parties may even be able obtain personal information that visitors voluntarily provide regarding personal health.[32]

Privacy advocates argue that the problem will grow even larger as violations of privacy become increasingly invasive. For example, some fear that Web marketers will formulate behavioral profiles that could be sold to any party willing to pay. Further, consumer behavior on the Web might be compiled into electronic dossiers and subpoenaed for court cases, such as divorce or custody suits.

In 1999, DoubleClick.com announced plans to correlate information gathered from Web site users with actual names, phone numbers, home addresses, and a host of other personal information. After DoubleClick purchased Abacus Direct, which operates a huge database of consumer purchasing data consisting of almost 3 billion transactions, a firestorm of concern erupted. The controversy caused the *Wall Street Journal* to conclude, "the online-advertising colossus [DoubleClick] has rapidly gone from a dot-com darling with an inside track on e-business to an Internet-privacy pariah."[33] The public outcry finally forced DoubleClick to stop its efforts to tie Web information to consumer data until industry and government agreed on privacy standards. As a result of the controversy, DoubleClick now has a strong privacy policy, including allowing customers to opt out of "**cookies**." The United States Federal Trade Commission, which investigated DoubleClick's data collection practices, indicates that only 41 percent of the most popular Web sites adequately inform customers of their privacy policies, and only 20 percent of Web sites live up to all of the "fair information practices" the FTC is pushing the on-line community to adopt.[34]

The level of concern generated by DoubleClick's plans illustrates that e-businesses ignore customer privacy concerns at their peril.[35] If consumers fear that their privacy will

---

Text Box 4.13 The Coveted E-Mail Address

The *Wall Street Journal* reported that Sony Music Entertainment, a division of Sony Corporation and owner of a popular Internet newsletter service called InfoBeat, sent e-mail addresses of people who receive its newsletter to advertisers in spite of a promise of confidentiality, which reads as follows: "We will NEVER release, sell, or give a subscriber's name or e-mail address to any other party or organization, without the subscriber's explicit permission." Online shoppers who did not give consent to have their e-mail addresses released were unable to maintain the confidentiality of their e-mail addresses if they clicked on the ad banners of two advertisers. A computer security consultant in Massachusetts was the person to bring the e-mail address leakage to the attention of InfoBeat. This same consultant also found another security problem with InfoBeat's newsletter. By looking at the source code on the newsletter he received, he found his date of birth, which he was required to give to InfoBeat in order to subscribe to the newsletter. This meant all the personal information of InfoBeat customers was available to all subscribers—including street addresses, phone numbers, and even the stocks the individual customers requested to follow in their personal newsletter.

Adapted from: "Sony's Infobeat Leaked Data On User E-Mail To Advertisers," *Wall Street Journal*, November 8, 1999.

not be protected, they will be less willing to interact with businesses over the Web. E-businesses that fail to protect customer privacy may also face legal liability and litigation. For example, in March 2002, Citibank agreed to pay $1.6 million to settle complaints by 27 states that it had been providing private data to telemarketers who were using that data to trick customers into unwittingly buying club memberships, roadside assistance, and dental plans.[36]

Cookies are small files generated by Web sites (see Text Box 4.15, p. 98, and further discussion on cookies in Appendix B, a toolbox on Web technology). Through a facility built into the online shopper's Web browser, cookies are saved, often without the PC user's knowledge, to the hard drive of the user's PC. When a user requests a Web page from a server, any cookies that have been marked for transmission to that server are first sent. Cookies are usually used to store a marker that helps a Web site identify the user on a return visit. Some firms use cookies to enhance efficiency for the user. For example, Amazon.com uses cookies to automatically identify you when you return to their site, so it is faster to complete a purchase. By using cookies to uniquely identify visitors, Web sites can more accurately track customer buying habits and preferences. Using this information, the sites can tailor advertisements and Web page content for each user.

A subtle aspect to cookies that is not appreciated by most users is that they can be used to track user visits across multiple Web sites. For example, consider the sites that display DoubleClick-brokered banner ads. The banner ad is served from a DoubleClick Web server, and this gives the DoubleClick server an opportunity to place a cookie on the user's PC. Each request to download a DoubleClick ad indicates the uniform resource locator (URL) of the Web page that contains the ad. By recording the URL's of all Web pages for a user and using cookies to uniquely identify users, DoubleClick can tell where a particular user has traveled in cyberspace within the Web sites served by DoubleClick ads. By sharing information with one another, advertising agencies have the capability of building comprehensive databases of user activities.

One of the major concerns about the use of cookies stems from the fact that some businesses using cookies sell information about their customers to other organizations. Information about users is typically restricted to a unique identification number unless the user volunteers other information, such as name, e-mail address, or credit card number. However, if the user does volunteer such information, all subsequent interactions with

---

Text Box 4.14 Cable Company Stops Recording Customer Activities

Comcast Corp., the nation's third-largest cable company, pledged to immediately stop recording the Web-browsing activities of each of its one million high-speed Internet subscribers.

Comcast said in a statement that it will stop storing the information "in order to completely reassure our customers that the privacy of their information is secure." The Associated Press said that Comcast had started recording each customer's visit to a Web page as part of an overhaul to save money and speed up the network.

Comcast reassured customers yesterday that the information had been stored only temporarily, was purged automatically every few days and "has never been connected to individual subscribers."

Adapted from: "Comcast Plans to Stop Recording Activities Of Internet Subscribers," *Wall Street Journal*, February 14, 2002.

that Web site can be linked with personal identity, and even sold to other marketers. Further, as previously mentioned, some companies have begun the process of correlating information gathered by Internet cookies with other personal consumer information.

Controlling the Risks Associated with Compromised Privacy

As discussed above, privacy risks are of concern to e-businesses because (1) consumers who are not confident that their personal information will be kept secure and confidential are less likely to transact with an e-business enterprise, and (2) e-businesses that either purposefully or inadvertently "share" customers' personal information (e.g., e-mail addresses, names, ages, and other demographic data) with third parties may be exposed to legal liability and litigation. Savvy online shoppers can protect themselves by being careful with information they share online and through careful cookie screening. But e-businesses that want to inspire confidence in their customers must not take a "buyer beware" attitude toward privacy protection. Instead, they must develop and practice sound policies toward privacy protection.

Cookie Screening

Consumers can protect themselves against the risks of compromised privacy to some extent by screening the cookies that are placed on their hard drives. Most Web browsers can be configured to notify users before a cookie is written to the computer's hard drive, or even to restrict cookies in certain ways. For example, the Netscape browser lets users specify that a cookie can be saved on the computer's hard drive only if the cookie will be visible just to the server that originated the cookie, and not to others. This particular restriction offers online shoppers a little control over the amount of information being collected by third-party e-business agents. Browsers also offer a mode in which the user is prompted each time a Web site wishes to store a cookie; however, the use of cookies is so pervasive that this prompt mode is extremely burdensome. Most users either allow cookies or disable them entirely.

Effective Privacy Policies

E-businesses interested in protecting the privacy of their customers should develop effectively designed and implemented privacy policies. A 1999 law requires all companies to

---

Text Box 4.15 Cookie Ingredients

Cookies are very small data files that are automatically created on an Internet user's hard drive. The data file is created in response to a command from a Web site that the user visits. The file usually contains a unique tracking number that can be read by the site on future visits. With each visit, additional information is added to the cookie, and sites use the information to "remember" visitors from one visit to the next. The cookie cannot contain personal information such as names and addresses unless the user volunteers that information.

Cookies usually do not contain sensitive information, such as credit card numbers. ***However, the company that manages the cookie file determines the information kept in cookies.*** Hence, if sensitive information is stolen out of a cookie file, the company that issued the cookie is at fault, and may be liable for damages. The greater risk does not lie in the cookie itself, which resides on the user's computer, but in Web site servers wherein corresponding cookie information is stored. If someone manages to break into the company's server, customers may become victims, and the company can be held liable for damages.

notify their customers of their privacy policies once per year, and a growing number of privacy regulations, laws and guidelines are being implemented. Businesses and their trusted advisors must be aware of the legal requirements relating to privacy in each industry. For example the Gramm-Leach-Bliley Act was recently enacted for the financial services Industry, and HIPAA for the U.S. healthcare industry. Legal requirements aside, companies are wise to increase the confidence of their customers with respect to their privacy concerns.

Delta Airlines engages in e-business by selling airline seats directly to customers through its Web site. Part of Delta's privacy policy is reproduced in Text Box 4.16 (p. 100). As you can see from this example, a privacy policy declaration can be very explicit and thorough. However, e-business privacy policies should also include explicit and thorough practices that continuously monitor compliance with the publicly stated privacy declaration at all levels of the organization.

Privacy concerns create assurance opportunities. A recent survey indicates that more than 90 percent of consumers say they would do more business with a company if that company had its privacy practices verified by a third party, such as accountants.[37] Given the fact that many e-businesses are guilty of violating their explicit privacy policies, e-businesses that are serious about enhancing customers' confidence sometimes purchase independent third-party assurance services. Such services can enhance online customers' confidence in the level of security and privacy in transacting with an e-business enterprise. Since the CPA profession is attempting to become a prime provider of such assurance, this topic is discussed in the next chapter

Destructive Codes and Programs: Risks and Controls

Risks Associated with Destructive Codes and Programs

Regardless of their origins, harmful codes and programs have the potential to shut down entire networks and incur huge costs in the form of lost sales and productivity. Most people who are familiar with computers understand the need to be wary of what types of information and programs are introduced into the computer system—the biggest worry stemming from infectious little programs, known as viruses. **Viruses** are software programs capable of infecting computer files and replicating themselves across systems. Simply downloading a virus does not mean the virus has done any damage. A user must execute the file or code containing the virus (often found in the form of an attachment to an e-mail) in order for the virus to be activated. Several types of viruses exist, including macro viruses, boot viruses, and file viruses.

A **macro virus** is created using the macro language in a program such as Microsoft Word and spreads as files containing the virus are transferred from one system to another. The Melissa virus, which infected thousands of computers throughout the world in late March 1999, was a macro virus that spread through electronic mail and caused some companies to take their mail systems off line. The following year, the similar but more destructive Love Bug virus struck (see Text Box 4.17, p. 101), along with a host of "copycat" viruses in subsequent years.

Text Box 4.16 Delta Airlines Web Site Privacy Policy

We are always conscious and respectful of your personal privacy.
At Delta, we recognize the importance of protecting your personal information. This Privacy Policy will answer your questions about the kind of information we collect and how we use it. We have also included information on how to prevent your personal information from being collected or shared when you visit our Web site, respond to our Web-based advertisements, or send us e-mail. We reserve the right to modify this Privacy Policy at any time without prior notice. If we change or update our Privacy Policy, we will post the revised policy here, and any changes will apply to all information collected by Delta, including previously collected information.

What information do you gather and how do you use it?
We collect information about your visits, such as service provider, browser type, operating system, pages accessed on our Web site and the date and time of access to optimize your user experience and enhance your time spent with us online. We also receive information telling us what site you came from. When you send us an e-mail using the E-Mail Us page, we will retain the content of the e-mail, your e-mail address, and our response in order to handle any follow-up questions you may have. We also use this information to measure how effectively we address your concerns.

When using delta.com (purchasing travel, enrolling in the SkyMiles program, registering for promotions, etc.), we may ask for, among other things, the following information: Name, Address, E-mail address, Credit/Debit card number and expiration date, Billing address, Phone/fax number, and SkyMiles account number.

We retain your flight information and account and bonus mile information. We may ask you to voluntarily provide us with information regarding your personal or professional interests, demographics, experience with our products, and contact preferences. This information may be combined with information about you, which we gathered from other sources. We use the information to design offers customized to your interests. For example, you may receive a special offer for your most frequently traveled destinations.

Who do you share my personal information with?
We do not sell your name or other private profile information to third parties, and do not intend to do so in the future. We routinely share your information with our SkyMiles Partners and Promotional Partners. From time to time, we may engage third parties to process information on our behalf; however, Delta requires that these third parties comply with Delta's privacy policies when processing this information. When you purchase services or products through Delta that are to be provided by another party (for example, a travel segment on another carrier, hotel accommodations, rental car, etc.), we share your information with the third-party so that the third-party can provide the services or products you requested. We may also receive information about you from the third-party providers. We may share anonymous, aggregated information about all our users with third parties.

How does delta.com use cookies and similar technologies?
Delta uses cookies, tags, and other similar technologies to improve your experience on our site. These technologies allow us to recognize your preference information, keep track of your purchases, remember your SkyMiles number, and facilitate effective site administration. We use the information we collect to enhance your visit to delta.com and provide you with information tailored to your needs. You may elect to refuse cookies. Please refer to your browser Help instructions to learn more about cookies. Delta has engaged third parties acting on Delta's behalf, such as CentrPort™, to track and analyze your usage of our site. If you wish, you may opt out of CentrPort tracking.

How do I tell Delta that I don't want to be contacted for promotional purposes?
We only send promotional e-mail messages to you if you have voluntarily provided us with your e-mail address. Occasionally, a third party will act on Delta's behalf and send an e-mail message for Delta. You may request to be removed from Delta's e-mail subscription list or designate e-mail preferences by visiting our E-mail Programs.

Source: www.delta.com, May 2002. Used by Permission.

> ### Text Box 4.17 The "Love Bug" Virus
>
> On May 4, 2000, a computer virus known as the "Love Bug" maliciously damaged millions of computers worldwide. The assault began in Asia and quickly spread to Europe and then the United States. It was known as the "Love Bug" because it spread in the form of an e-mail message with the phrase "ILOVEYOU" in the title. Attached was a .vbs (Visual Basic Script) file called "LOVE-LETTER-FOR-YOU".
>
> The virus was designed to attack users of the Microsoft Outlook mail program. When a recipient opened the attached file, the virus mailed itself to everyone in the victim's address book, displaying the victim as the sender of the message. Because the virus was spread in this manner, it gave the message the appearance of validity to new recipients since it appeared to come from someone they knew.
>
> Once opened, the virus also attacked computer files on the recipient's hard drive. It erased art and photograph files ending with the letters .jpg and .jpeg, and made .mp3 music files inaccessible. The virus also searched the victim's hard drive for user IDs and passwords and e-mailed them to the Philippines.
>
> The day after the virus attack, the *Wall Street Journal* estimated that tens of millions of computers worldwide were infected with the virus and that damages would be substantial. The following week, the *Wall Street Journal* quoted Computer Economics, Inc.—an economic research firm with close ties to anti-virus software vendors—which listed damages at $2.61 billion.
>
> Adapted from: "Virus Gives 'Love' a Bad Name," *Wall Street Journal*, May 5, 2000; and "Digital Tips Help in Probe Of Bug Creator," *Wall Street Journal*, May 8, 2000.

A **boot virus** infects the boot sector of a system's hard drive, replacing the boot code with infected code, thereby usurping control of the computer the next time the machine boots. Approximately 75 percent of reported viruses are boot sector viruses. A boot virus generally infects a computer when an infected floppy disk is used on the system.

A **file virus** infects executable files in a system (for example, files ending in .COM, .EXE, or .OVL on a Windows PC). File viruses, like boot viruses, may replace original file instructions with virus code. A file virus may also change a file extension and then create a new file with the same name as the original file but with a different extension and with the infectious characteristics of the virus. Infected executable files can contain altered instructions ranging from relatively harmless screen messages to very damaging system functions, such as reformatting and erasing critical storage devices.

A **Trojan horse** is similar to a virus but it does not replicate itself. Like the Trojan horse of Greek mythology, which the citizens of Troy believed to be harmless, a computerized Trojan horse takes the form of a legitimate program—such as a game or attractive graphic. The user downloads the Trojan horse unknowingly and, just as the city of Troy was destroyed by the Greek soldiers hidden in the Trojan horse, the user falls victim to the deceptive and disruptive program code hidden within the baited program.

These and other types of malicious codes that can harm systems are listed in Table 4.2 (p. 102), along with identifying characteristics of each program.

Controlling the Risks Associated with Destructive Codes and Programs

McAfee.com, a company specializing in computer virus protection and prevention, estimates that there were at least 57,000 different computer viruses in existence as of April 2002. Several new viruses are discovered every day. With the incredible number of malicious programs circulating on the Internet, a company engaging in e-business cannot af-

Table 4.2 Quick Reference of Destructive Programs

Name	Characteristics/Related Facts	Example
Virus	Software designed to replicate itself and spread from location to location without user knowledge. A virus usually attaches to the system in such a way that it is activated when a part of the system is activated. The replication properties of a virus allow it to infiltrate a network very quickly.	Although viruses are usually considered dangerous, some viruses may simply be annoying. Consider the "Stoned" virus—a program that merely writes "Your computer is stoned" on the screen.
Worm	Worms are similar to viruses except that worms do not replicate themselves. Worms are created to destroy or change data within a system. Although a worm may be hunted and eliminated, the program embedded in the worm, for example "delete files," may remain active—files may continue to be deleted after the worm itself is eliminated.	The Morris Internet Worm incident may be the most famous worm encounter in history. Effects from the worm overloaded more than 6,000 Internet servers. This event occurred early in Internet history (1988) and damages amounted to $10 million.
Trojan Horse	A malicious program that appears to be a legitimate program or file. When the "legitimate" file is activated, the program (usually harmful) is activated, detaches, and damages the system that activated it. Trojan horses do not replicate themselves but can contain viruses.	While one system administrator played a game of chess with another party, Trojan horse software enabled perpetrators to gain access to sensitive files. In another incident, a company executive copied a graphics-enhancing program off a bulletin board. The executive lost 900 files due to the virus embedded in the Trojan horse program.
Hoax	A file or message that is sent out claiming to be a virus but that is not really a virus. The idea is to cause a scare because of the difficulty in differentiating a hoax from a real virus. Just like a real-world bomb scare hoax, authorities and administrators must take threats seriously.	A Valentine's Day Hoax read as follows: "Read this immediately...on February 14, 2000, you may receive an e-mail that says 'Be My Valentine.' Do not open it...it contains a deadly virus...it will erase your windows along with many other program files."
Logic Bomb	Code inserted into an operating system or application that causes a destructive or security-compromising activity whenever specific conditions are met. Logic bombs are sometimes known as time bombs and may be used in conjunction with a virus.	The famous Michelangelo virus was embedded in a logic bomb. The virus was triggered on the artist's birthday, March 6.
Trap Door	Illegitimate means of access created by programmers enabling easy navigation through software programs and data without going through normal security procedures. A trap door (also called "back door") allows access to a system without the use of a password.	A popular database product was vulnerable for seven years to security break-ins. The trick was to log-in with username "politically" and password "correct." This trap door was not created maliciously, but it was still alarming.

ford to operate without effective protection against malicious code. However, the purchase of effective software does not guarantee complete protection. Even if a company uses a virus protection program, it is never fully protected from all viruses, because of the vast number of viruses that are created every year. In order for the virus protection software to be effective, it must be updated frequently. There are many companies that provide antivirus programs, and most of them offer free updates through their Web sites. Other kinds of programs, such as intrusion detection suites (described earlier), are also available to protect against other forms of malicious code.

Human Factors in E-Business

People—The Weak Link

Figure 4.1 (p. 80) illustrates that the human factor is a pervasive problem playing a role in most of the other e-business risk factors. Indeed, the human factor plays a significant role in each of the risks discussed up to this point. For example, despite strong password policies and procedures, people sometimes make careless mistakes and allow passwords to be compromised. Employees are often ultimately the weak link in an otherwise secure e-business chain. This is because people frequently do not comply with control procedures. For example, they may download valuable proprietary information in unencrypted form onto a laptop, which is then stolen at an airport. They may not follow prescribed password policies, or they may fail to update virus protection programs on a regular basis. Sometimes systems and policies are so complex and change so rapidly that it is unreasonable to expect individual workers to keep up with it all. Thus, the human factor is pervasive in all areas of e-business risk.

Text Box 4.18 Janet Reno: The Internet as Facilitator of Good… and Evil

"A real world terrorist, in order to blow up a dam, would need tons of explosives, a delivery system, and a surreptitious means with the aid of armed security guards. Cyber terrorists could achieve the same devastating result by hacking into the control network and opening the floodgates. There is a dark side. A dark side in terms of traditional crime, of threats, child pornography, fraud, gambling, stalking, and extortion.

"They are all crimes that, when perpetrated via the Internet, can reach a larger and more accessible pool of victims, and can transform local scams into crimes that encircle the globe. By connecting a worldwide network of users, the Internet has made it easier for wrongdoers to find each other, to congregate, to socialize, and to create an online community of support and social reinforcement for their antisocial behaviors."

Source: Janet Reno, United States Attorney General, speech at Stanford University, www.usdoj.gov/archive/ag/speeches/2000/011000naagfinalspeech.htm, January 10, 2000.

Employees constitute a weak link in the security of an e-business environment not only through their neglectfulness; they are also often the targets of malicious outsiders seeking to gain access to systems. **Social engineering** is based on the simple idea that most people working in an organization are prone to be helpful—too helpful—even when discretion is appropriate. Playing on this notion, hackers sometimes use phone calls and e-mail to pry passwords and other important data from unsuspecting personnel. A **social engineer** may try to persuade others to divulge information by making them feel that they need to be loyal to their coworkers and that they should do what they can to keep the operations of the company moving smoothly (see Text Box 4.19, p. 104). In addition to social engineering, **dumpster diving**—sifting through a company's or an individual's

---

Text Box 4.19 Please Help Me Hack Your System!

Kevin Mitnick, notorious convicted hacker, told U.S. senators at a March 2000 congressional hearing that he had penetrated Motorola's information systems by persuading employees to divulge passwords. How? He simply told the employees that he was one of them and needed their help. He also obtained confidential information from the IRS and the Social Security Administration through similar means.

Adapted from: "Top Hacker Gives Senate Panel Tips On Computer Security," *Chicago Tribune*, March 3, 2000.

---

garbage—may help hackers find useful information. Sometimes information gathered through dumpster diving is used make attempts at social engineering more credible.[38]

No one wants to be thought of as being paranoid or too cautious. People working at the help desk in an organization are likely to receive several calls each day that relate to password information. Should the help desk give out such information over the phone? A good policy is that no one in the organization should ever be required to reveal password information—not even to the network administrator or department manager. These people, if their job requires it, will already have suitable access, so there should never be a need to ask for user passwords. One of the authors of this text changed Internet service providers when a service representative asked for his password in order to update the account; this was a strong indication that the provider was immature in its security management. We repeat: a business process should *never* require that a password be revealed. This issue should be addressed explicitly in the security policy of an organization. Passwords are not the only target of a social engineer—bank account numbers, personal identification numbers, and credit card numbers are also high-risk targets.

Responsible Personnel

Effectively managing risks in an e-business environment involves more than just well-designed controls and a disaster-recovery plan. It must also include competent and honest IT staff to ensure that control systems are functioning properly. It must include employees who conscientiously comply with control policies and procedures. Along these lines, the IT department must be adequately staffed to ensure that updates and changes are made to the system in a timely manner. If the IT department is understaffed, changes will not be made in a timely manner and the risk that harm will occur and go undetected for long periods of time is greatly increased. In the e-business environment, threats can arise so quickly that adequate monitoring of the system and timely updates to software security measures are critical to the integrity of information contained in and recorded by the system.

Two keys to increasing the likelihood of having responsible personnel are effective *hiring* and *training* practices. Thorough background checks should be conducted on potential candidates, especially for positions where the individual may eventually have access to important files and valuable company resources. Obviously, some undesirable hires may slip through the cracks. And under certain situational pressures, even people with strong moral values, good character, and no previous history of wrongdoing may succumb to temptation. Nonetheless, a careful hiring policy can prevent numerous sorts of losses. Training is also important because well-designed control policies and procedures are ineffective unless they are properly carried out. Employees must be instructed on the nature of the company's controls, and on how to properly comply with them. Even after employees have been trained, regular reminders are often necessary to maintain a high level of compliance. And it is always vital to audit systems (manually and automatically) to ensure adequate levels of compliance.

However, an attitude of dictation and enforcement is not likely to be successful. A control that seems reasonable in theory can prove to be burdensome in practice. As a result, individuals sometimes look for ways to "route around" control procedures. Controls need to be designed with overall balance in mind. Security is a study in balancing convenience and safety. Recognizing that many people will circumvent burdensome controls, process designers must also be responsible by making reasonable decisions about what controls to put in place. Finally, an e-business enterprise must provide thorough training that teaches not only *how* to follow business processes, but also *why* the various controls are necessary; this will promote better individual acceptance of the controls. For example, all firms should make sure their employees understand why the Love Bug virus was able to do its damage, and institute a policy of skepticism regarding executable files attached to e-mail.

Action Plan for Breach of Security

It is simply an unavoidable fact that people sometimes make mistakes or intentionally do wrong. E-businesses should have a formal policy for what to do when control policies have been violated. Employees should know exactly what to do and whom to contact if they feel their passwords have been stolen or if someone has gained unauthorized access to the system. Network managers and administrators should be aware of the potential ways that an intruder can gain access to the system and what to do if unauthorized access is detected. An intrusion response plan needs to be in place to handle suspected attacks. Such a plan includes at least the following elements: preparation, incident detection, and immediate reaction to limit damage, detailed analysis, recovery, and follow-up monitoring. A good communications infrastructure is necessary, and in some cases law enforcement authorities should be notified.

Company policies should also ensure that system access is terminated whenever an employee terminates employment for any reason. The employee's computer and building access should be immediately revoked. The employee's computer files should be placed under the control of the network administrator, and all passwords, access codes, and dial-up connections to which the employee might have had access should be changed.

System Interdependencies

As Figure 4.1 (p. 80) indicates, the presence of system interdependencies exposes e-business enterprises to risks that come from outside traditional organization boundaries. E-business often involves highly interdependent partnerships with customers, suppliers, and various electronic service providers. Thus, the very nature of e-business often requires linking up information systems in ways that transcend organizational boundaries. Several examples of these highly interdependent partnerships have been discussed in pre-

---

Text Box 4.20 The Importance of Strong E-Business Partners

Garden.com, an acclaimed e-tailer specializing in garden-related products, at one point turned to a logistics outsourcer to help with order fulfillment. Unfortunately, the outsourcer did not understand the nature of e-business order fulfillment. When Garden.com featured a popular terra cotta planting pot on its Web site, the outsourcer was unable to keep up with the speed at which e-business shifts the logistical landscape. Thirty percent of the pots were broken when the customers received them, the boxes in which they were shipped were wrong-sized and sloppily taped, and the packing material was dirty. The sloppy appearance of the packaging affected customers' perception of the pot itself, and gave the mistaken impression that Garden.com was cutting corners. When Garden.com complained, the outsourcer said that it just could not keep up with the "velocity of change" that comes when items are being added, dropped, ordered, cancelled, and returned in real time. Meanwhile, though Garden.com was generally conscientious and had an excellent overall order fulfillment record, some customers simply clicked to the firm's competitors. Although not only due to this order fulfillment fiasco, Garden.com has ceased operations.

Adapted from: Tom Kaneshige, "Choose Your Allies Carefully," *Upside Today*, May 24, 2000.

---

vious chapters, such as the Wal-Mart and Procter & Gamble EDI linkage discussed in Chapter 2 or the Dell and Ford/GM/Chrysler extranets in Chapter 3. These partnerships are vital, and many e-business companies are sacrificing today's profits in order to develop strong partnerships that they hope will prove profitable in the future. But the interdependent nature of these partnerships means that the risks an enterprise faces are at least partly determined by how well partners are identifying and mitigating risks to their systems (see Text Box 4.20).

Because the quality of a partnership depends heavily on the quality of each partner's information systems, as well as on the communication system between partners, organizations must ensure that their information systems are well managed and controlled. An organization engaging in e-business must ensure that not only its own information system, but also those of its critical partners, allow for the safe acquisition, processing, storage, and communication of important information.

More specifically, it is essential that companies engaged in e-business design their IT infrastructures to accomplish at least four fundamental objectives for every transaction conducted with customers or business partners:[39]

- **Authentication**—establish identity before transacting or allowing access to assets or information.
- **Integrity**—ensure data is accurate and not vulnerable to inappropriate changes.
- **Confidentiality**—restrict data access to authorized parties.
- **Non-repudiation**—conclusively trace an action to an individual so that accountability can be established and transactions cannot be repudiated.

In an e-business environment, organizations must realize their responsibility to ensure that their trading partners are using effective risk identification and management processes to protect the strength and integrity of individual transactions and of the entire network of interdependent enterprises. How can they do this? As we discuss in Chapter 5, assurance providers can play an important role in facilitating e-business by giving enterprises the confidence they need to establish interdependent partnerships with trading partners.

Anticipating and Managing E-Business Risk

We have discussed some important examples of the risks associated with e-business, but the information contained in this chapter is not exhaustive. In fact, managers, account-ants, and assurance providers should understand that perhaps the most dangerous risk category is what we might call **emergent risks**: threats that have yet to be identified. Emergent risks test the effectiveness of a risk management program and determine how quickly and how effectively an organization is prepared to respond and adapt to new threats. For example, hackers are constantly working to invent new ways to exploit pre-viously unknown vulnerabilities in operating systems and firewalls, and to create new vi-ruses that are increasingly destructive and communicable. Plugging all the gaps that make operating systems vulnerable is a difficult, on-going process (see Text Box 4.21).

An e-business enterprise can never justifiably feel complacent that it has effectively ad-dressed all known risks. In the e-business world, the risk that is most likely to hit you hard is the one you did not know existed. Emergent risks are inherently difficult to man-age. But an e-business company that does not make a significant investment in continu-ously monitoring and mitigating emerging threats is certainly less than secure. A good risk management program should include an explicit effort to stay on top of emerging risks, for example by checking vendor sites regularly for updates on software programs, staying current on topics in the area of computer security, and working to promote a workplace attitude that security is everyone's responsibility. Best practices in risk man-agement require a commitment that seems paranoid to the casual observer.

Comprehensive risk management is as important in e-business enterprises as in any other organization. But there are areas in which e-business enterprises should focus additional attention. Given the risks that are either unique or greatly heightened in an e-business environment, companies should work diligently to achieve and maintain a secure IT in-frastructure, practice effective internal control, develop strong partnerships with other e-

---

Text Box 4.21 Sometimes a "Patch" Creates More Holes

A Microsoft Corp. technology for plugging a common security hole is vulnerable to the very attack it was designed to prevent. The timing of the discovery is doubly embarrassing, coming only a month after Mi-crosoft Chairman Bill Gates announced a company-wide commitment to improving the security features of its software.

Researchers at Cigital said they discovered the problem in a compiler that comes as part of Visual C++.NET, a new version of a popular Microsoft programming tool. Compilers help translate code that programmers write into a language that computers understand. Microsoft modified the compiler to help prevent what are called buffer overflows, a common hacker attack that makes it possible to replace in-structions in a program with malicious code.

The modifications that Microsoft added to the compiler have some relatively well-known weaknesses that would allow a skilled attacker to sidestep the safeguards. That means that Visual C++.NET is not actually safer than earlier versions; in fact, it could lead programmers who use it to create more programs that con-tain vulnerability to buffer-overflow attacks.

"They were trying to avoid flaws, but instead managed to create a flaw seeder," Gary McGraw, Cigital's chief technology officer, said.

Adapted from: "Cigital Says Microsoft Program Isn't Secure," *Wall Street Journal*, February 14, 2002.

Text Box 4.22 Ten Best Practices for E-Commerce Self-Defense

- Conduct a risk assessment of the enterprise before implementing technical controls to eliminate costly adjustments after implementation
- Develop and communicate security standards to employees to establish responsibilities
- Test defenses—especially firewalls—to identify potential weak points
- Get an independent opinion of security measures to evaluate overall online security
- Limit access to e-commerce controls to the fewest people and the fewest systems possible for the minimum time it takes to perform essential functions
- Use firewalls to block intrusions
- Monitor employees' online activity through the use of systems management tools to enforce security policies
- Monitor networks for unusual activity
- Consult the Internet service provider to determine whether the ISP can block attacks before the attacks reach company systems
- Inform the proper authorities when systems are violated

Adapted from: American Institute of Certified Public Accountants, "Best Practices for E-Commerce Self-Defense," *Journal of Accountancy* (April 2000): 12.

---

businesses, stay on top of the human factor, and make use of independent assurance providers to stay on top of risks that stem from system interdependencies.

Recently, the AICPA released a list of the "ten best practices for e-commerce self-defense." You will see that the list represents a summary, of sorts, of many of the concepts covered in this chapter. We present the AICPA's list in Text Box 4.22.

Summary

As mentioned in the beginning of this chapter, understanding risks helps to create a secure business environment and develop and maintain strong partnerships, which are critical to achieving success in e-business. Accounting professionals who understand the risks of e-business, and how to efficiently and effectively control those risks, have an excellent opportunity to help organizations engage and succeed in the e-business environment both through consulting and assurance services. For example, by being involved in the design phase of an e-business enterprise's security policy, accountants can help management design control policies, procedures, and tools that will mitigate many of the risks discussed in this chapter. It is also critical for auditors to understand these risks in order to conduct an efficient and effective financial statement audit.

This chapter discusses some of the risks confronting e-business enterprises. From an assurance provider's perspective, there are risks inherent in providing services to e-business firms, such as the financial accounting risks arising from new accounting practices associated with new business models. Auditors are beginning to be named in e-business lawsuits involving unique accounting practices, suggesting a unique "e-business" risk for auditors. There are also substantial auditing risks associated with start-up failures, lack of controls, and breaches in security. Many Internet start-ups came about at Internet speed. Unfortunately, many of them have also disappeared just as quickly, and more will surely fail in the near future. The fact that many e-businesses will eventually fail represents a major audit risk.

Assurance providers must understand the risks facing e-business firms in order to properly assess client business risk. Additionally, accounting professionals must understand the risks of providing e-business services in order to set acceptable engagement risk. At the same time, e-business presents accounting professionals with tremendous new opportunities. The implications and opportunities of e-business for accountants and assurance providers are discussed in Chapter 5.

 For more information, please visit the Companion Website at www.prenhall.com/glover.

Review Questions

4-1 While four distinct categories of e-business risk have been identified in this chapter, only managing the risks within these categories is not sufficient to manage all of the risks associated with e-business. Identify and describe the two overarching elements that contribute to the risk exposure of an e-business.

4-2 Describe some of the vulnerabilities of an e-business system that can be attributed to IT infrastructure.

4-3 Describe the difference between a hot and a cold site. Why would a company want either? Might a company wish to have both? Why do you think companies often fail to test these sites adequately?

4-4 Stealth technologies are able to capture data transmitted in electronic pulses through copper wires without ever breaching the protective covers of the wire. What technologies protect against such stealth technologies and assist e-businesses in maintaining the confidentiality of information they send over insecure lines? Would you consider the wireless Internet more or less vulnerable to stealth technologies? (Also see the Technology Toolboxes.)

4-5 The government e-mail sniffing system, Carnivore, is introduced in this chapter. What are some possible privacy implications of firms using a similar technology in monitoring employee e-mail and Internet activity?

4-6 With all of the effort that is expended on developing a secure e-business environment, many individuals are surprised to learn that the weakest link in e-business security is not technology—it is people. One of the most useful tools of a hacker is social engineering. Describe social engineering and discuss why it is so effective.

4-7 E-businesses that are engaged in B2C e-commerce through a Web site often create an electronic shopping cart to store items the customer has selected from a Web catalog. This electronic shopping cart works by using a technology that allows the e-business to specifically identify the customer each time the customer visits the electronic store. What Web technology allows the electronic store to track which customer is requesting information? How does this technology affect the individual's privacy? Can an individual respond in some manner to eliminate or reduce the use of this technology?

Discussion Cases

4-8   Engaging in e-business to expand potential business opportunities typically changes the nature of a company's risk and often increases the risk. Assume you are a local custom furniture entrepreneur and are considering integrating the Internet into your operations. Identify risks that are likely to be eliminated, decreased, increased, or created through engaging in e-business.

4-9   In hiring new employees, companies invest significant amounts of resources in training. How should companies better educate their new employees to the dangers of social engineering?

4-10 Annie Chapman has been hired by your company to evaluate the risks associated with information security in your company. She begins her evaluation by reviewing IT infrastructure and information security policies and procedures. Next, she looks for a disaster recovery plan and evaluates whether it is viable; specifically, she re-quests records of the last testing of the plan. At this point, she declares that ade-quate control procedures are in place and that the company needs not worry further about information security. As the company's accountant, you are not confident that her evaluation of risks and the appropriate mitigating controls is complete. You draft an e-mail to the company president outlining your concerns about what Annie might have missed. What elements would you include in this e-mail?

Research Cases

4-11 Microsoft has publicly asserted that they are making a serious effort to secure its operating and other software systems from unwanted access and use. What are some of the implications of Microsoft's public stance on the security of its systems? What is the recent track record of Microsoft's added security awareness?

4-12 Generate a list of potential passwords that you believe would be fairly secure. Search the Web for a password-cracking program. Follow the instructions that ac-company the program to run the program on the list you generated. Report on the success of your list of passwords.

4-13 Visit the homepage of a favorite company and find their privacy and security state-ments. Compare their statements with those of Delta (p. 100), and discuss the ade-quacy of disclosure and of assurance offered by the statements.

Notes

1.   Patrice Rapalus, Director, Computer Security Institute, in press release summarizing *2002 Computer Crime and Security Survey*, April 7, 2002.

2. *Chicago Tribune*, March 2, 2000. Also see *The Economist*, February 19, 2000.

3. "Past Hack Attacks," *Christian Science Monitor*, May 5, 2000, p. 3.

4. See Brian Sullivan, "Internet Fraud Cost $17.8 Million in 2001, Federal Study Says," *ComputerWorld*, April 10, 2002; and FBI Internet Fraud Complaint Center Web site, statistics section, at www.ifccfbi.gov.

5. Ernst & Young, *Global Security Report* (2002): p. 1.

6. Deloitte and Touche LLP, *Enterprise Risk Services* (1998): 7–8.

7. Let us know when you've figured out all the details of Enron's complex business model. From all indications, Enron appears to be a study in e-business risks "coming home to roost."

8. As of this writing, the Committee of Sponsoring Organizations (COSO) is developing a comprehensive "Integrated Enterprise Risk Management" framework to guide organizations' risk management efforts, including those related to technology and e-business. See COSO's Web site for further information (www.coso.org).

9. Institute of Internal Auditors, *Tone at the Top*, no. 12 (November 2001).

10. "Hackers Crack Egghead.com," *CNet News.com*, www.news.com, December 22, 2000.

11. Linda Rosencrance, "Update: Egghead.com Says Customer Data Not Compromised," *Computerworld*, January 8, 2001.

12. "Egghead Says Hacker Didn't Get Access to Cards," *CNET News.com*, www.news.com, January 8, 2001.

13. Microsoft doesn't call them "patches." They prefer the terms "update" and "service pack." Microsoft's excellent Windows Update Web site (windowsupdate.microsoft.com) accessed May 20, 2002, divides its downloadable software categories for Windows 2000 updates into "Critical Updates and Service Packs," "Picks of the Month," "Advanced Security Updates," "Recommended Updates," "Additional Windows Features," and "Device Drivers."

14. Robert Lemos and Ben Charny, "Egghead Cracked: Data at Risk," *ZDNet News*, www.zdnet.com, December 21, 2000.

15 See www.cert.org; and Robert Suro, "FBI Cyber Squad Falling Behind Rise in Computer Intrusions," *Washington Post*, October 7, 1999.

16. See Paul Saffo, of the Institute of the Future, *Newsweek*, December 25, 2000.

17. Jaikumar Vijayan, "Denial-of-Service Attacks Still a Threat," *Computerworld*, April 8, 2002.

18. Ibid.

19. See www.cybersource.com.

20. *Chicago Tribune*, August 17, 1999.

21. Margaret Mannix, "High-tech Card Fraud Goes on Right Behind Your Back," *U.S. News and World Report*, February 14, 2000, pp. 54–56.

22. *The Kansas City Star*, June 12, 1999.

23. See www.icsa.net.

24. We invite the reader to look at the patch situation for Corel's WordPerfect 8 Suite (http://www.corel.com/support/ftpsite/pub/wordperfect/wpwin/8/cwps8.htm) May 20, 2002. One of the links is a program that helps the user figure out what patches need to be applied.

25. *Newsweek*, May 13, 2002.

26. *The Guardian*, February 2, 2000.

27. Dan Carney, "Fraud on the Net," *BusinessWeek*, April 3, 2000.

28. PricewaterhouseCoopers, *Risk Management Forecast: 2001,* p. 185.

29. A.K. Jain et al., "Biometrics: Personal Identification in Networked Society," 1999 as presented in PricewaterhouseCoopers, *Risk Management Forecast: 2001*, p. 204.

30. Other concerns about online shopping: not being able to physically inspect the product, being unfamiliar with the purchase process, and having to wait for delivery.
31. See Heather Green, "1984 in 2000: Getting Too Personal," *BusinessWeek*, February 7, 2000.
32. John Schwartz, "Online Health Sites to Unveil Standards; New Guidelines on Ethics, Privacy Will Offer Consumer Safeguards," *Washington Post*, May 7, 2000. Also see *Chicago Tribune*, March 12, 2000.
33. Andrea Peterson, "A Privacy Firestorm at DoubleClick," *Wall Street Journal*, February 23, 2000, p. B1.
34. *Wall Street Journal*, May 23, 2000, p. A1 FM.
35. A recent survey indicates that the elements of a company's privacy policy that consumers most want verified by a third party are adequate security procedures, no release of personal data without permission or unless required by law, limited access within the company, collection of only customer information that a company's privacy policies say it is collecting, and use and sharing of information only according to stated privacy policies. Over 80 percent of the respondents to the survey indicate they believe independent verification of company's stated privacy policies should be required by law. Europe tends to be more strict than the United States with respect to this kind of legislation.
36. *Newsweek*, April 8, 2002, p. 59.
37. *The CPA Letter*, April 2002.
38. "Cybercrime", *BusinessWeek*, February 21, 2000, p. 40.
39. PricewaterhouseCoopers, *Risk Management Forecast: 2001*, p. 186.

Chapter 5: Implications and Opportunities of E-Business Assurance

In Chapter 4 we identified several risks related to e-business and discussed internal controls to mitigate these risks. However, even with effective internal controls in place, there are important risks that cannot be completely "controlled away" in an e-business environment. For example, e-business typically exposes a company to additional risk based on the quality of the controls of their electronic partners. Further, the rapidly changing e-business environment constantly adds new potential risks to firms and consumers. This creates demand for external parties who can provide e-business assurance.

Before we discuss the opportunities and risks assurance providers face in an e-business environment, we should first define what we mean by "assurance." According to the Special Committee on Assurance Services (discussed later on p. 127), **assurance services** are "independent professional services that improve the quality of information, or its context, for decision makers." As you can see, this definition expands the potential role of the independent assurance provider far beyond the traditional role of financial-statement auditor to include almost any service that has to do with information. In fact, the definition was purposefully crafted to be very broad and inclusive so as not to unnecessarily limit the frontier of opportunities available to assurance providers.

Over the past century, the assurance provided by certified public accountants (CPAs) has been centered primarily in providing assurance to external parties regarding the reliability of a company's financial statements. This assurance is provided in the form of an audit opinion as to whether the financial statements are fairly stated in all material respects, in accordance with generally accepted accounting principles (GAAP). Financial-statement auditors are generally highly skilled in the planning and performance of financial-statement audits—a service that continues to be critically important to the efficient functioning of the modern economy, perhaps even more so in the wake of the Enron debacle.

The advent of information technology (IT) in the past two decades has brought revolutionary changes to the business world. A rapidly increasing number of companies and individuals rely on computers and databases to store, process, interpret, communicate, and report data in ways never before imagined. As has been discussed in preceding chapters, these technological developments have allowed enterprises to conduct business with customers and suppliers electronically.

These incredible technological changes have also brought dramatic changes to the accounting profession. Accountants are actively reevaluating their core competencies and analyzing how these competencies fit in with the new assurance challenges and opportunities brought by the advent of e-business. Currently, e-business has implications in three primary respects for the assurance services CPAs provide:

1. CPAs must consider the impact of e-business when conducting financial-statement audits.
2. Demand exists for independent assurance about the integrity of the information systems e-business enterprises rely on to conduct their business electronically.
3. Demand exists for assurance on the communication of information through electronic channels in the course of conducting e-business.

Financial Statement Assurance in an E-Business Environment

The financial-statement audit retains a vital role in today's business world, and the emergence of e-business does not change this reality. On the contrary, the financial-statement audit is as critical to the functioning of the capital-markets system in the United States as it has ever been. Without the financial-statement audit or another similar form of assurance to replace it, our economy simply could not function in its present form. Businesses in need of large amounts of capital to expand or initiate new ventures would have difficulty convincing potential investors or creditors of the reliability of their financial statements. Investors would thus demand a much larger premium for the increased **information risk** they would bear. Enterprises would be unable to acquire capital at a reasonable cost, and the economy would, at a minimum, function less efficiently. Further, revenues to accounting firms from financial-statement audits in the United States are significant (current estimates place this number around $8 billion annually).

Although the basic concepts underlying a traditional audit are still relevant in an e-business environment, auditors must modify their specific approaches to account for the risks unique to an e-business environment. These risks will almost certainly be characterized by complex technology and highly networked information systems. For financial-statement auditors, one of the primary implications of e-business results from the complex information technologies that make e-business possible. In an e-business environment, large and highly networked database-driven systems take on the role of processing and storing a company's data, different portions of which are made available to different stakeholders depending on their respective functions and information needs. From payroll information and sales transactions to customer information and marketing techniques, an e-business enterprise's information is typically stored, processed, and communicated electronically. If traditional, paper-based audit trails can no longer be followed, new audit techniques must be employed. Further, because electronic data are easily manipulated, effective internal controls become very important. In fact, the conventional idea that an auditor can rely primarily on substantive tests when controls are inadequate may not be valid when the majority of audit evidence is electronic in nature.[1]

As businesses conduct and record their transactions electronically, the financial-statement auditor must address the additional risks e-business creates. Information integrity and security become a major concern when the information is widely distributed and readily accessible in highly networked environments. As companies open themselves to various stakeholders, they also become vulnerable to unwanted intrusions (for example, see Text Box 5.1). Data integrity and data security become extremely difficult to manage and maintain in such an environment. Managing these new risks consumes a significant portion of the efforts and resources of these enterprises. Client's management of e-business risk is of vital concern to the financial-statement auditor.

In addition to the risks brought about by the nature of the technology used, auditors must be aware of other implications of e-business for the financial-statement audit. Some of these risks include interdependence between entities' information systems, increased possibilities for obsolescence, and, in fact, essentially all of the risks discussed in Chapter 4.

Text Box 5.1 Technology Enables *All* Kinds of E-Business!

Technology has revolutionized business by enabling all kinds of activities not previously possible. In the process, many "traditional" business risks relevant to assurance providers have been mitigated, but new ones have arisen. In January 1998, Vladimir L. Levin admitted to using stolen passwords to illegally transfer money from Citicorp customer accounts in the summer of 1994. Mr. Levin, who was only 26 years old at the time, succeeded in illegally transferring $12 million from customer accounts and actually withdrew over $400,000. Financial frauds have occurred for hundreds and even thousands of years. What is novel about this particular fraud is that information technology enabled Mr. Levin to carry out the e-business theft while sitting at a computer terminal in his apartment in St. Petersburg, Russia!

Adapted from: Dean Starkman, "Russian Hacker Enters Fraud Plea in Citicorp Case," *Wall Street Journal*, January 26, 1998.

In fact, most of the surviving e-businesses born within the last few years are struggling, and, of course, many well-known dot-coms disappeared as quickly as they were conceived. More will likely follow, and their auditors will bear a significant risk of being a target of litigation in the wake of the bankruptcies. Even auditors of more traditional business clients must be aware of the broader implications of e-business. What if, for example, a client is operating with a business model that is in danger of being undermined or even becoming obsolete given the advent of a competing e-business paradigm? Such circumstances could have enormous implications for the fairness of the client's accounting representations. For example, the client's long-lived assets, or its inventory, may not be valued appropriately given the impending threats to its way of doing business. In some cases, these threats may even have serious implications for whether the client is likely to continue as a going concern.

E-business has pervasive implications for the auditor and the financial-statement audit—that much is clear. Let's take a closer look at the implications of e-business for the financial-statement audit and the ways auditors are adapting their services to meet new demands created by e-business. We will limit our discussion of these implications to two general areas—the IT environment common to e-businesses and other characteristics of e-businesses that contribute to financial-statement risk.

IT Environment

A financial-statement auditor's primary objective is well defined—to express an opinion on the fairness of the client's financial statements in accordance with GAAP. Although auditors have traditionally looked for opportunities to provide further consulting and assurance services to clients, expressing an audit opinion is their primary objective. Thus, in the context of a financial statement audit, the assurance provider is most concerned with e-business risks that may lead to material misstatements in the financial statements.

As mentioned previously, one of the obvious characteristics of an entity heavily involved in e-business is that it, of necessity, operates in a highly networked IT environment where information is stored, processed, and communicated electronically. In fact, many of the risks associated with e-business stem from the heavy reliance on IT systems that e-business requires. A primary concern of the auditor when dealing with an e-business setting thus becomes how to effectively audit in an IT environment. IT systems have been around for a number of years, and auditors have developed a significant amount of experience in dealing with IT-related risks and performing audits in IT environments. Though this chapter is in no way intended to provide a complete discussion of IT auditing (a complete discussion could fill volumes!), we will briefly review some of the standard steps employed and the primary issues that arise when auditing in an IT environment. You will quickly recognize that the steps involved are the same as the steps used in any financial-statement audit; however, our discussion will illustrate that the *issues* involved are sometimes quite unique. The relevant management assertions that the auditor will attest to are the same whether the client uses a manual accounting system or a highly sophisticated IT system that enables the conduct of e-business—existence, completeness, rights and obligations, valuation or allocation, and presentation/disclosure.

Step One: Understand IT Internal Control System

As in all audits, the auditor must gain a sufficient understanding of the client's internal control system to plan the audit. As auditing standards indicate, a client's control system includes the enterprise's control environment, ongoing risk assessment, control activities, information and communication, and monitoring activities (see Statement on Auditing Standard 78). One of the primary weaknesses of many IT systems is their failure to include many traditional controls, such as segregation of duties or matching of paper documents that might otherwise be present. Sometimes these traditional controls are replaced by electronic controls built into the software system. Even though some risks common to information systems that rely on manual processing and paper documents are mitigated in an electronic system, IT systems expose business enterprises to new risks.

To properly address these risks, the auditor must begin by evaluating the internal controls relating to the company's IT system. In a networked IT environment, a company will place its main emphasis on software-based controls. For example, password-based access controls are typically relied upon very heavily in a networked IT environment; thus, the soundness of an enterprise's password policies and procedures is often central to an auditor's examination of the entity's control system. Through flowcharting, interviewing, and reviewing organizational manuals, the auditor can achieve an overall understanding of the strengths and weaknesses of the control system. When dealing with relatively sophisticated systems, auditors often rely on the help of IT specialists who are experts at understanding software- and hardware-based controls (see Text Box 5.2). The specific e-business controls discussed in the prior chapter will help give you an idea of the types of controls the auditor must understand in an e-business client's IT system.

Step Two: Assess Control Risk Based on Understanding of Internal Controls

To plan an effective and efficient audit, the auditor must assess the client's level of control risk, or the risk that the client's controls will fail to prevent or detect a material misstatement that may arise. As in any financial statement audit, this assessment will heavily influence the nature of procedures to be performed throughout the remainder of the audit.

If the auditor perceives that control risk can be assessed at a low level, he or she might choose to take a "reliance" approach to the audit. Under this approach, the auditor feels confident enough about the controls within the IT system that, after adequately testing

---

Text Box 5.2 IT Audit Specialists

All of the large national and international accounting firms rely on teams of IT experts to assist financial statement auditors in assessing the reliability of a client's IT controls. Here is a look at how these IT experts add value.

IT experts possess an understanding of risks and controls that is useful in assessing the reliability of a network computer system. IT experts aid financial-statement auditors in gaining an understanding of a client's IT controls and assessing control risk for the audit based on this understanding. IT experts are not necessarily experts in financial-statement auditing. Instead, these intermediaries facilitate the service performed by the accounting firm by using their skills and knowledge to adequately and efficiently assess the reliability of a client's IT controls.

For example, Ernst & Young, LLP (E&Y) offers IT internal audit and effectiveness services through its Technology and Security Risk Services (TSRS) group. For enterprises operating on client/server Enterprise Resource Planning (ERP) application suites, E&Y provides ERP Integrity services (ERPIS), a service geared toward maximizing control efficiency while minimizing IT risk for clients with ERP systems.

---

controls, the auditor will reduce assessed control risk below the maximum and rely on the control system to reduce the level of more costly substantive audit procedures. The auditor will rely on data extracted from the system, as the auditor has concluded that the system has the necessary controls in place to produce reliable information.

However, if the auditor assesses a high level of control risk, he or she will choose to take a "substantive" approach. With this approach, the auditor concludes that the system's controls are not adequate to justify reliance on the integrity of the data the system produces. As a result, the auditor will increase the level of substantive testing, relying to the extent possible on evidence that originates outside of the client's system, such as confirmation of receivables and payables. In the absence of adequate internal controls in an e-business environment, the auditor may even be forced to conclude that the system is not auditable because the electronic data produced by the system is not reliable. During this phase of the audit, IT specialists often assist the auditor in assessing the client's control risk, and in determining whether testing the control system to justify a further reduction in the control risk assessment is likely to be efficient. Network security assessment software is sometimes used to assess critical network controls (see Text Box 5.3, p. 118).

Step Three: Test the Controls

Assuming the auditor decides that a reliance approach is justified, the next step is to perform tests of the client's controls. In an e-business environment, this will often include testing monitoring controls, general computer controls, and application controls. **General computer controls** are controls used by management to ensure IT activities and the overall computer environment are adequately handled. They relate to the effective development and implementation of new IT systems, maintenance of existing systems, and oversight of computer operations to maintain the security and integrity of information. For example, one general computer control might be to restrict modification of software programs to authorized parties.

Monitoring controls refer to management review of various items or activities designed to detect incorrect or improper handling of data or information. For example, a client might have a policy requiring that an appropriate manager regularly compare sales re-

---

Text Box 5.3　Network Security Assessment

As discussed in the previous chapters, e-business brings new risk in large part because e-business often involves widespread access to information and opens countless potential new "windows" into an e-business enterprise's networked IT systems. The associated risks are potentially of both indirect and direct interest to the financial statement auditor. Thus, in many cases, adequately testing controls will include testing controls relating to network security. As discussed in Chapter 4, they include such software-based controls as firewalls, intrusion detection programs, and security suites.

Software programs have been developed to help auditors efficiently and effectively test network security controls. Three of the most commonly used security assessment software packages are:

- Cybercop Scanner 5.5 (www.nai.com)
- Internet Scanner 6.2.1 (www.iss.net)
- Symantec NetRecon 3.5 (www.symantec.com)

Each of these software programs provides auditors the ability to identify network weaknesses in a company's computers, routers, firewalls, Web servers, and other communication devices. Once weaknesses have been identified, each software program provides an analytical report identifying areas requiring additional attention. Auditors can then classify risk levels as low, medium, or high, based on the software's assessment of network security.

---

ports generated *outside* the accounting system with system-reported revenues. Such management monitoring controls are usually considered a vital part of an effective control system and can provide comfort that the information system is capturing, summarizing, and reporting reliable data.

Finally, **application controls** are manual or automated control procedures that are applied to specific business processes or transactions to ensure the integrity of data and information. For example, an e-business sales order software application might prevent a customer order from entering the system in the absence of a valid credit card number.

The purpose of testing a client's controls is to decide how much reliance to place on the system that is responsible for generating reliable financial information. The results of the auditor's tests will then determine the amount of substantive testing to be performed. While many control tests used in a more traditional setting are also applicable in an IT environment, there are several control tests that are applicable only in an IT environment. The auditor—with help from an IT specialist, if necessary—must decide which tests are most appropriate for the client's unique system. Below are a few examples of the many techniques available for testing the reliability of controls in an e-business environment.

Test Data Approach. The **test data method** evaluates the integrity of the application by processing a sample of test data through the application under review. Test data are carefully prepared and can include seeded errors of various types. Expectations are formed as to the nature of the results. After the data have been processed, the actual results are compared to the expected results to form a conclusion regarding the application's integrity. If performed correctly, test data techniques can produce detailed information on the system's functionality with little or no disturbance of the organization's operations.

Parallel Simulation. **Parallel simulation** techniques involve creating a program that replicates key processes of the application to be tested. The auditor first must gain a thorough understanding of these key processes. This knowledge is then used to create a program that simulates the original application. The auditor then gathers previously processed data from the client's records and processes the data through the replica system. The results of the test are compared to the results when the data was originally processed through the actual system to gain evidence on the functionality of the application under review.

Integrated Test Facility. The **integrated test facility (ITF)** is a function created within a software application that allows test data to be processed concurrently with actual data. When an application is created, an ITF is developed as an integral part of the system. These test facilities produce "dummy" or "test" files that are integrated with legitimate data. As actual transactions are performed during normal operations, the test transactions are also processed and the results are compared against expected results. The benefits of this test are that it can be performed in an on-going manner without disrupting the company's daily operations. Care must be taken, however, to ensure that test data are not allowed to be left in the system and corrupt the client's actual data. This type of software-based testing is considered a key component to emerging "continuous auditing" approaches that are possible in an electronic environment.

Step Four: Reassess Reliance and Substantive Testing Levels

At this point, the auditor will evaluate the evidence produced from the control tests and determine the amount of reliance to place on the system's controls. The auditor's conclusion will determine the nature, extent, and timing of substantive tests to be performed. If the controls can be heavily relied upon, then the auditor will perform more extensive tests of controls and fewer substantive tests of transactions and detailed tests of balances. Likewise, if the controls cannot be heavily relied upon, then the auditor will likely decide to invest more heavily in substantive testing.

Step Five: Perform Substantive Tests that Address Management Assertions

With the control testing already performed and the amount and type of substantive tests determined, the auditor can now focus on performing substantive audit tests. In doing so, it is important that the auditor focus on addressing management's assertions, just as in the audit of a more traditional client. The type and depth of audit procedures should be sufficient to provide the auditor with a basis for reporting on management's assertions within the financial statements.

To facilitate substantive testing, auditors can utilize several types of generalized audit software packages. These packages are developed specifically for audit use and allow the auditor to perform various evidence evaluation and testing functions. Usually, these programs are developed in a manner that allows the average user to easily be trained in their use—little previous training with technical IT functions is required. The greatest benefit is that these programs can be used to perform a wide variety of audit functions from data extraction and selection to sampling and manipulation. The use of such software can significantly enhance the efficiency of an audit. Tasks that traditionally took many man-hours to perform can often be executed with a few clicks of the mouse. Where previously only a sample of data could be tested, in some cases the auditor can test *all* of the data in a fraction of the time (see Text Box 5.4, p. 120; and Text Box 5.5, p. 121).

Text Box 5.4 Audit Data Extraction and Analysis Software

As the environment in which auditors' work becomes more and more electronic, it becomes necessary to trade in traditional paper-based audit tools for electronic audit tools. Below, we outline two particular audit data extraction and analysis software programs currently in use by auditors.

ACL—Recently voted the preferred software application for continuous monitoring, data extraction, and fraud detection, ACL is powerful, yet easy-to-use. Incorporating built-in audit functionality and simple, English-like commands, ACL helps auditors access, analyze, and report on data from nearly all computing environments. It offers practically unlimited file size capabilities, excellent processing speed, batch automation features, and comprehensive graphing tools. Available for Windows and mainframe systems, ACL is easy and intuitive to use and doesn't require extensive training. (See ACL's Web site at www.acl.com. Used by permission.)

CaseWare IDEA 2002—Interactive Data Extraction and Analysis (IDEA) was developed under license by the Canadian Institute of Chartered Accountants. IDEA is intuitive to use and can extract data from a wide variety of file formats, thus allowing the auditor to reduce its reliance on the IT department. According to the company, "With IDEA, you can read, display, analyze, manipulate, sample, or extract from data files from almost any source. IDEA has functions and features not found in any other product, to help you work more efficiently, effectively, and with more value." (See www.caseware-idea.com. Used by permission.)

XBRL. Perhaps the most substantial recent innovation in financial statement auditing with relation to e-business is Extensible Business Reporting Language (XBRL). XBRL is adapted from XML (Extensible Markup Language—discussed in Chapter 2) to fit the specific needs of businesses. Essentially, XML is similar to the common HTML language of the Internet, with one major exception: XML allows users to identify information in documents with user-defined tags, allowing for enhanced online information communication. XBRL is an effort by international industry leaders in accounting, and financial reporting and accounting software developers to develop a common set of XML tags to be used in business and financial reporting.

One of the primary advantages to XBRL is that it allows for financial statement users to "grab" specific online financial statement information and import it directly into a spreadsheet or other software application without jumbling the numbers. Minor differences in the format of financial statements of different companies can be eliminated by end-users because all components of the statements are individually labeled to allow for appropriate restructuring to the user's preferred format.

From an auditor's perspective, such capabilities will allow for more automation of the audit process. Numbers can be downloaded the instant they are available from the client, and can be processed for potential errors immediately. This real-time auditing may allow for more efficient and timely audits.

Benefits to preparers of financial statements are also evident. First of all, clients can expect to see some of the savings that result from audit efficiencies. Second, for organizations with a significant number of reports to generate, some experts estimate that the

---

Text Box 5.5 DATAS: Error and Fraud Detection Software and Benford's Law

DATAS (Digital Analysis Tests and Statistics) is a powerful software application used for detecting errors and fraud. Among other things, DATAS incorporates a mathematical principle known as Benford's Law. This law states that the individual digits 1 through 9 will appear with predictable frequency in a group of random numbers (random meaning randomly selected from society, such as from baseball statistics, financial statements, etc.). For example, a 1 will appear as the first digit in a number 30 percent of the time, while a 9 will be the leading digit only 4.6 percent of the time. Because all numbers follow this predictable pattern, fraudsters attempting to generate numbers that are random in appearance (say, with 7's and 2's appearing as a leading digit with random frequency) can be easily exposed. As counterintuitive as it may seem, Benford's Law can immensely helpful in identifying fraud. The IRS is one of the many organizations that has shown a great deal of interest in this phenomenon—seeing it as potential tool for detecting tax fraud.

DATAS analyzes numeric data for patterns that do not conform to Benford's Law and reports these anomalies to the user for further investigation. Even though the mathematical theory behind the software may seem complex, the software itself is easy to use. It can be used as an add-in tool with ACL, IDEA, Excel, and SAS.

---

standardization and compatibility of XBRL statements will reduce Web publishing costs by 30 to 60 percent annually.

However, XBRL is not without opposition. While many see it as the future of electronic financial reporting, it is a big step to take. Currently, only a small number of companies have converted to using XBRL for online financial statement publishing. Some companies worry about liabilities that may arise because of inaccurately tagged numbers. Others are concerned by the initial cost of the change.

XBRL and real-time reporting represent a significant change in a profession with a long history of carefully prepared formal reports generated weeks or months after a reporting period ends, so some reluctance is probably to be expected. However, many knowledgeable observers believe XBRL is the best available tool for enhancing information interchange in e-business and see the reluctance as temporary.[2]

Other Financial Statement Risk Factors in E-Business

In addition to the concerns that stem from the use of complex, highly networked IT systems used in e-business, there are several other areas on which the auditor must focus to completely address all of the additional risks in an e-business environment. Chapter 4 addresses the risks typically facing businesses and customers engaging in e-business. But the heightened risks associated with e-business do not all relate to the underlying information technology. For example, in Chapter 4, we discussed the fact that enterprises engaging in e-business tend to have risk-increasing characteristics such as rapid growth, frequent mergers and acquisitions, formations of new partnerships that tend to be highly interdependent, initial public offerings and other significant financing transactions, complex information systems, and increasingly complex business models and processes.

These risks are of interest not only to management, but also to the financial statement auditor because most risks that an enterprise faces can either directly or indirectly affect the fairness of an enterprise's financial statements. For example, even risks that may not directly affect the financial statements can put pressure on management in ways that can affect the company's control environment.

Enterprises engaging in e-business can present unique challenges to auditors simply because of the unique business models and performance measures created and emphasized in the world of e-business. Although any business must ultimately generate positive cash flow and profit to survive, analysts, managers, and investors at times have been less concerned with traditional financial measures such as net income during the early stages of an e-business. They sometimes have been more concerned with measures such as revenue growth and gross profit margin. This shift in important measures is caused by the need to value e-businesses that are not profitable and that may be pursuing an entirely untested business model. These companies are often evaluated in terms of their potential to grow into a successful player in the market.[3]

The differences in e-business and traditional business models and the emphasis on different performance measures present new challenges for auditors. For example, virtual companies may not have material traditional assets such as inventory or accounts receivable. Also, current accounting standards do not always clearly address how to appropriately account for e-business transactions, raising difficult revenue recognition and expense classification issues. Finally, taxation of Internet transactions promises to be a very complex endeavor.

To illustrate, consider drugstore.com, a rapidly growing company specializing in the sale of health, nutrition, personal care, beauty, and pharmaceutical products over the Internet (see Figure 5.1). Drugstore.com's original business model did not require traditional inventory. Instead, customers ordered products online and drugstore.com relied on one of its many partnering distributors to fill the orders. In 2000, drugstore.com opened its own distribution center, moving away from its initial "pure-play" e-business status to become a little more like its "bricks-and-mortar" competitors. Like many of the surviving dot-coms, drugstore.com is now what some would call a "clicks-and-bricks" e-business company. However, a portion of the company's revenues is still generated through its e-business activities with distribution partners, including Rite Aid Corporation.

Customers can log-on to drugstore.com and order prescriptions for pick-up at their local Rite Aid store. While this seamless transaction may seem simple to consumers, this segment of drugstore.com's business presents some interesting challenges for auditors. While the fundamental concepts of financial statement auditing still apply, the nature of drugstore.com's business model changes the nature of the audit issues that arise relative to those typically present in a traditional company. Although a complete discussion of the issues is beyond the scope of this book, below we discuss a couple of examples illustrating how e-business business models affect the nature of the auditing issues faced by the company's financial statement auditor.

Inventory. While auditors of traditional retail clients typically spend a significant portion of budgeted audit hours auditing inventory, management assertions relating to inventories represent less of a concern with drugstore.com, at least in a traditional sense. Drugstore.com indirectly deals with a tremendous variety of inventories, but owns and ware-

Figure 5.1 drugstore.com™ Home Page, May 2002

houses only a portion of it. Instead, many orders that are placed with the company are filled directly by its partnering vendors, such as Rite Aid. Nonetheless, drugstore.com, inc.'s success as a retailer depends critically on the company's ability to provide customers with reliable and efficient access to a large variety of inventory that they do not own. So, while the company carries relatively little inventory on its balance sheet, and therefore does not present many of the usual inventory auditing issues, inventory is a central concern in an unusual way—the auditor's concerns about inventory will center on the nature and reliability of the company's partnerships.

As this example illustrates, one of drugstore.com, inc.'s most significant assets consists of the company's partnership with vendors. With this network of partners, the company has an unprecedented ability to supply customers with an almost endless variety of products. Without these relationships, the business has little more than an attractive Web site. Like many e-business enterprises, the company's interactions with both customers and vendors are entirely dependent on an IT system that is Internet-enabled. These assets cannot be found on the balance sheet, but because the enterprise's success depends on them so critically, auditors ignore them at their peril. Further, due to its fast rate of growth, the company is essentially a very different company in terms of size and other characteristics each year. Thus, the auditor must be careful to reassess risks and fundamentally recreate the audit program for each year's audit.

Revenue Recognition. At what point should drugstore.com recognize a sale as revenue on the books? Since the company usually doesn't transfer the goods to the customer, when can drugstore.com consider the earnings process to be substantially complete and to have a valid promise to pay? Does this happen when the order is placed or when the partnering vendor ships the product to the customer? Should the gross price of the products be recognized as revenue, or should drugstore.com's markup be considered essentially a sales commission such that only the net markup is recognized as revenue? These questions, which again hinge on the nature of drugstore.com's partnering arrangements (e.g., specification of who is responsible if the customer does not pay, who suffers the risk of loss in transit, etc.) are crucial to the company's financial reporting.

Drugstore.com's annual report states, "Title to products ordered by customers and shipped or delivered by a fulfillment partner passes to the Company at the fulfillment partner's distribution center or, for certain pharmaceutical sales, when the pharmaceuticals are made available for customer retrieval at a Rite Aid store." Drugstore.com assumes title to the products at the shipping point and assumes all the "risks and rewards" associated with ownership for these shipments. Thus, the company reports revenues on a gross basis (citing that they believe this practice to be in accordance with EITF 99-19). Revenue is recognized for the full amount of the sale and cost of goods sold is reported as the amount paid to the vendor who actually ships the product.

Amazon.com, another online company that relies heavily on partnerships in its retailing business model, recognizes revenue in a similar fashion. In its annual report, Amazon cites EITF 99-19, indicating that in transactions where Amazon is subject to inventory risk, is the primary obligor, or has control of the setting of the sales price for merchandise, it recognizes revenue at gross. However, when these characteristics are not present in a transaction, revenue is booked at net.

Revenue recognition has become a central accounting and auditing issue for e-business enterprises due to the emphasis on revenues in stock valuation, which creates the incentive to "gross-up" revenues. The FASB has labeled revenue recognition as "the largest single category of fraudulent financial reporting and financial statement restatements."[4] Not surprisingly, dot-com companies have a history of employing non-traditional revenue recognition policies. In response to these troubling revenue recognition practices, the Securities and Exchange Commission (SEC) released Staff Accounting Bulletin (SAB) 101, *Revenue Recognition in the Financial Statements*, in December 1999, which, among other issues, specifically addresses the issue of recognizing revenue on a gross or net basis. Text Box 5.6 is an outtake from SAB 101. In explaining accounting guidelines, the SEC often provides "hypothetical scenarios," such as the one sited in this Text Box. The important take-away from this example is that, in determining which method of revenue recognition is appropriate, the SEC concluded that the issue revolves around whether the company acts as a principal in the transaction, takes title to the product, or has risks and rewards of ownership. In the SEC's view, when these conditions are present it is appropriate to recognize revenue on a gross basis with an offsetting cost of goods sold. However, if the company instead acts more like an agent or broker, then the company's markup should be considered a sales commission and revenue should be recognized on a

---

Text Box 5.6 SAB 101, Question 10

Facts: Company A operates an Internet site from which it will sell Company T's products. Customers place their orders for the product by making a product selection directly from the Internet site and providing a credit card number for the payment. Company A receives the order and authorization from the credit card company, and passes the order on to Company T. Company T ships the product directly to the customer. Company A does not take title to the product and has no risk of loss or other responsibility for the product. Company T is responsible for all product returns, defects, and disputed credit card charges. The product is typically sold for $175 of which Company A receives $25. In the event a credit card transaction is rejected, Company A loses its margin on the sale (i.e., the $25).

Question: In the staff's view, should Company A report revenue on a gross basis as $175 along with costs of sales of $150 or on a net basis as $25, similar to a commission?

Interpretive Response: Company A should report the revenue from the product on a net basis. In assessing whether revenue should be reported gross with separate display of cost of sales to arrive at gross profit or on a net basis, the staff considers whether the registrant:

1. Acts as principal in the transaction
2. Takes title to the products
3. Has risks and rewards of ownership, such as the risk of loss for collection, delivery, or returns
4. Acts as an agent or broker (including performing services, in substance, as an agent or broker) with compensation on a commission or fee basis.

If the company performs as an agent or broker without assuming the risks and rewards of ownership of the goods, sales should be reported on a net basis.

Source: SAB 101, *Revenue Recognition in the Financial Statements*, December 1999.

---

net basis. It is important to note that under either method the bottom line is the same, but the "gross" method allows companies to report much higher revenue figures than does the "net" method (see Text Box 5.7). Because of the focus of e-business on revenue growth, the SEC is cracking down on companies that, in the Commission's view, inappropriately "gross up" revenues.

Another way e-businesses have been "grossing up" revenues is through barter transactions—exchanging services for services and booking the value of the services received as revenue. A hypothetical example of this type of transaction would be if Amazon.com and drugstore.com agreed to trade advertising on their respective sites without any money changing hands. Each company would then recognize advertising revenue for the

---

Text Box 5.7 Priceline.com

Priceline.com is a popular Web site that lets customers "name their own price" for airline tickets, hotel reservations, and more. When Priceline arranges for customers to purchase, for example, airline tickets, it recognizes the entire amount the passenger pays for the ticket as its own revenue. Critics claim that Priceline is nothing more than a glorified travel agent; thus, recording revenues for the gross amount of an airline ticket is inappropriate. Priceline contends that it bears the risk of losing money if its customers default on purchases; but critics counter Priceline does not really bear any risk, because it only buys tickets when it has a firm credit card order.

The question of whether to record revenues at the gross or net amount is a serious issue in the e-business world. On a net basis, Priceline's revenues would be significantly smaller. Worried that some Web companies are manipulating revenues, the Emerging Issues Task Force (EITF) of the FASB issued EITF 99-19 in 1999, and the Securities & Exchange Commission (SEC) issued SAB 101 in 2000.

amount they would charge a normal customer to post an advertisement, and an offsetting entry to advertising expense for the same amount. Thus, without ever exchanging cash, both companies could boost recorded revenues. The SEC called for a halt to this practice in SAB 101.

MicroStrategy represents perhaps the biggest debacle involving nontraditional revenue recognition policies of e-business enterprises to this point. The company's stock price climbed from around $7 per share to over $300 per share between April 1999 and March 2000. However, when SAB 101 was issued, the company was forced to restate revenues. As a result, reported net income dropped from a net profit of $12.6 million to a net loss of $33.7 million for 1999. Microstrategy's stock price quickly followed suit, dropping over 90 percent in price between March and April 2000. Several lawsuits ensued, the majority of which were consolidated into a class action lawsuit against MicroStrategy. In its 2001 Annual Report, MicroStrategy reported the outcome of this lawsuit as follows:

> "Under the settlement agreement, class members will receive: (1) five-year unse- cured subordinated promissory notes issued by MicroStrategy having an aggre- gate principal amount of $80.5 million and bearing interest at 7.5 percent per year; (2) 2,777,778 shares of our class A common stock; and (3) warrants to pur- chase 1,900,000 shares of class A common stock at an exercise price of $40 per share with the warrants expiring five years from the date they are issued."

As of July 2002, MicroStrategy's stock price has yet to recover from its precipitous drop in 2000, selling at the time of this writing for about $1 per share.

Expense Classification. Because of the increased focus the e-business environment places on gross margin as a performance measure, management has an increased incen- tive to reclassify costs in order to create a better gross margin percentage for the com- pany. Amazon recently came under review by the SEC for this reason. Critics argue that in an effort to inflate gross margin, the company was including warehousing costs, ship- ping costs, and customer service costs as part of their marketing expenses, thus overstat- ing marketing expense and understating cost of goods sold. Whether the allegations against Amazon are true or false, the focus on gross revenues and gross profit margin has created incentives to engage in creative accounting practices in the e-business world.

Taxation. The taxing of online purchases has been and continues to be a hotly debated issue. State and local governments contend that they are missing out on a great deal of potential tax revenue if e-businesses are not required to pay local sales taxes as are brick- and-mortar companies. However, e-business owners argue that the cost of tracking and collecting taxes for what could amount to virtually every local municipality in the coun- try would far outweigh the taxes they would be able to collect.

Under a 1992 Supreme Court ruling, mail-order companies are not required to collect sales taxes in states where they do not maintain a physical presence, or **nexus** (i.e., stores, warehouses, etc). To this point, e-business companies have benefited from this same rul- ing. However, the big issue may rest on the definition of what "nexus" means for an e- business company. Is a "physical presence" a building or could it be something smaller such as an individual Web server? This could mean that, for an e-business company, locating a Web server in a particular area for operational objectives could cause undesirable tax consequences. These issues are of potential importance to assurance providers in auditing reported tax expenses and liabilities, as well as to accountants specializing in tax compliance and planning services.

There is little doubt that e-business models and emerging technologies have had and will continue to have significant effects on accounting standards and on traditional financial statement audits; however, our discussion of these issues is of necessity limited. The financial statement audit and GAAP are no less important in an e-business environment, but to completely discuss the impact of technology and changing business models on these issues would fill a college textbook. You might take an entire course devoted to the study of auditing in an IT environment. Therefore, the rest of this chapter is devoted to a discussion of the new opportunities accountants have to provide new kinds of assurance services, beyond the financial statement audit, in the emerging e-business environment.

New Forms of Assurance to Facilitate E-Business

The emergence of new technologies has enabled new forms of commerce but has also brought about new forms of risk. Auditors face new challenges and new opportunities to provide innovative assurance services in this new environment. The definition of assurance mentioned previously expands the potential role of the independent assurance provider far beyond the traditional role of financial statement auditor to include almost any service that has to do with information.

The profession is proactively pursuing new opportunities to expand the breadth of professional service offerings of assurance providers. As part of this effort, the AICPA formed the Special Committee on Assurance Services (SCAS) in 1994. After a careful analysis of demographic and other trends, this committee concluded the following:[5]

> *Your marketplace is changing. Multibillion-dollar markets for new CPA services are being created. Investors, creditors, and business managers are swamped with information, yet frustrated about not having the information they need and uncertain about the relevance and reliability of what they use. CPA firms of all sizes—from small practitioners to very large firms—can help these decision makers by delivering new assurance services.*

The Elliott Committee (named after its chair, Robert K. Elliott) identified six new service areas considered to have high potential for revenue growth for assurance providers:

1. Risk Assessment
2. Business Performance Measurement
3. Information Systems Reliability
4. Electronic Commerce
5. Health Care Performance Measurement
6. ElderCare

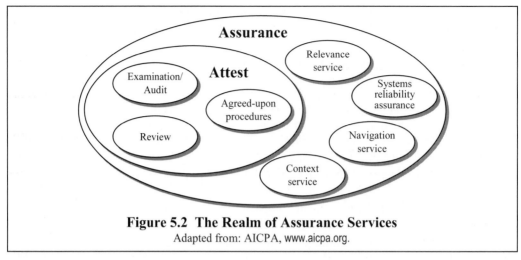

Figure 5.2 The Realm of Assurance Services
Adapted from: AICPA, www.aicpa.org.

The wide range of new services proposed by the Elliott Committee should give you a sense for the wide breadth of service offerings that the committee envisioned being offered by assurance providers. In addition to the six assurance services shown in Figure 5.2, the committee analyzed seven additional possible service areas and referred to hundreds more.[6] Figure 5.2 also illustrates the fact that the financial statement audit and other traditional attestation services are a subset of the much broader category of assurance services. The expanding realm of assurance services includes many additional service concepts.

The Committee also recognizes the potential for substantial expansion of the CPA role in providing assurance on risk assessment, business performance measurement, and information systems reliability. As illustrated in Figure 5.3, these three services intersect, forming a "new accountability domain," towards which the future of financial reporting and auditing may move.

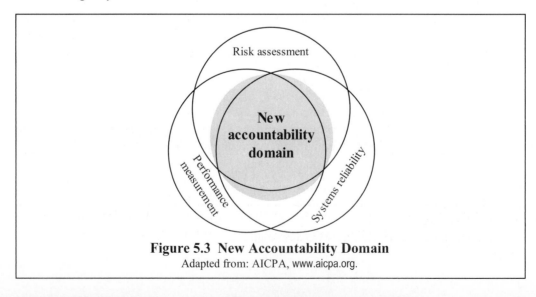

Figure 5.3 New Accountability Domain
Adapted from: AICPA, www.aicpa.org.

As previously discussed, e-commerce brings many new potential risks to the business environment and creates additional demand for accountability and assurance. These developments provide CPAs an opportunity to provide additional assurance services that go beyond the assurance provided by a financial statement audit. Here, we will focus on two of the six assurance services identified by the Elliott Committee—Information Systems Reliability Assurance and Electronic Commerce Assurance. While the two service areas are interrelated, an important distinction exists.

Information Systems Reliability Assurance. Systems reliability assurance services provide users with assurance that an enterprise's information systems are properly designed and are being operated in a manner that will deliver reliable data. Users of this assurance are divided into two groups: internal management and external users. The service provided to internal management provides assurance that the system produces reliable information necessary for management to make correct decisions and help the company achieve its goals. The service provided to external users provides assurance that the system on which external parties depend is reliably functioning. The ultimate goal is to provide real-time systems reliability assurance for data available over public networks.

Electronic Commerce Assurance. Electronic commerce assurance is the provision of assurance about the exchange of information and can be divided into two types of assurance services—integrity services and security services. In turn, integrity and security services can be applied in the context of both transactions and documents, and supporting systems. Table 5.1 briefly summarizes the essential concepts relating to security and integrity services. From this table, you can see that there is some overlap between e-business assurance and systems-reliability assurance, since e-business assurance includes some consideration of the reliability of supporting systems. Notice that these services directly address several of the risks discussed in Chapter 4.

Figure 5.4 (p. 130) illustrates how e-business and systems reliability assurance services provide assurance relating to the transactions and the supporting systems involved in the electronic exchange of information. Companies A, B, and C all rely on systems reliability assurance for both their internal systems reliability as well as for the reliability of the other two companies' interdependent systems. Electronic commerce assurance provides assurance on the transmission of transactions and electronic documents between the companies, along with some consideration of whether supporting systems can offer the necessary support for reliable electronic communication.

Table 5.1 Integrity and Security Services

	Integrity Services	**Security Services**
Transactions and documents	Elements were as agreed.	Parties are authentic. Transactions and documents are protected.
Supporting systems	Elements not altered through processing or storage.	Appropriate authentication and protection systems exist.

Adapted from: AICPA Web site, www.aicpa.org.

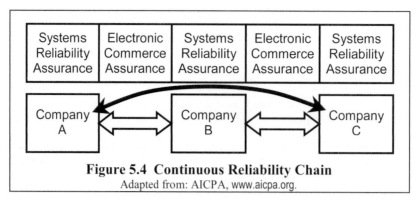

Figure 5.4 Continuous Reliability Chain
Adapted from: AICPA, www.aicpa.org.

In this new environment, CPAs can facilitate the functionality of e-business through providing assurance both between businesses and between businesses and customers. Now that we have discussed the general types of services CPAs can offer to facilitate e-business, we discuss some specific assurance services that CPAs have begun to offer to facilitate business-to-consumer (B2C) and business-to-business (B2B) e-commerce.

Business-to-Consumer Assurance

B2C assurance gives consumers comfort that in dealing with an e-business entity the various types of risks involved (e.g., risks related to infrastructure, authenticity, and privacy) are sufficiently controlled so that the interaction will be safe (e.g., no unauthorized use of credit card numbers), that privacy will be protected, and that transactions will be handled satisfactorily. The Internet has brought businesses and customers (who may be either individual consumers or other businesses) together in a new way, allowing customers to complete transactions at their own convenience. However, many feel that this type of e-business will never reach its full potential until online customers perceive that the additional risks of dealing online have been reduced to an acceptable level.

Even with the dramatic growth in Web commerce, a recent study shows that many consumers are still hesitant to perform transactions that require communicating personal information over the Internet (see Figure 5.5). To help e-business companies overcome this hesitancy and instill confidence in their customers, many companies and organizations, including the AICPA, have developed proprietary seals, which, when "stamped" on a Web site, certify the electronic privacy and security standards of that site.

Since the federal government does not mandate who can give digital seals, (as they do with financial statement audit opinions) the assurance provided by different seals may vary tremendously. The market for digital seals can be roughly separated into three different categories: CPA WebTrust, proprietary CPA firm seals, non-CPA firm seals.

CPA WebTrust

In response to growing need for B2C online assurance, the AICPA joined with the Canadian Institute of Chartered Accountants to create **CPA WebTrust**. As with other digital seals, a CPA WebTrust seal provides assurance regarding the online business practices of a particular company. The digital WebTrust seal is issued and maintained by a **trusted**

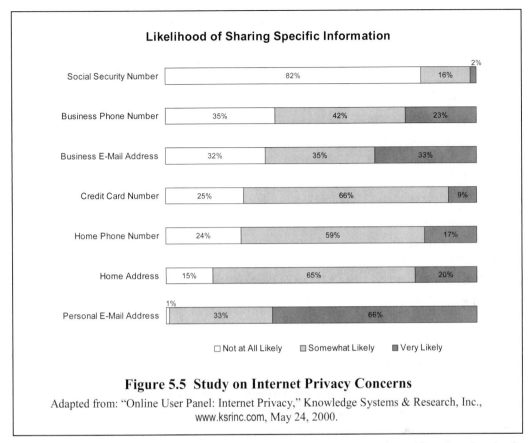

Figure 5.5 Study on Internet Privacy Concerns

Adapted from: "Online User Panel: Internet Privacy," Knowledge Systems & Research, Inc., www.ksrinc.com, May 24, 2000.

third-party service organization known as the seal manager, and certifies that the site in question meets the CPA WebTrust criteria.

Only a CPA who has been registered and certified by the AICPA to perform such evaluations can perform a CPA WebTrust audit. The CPA evaluates a company against a specific set of standards within each of seven main risk areas (see Text Box 5.8, p. 132).[7] Under each of the standards are various criteria specifically designed for the examination of B2C businesses, B2B businesses, service providers, and certification authorities.

If a client's business practices meet or exceed the WebTrust criteria, then the auditor provides the company's Web site with an electronic audit report. This report can be accessed via the CPA WebTrust seal placed directly on the company's Web site. Any online consumer can then click on the seal to view the attached report.

In order to verify that the company maintains its high standards of e-business integrity, each CPA WebTrust seal requires periodic reexamination. A CPA will review the company on a quarterly basis, or more frequently if needed, in order to evaluate any significant changes in the client's policies, practices, processes, and controls. Each seal of assurance is time-dated and requires an updated assurance report in order to remain active.

Text Box 5.8 WebTrust Primary Assurance Areas

1. **Online Privacy**—*The enterprise ensures that personally identifiable information obtained as a result of electronic commerce is protected as stated in its online privacy statement.*
2. **Confidentiality**—*The enterprise ensures that access to information obtained as a result of electronic commerce and designated as confidential is restricted to authorized individuals in conformity with its disclosed confidentiality practices.*
3. **Security**—*The enterprise ensures that access to the electronic commerce system and data is restricted only to authorized individuals in conformity with its disclosed security policies.*
4. **Business Practices and Transaction Integrity**—*The enterprise's electronic commerce transactions are processed completely, accurately, and in conformity with its disclosed business practices.*
5. **Availability**—*The enterprise ensures that e-commerce systems and data are available as disclosed.*
6. **Non-repudiation**—*The enterprise ensures that the authentication and integrity of transactions and messages received electronically are provable to third parties in conformity with its disclosed non-repudiation practices.*
7. **Customized Disclosures**—*The enterprise's specified disclosures (e.g., number of hits on the site in an established time frame) are consistent with professional standards for suitable criteria and relevant to its electronic commerce business.*

Source: AICPA, www.aicpa.org/webtrust.

Proprietary CPA Firm Seals

Several large CPA firms have created their own e-business audit services. In many ways, the proprietary, customized e-business assurance services being developed by large CPA firms are similar to the CPA WebTrust service. As with the CPA WebTrust service, the CPA firm provides assurance with respect to a client's e-business practices, but the assurance is tailored to meet the particular needs of each client. Again similar to CPA Web-Trust, the assurance provider typically performs tests to verify transaction integrity, information protection and privacy, and business practices. But because these engagements do not rely on the WebTrust criteria, assurance providers performing proprietary e-business engagements are able to compare their clients' e-business practices against flexible criteria that are tailored to their particular needs. When the auditors have finished their engagement, a proprietary seal bearing the CPA firm's name is placed on the client's Web site. The audit report can be accessed by clicking on the seal of assurance. Just as with CPA WebTrust, these seals must be periodically updated in order to confirm that the client continues to maintain their high standards.

Note that these e-business audits are performed separately from the traditional financial statement audit. While some of the procedures used might overlap, the two engagements produce two separate reports. In fact, it is not uncommon for an auditor to perform an e-business audit for a client that is not a financial statement audit client. However, at the time of this writing, the CPA does not jeopardize independence by performing both types of assurance engagements for a client.

Non-CPA Firm Seals

Perhaps the most prolific area of growth in the digital seal arena is seen among non-CPA firm seal providers. Keep in mind that while CPAs have a regulatory monopoly over financial statement audits, other types of assurance are open to competition! For example, the Better Business Bureau provides multiple seal types, including a privacy seal and a reliability seal (see Text Box 5.9). Currently, over 10,000 Web sites carry a BBB seal. One of the major advantages in choosing a BBB seal is cost. Because the seals are not based upon the results of an on-site audit, they can be offered for substantially less than seals offered by CPAs. Approval for a BBB seal is given based upon the answers to a Compliance Assessment Questionnaire. The BBB then allows the site to keep the seal unless customer complaints reveal privacy or security shortfalls.

TRUSTe, another non-CPA provider of digital seals, provides its digital seal to a number of well-known e-businesses such as eBay Inc. and Intel Corporation (which carries both the BBB OnLine Privacy seal and the TRUSTe seal). TRUSTe's mission is to "build users' trust and confidence in the Internet by promoting principles of disclosure and informed consent." Clicking on the TRUSTe "trustmark" on eBay's brings the users to a page informing them of the seal's meaning and how to proceed with privacy or security complaints. You may find it interesting to visit TRUSTe's Web site (www.truste.org) and compare their assurance product with the AICPA's WebTrust assurance product.

Text Box 5.9 Online Assurance Competition

The Better Business Bureau (BBB) is one of the largest competitors to the CPA WebTrust service. The BBB's Web site (www.bbbonline.org) states that the BBB's 90 years of trusted service provides additional assurance to the general public when its seals are seen. A Greenfield Online Survey in 2001 showed that "Just under 90 percent of online shoppers say they would feel more confident buying from a site displaying the BBB OnLine Reliability seal, than from one that does not." Its two most popular seals are the BBB OnLine Privacy and BBB OnLine Reliability seals, shown at left.

Each seal has specific standards that must be upheld by the Web site in order to maintain the seal. Approval to carry the BBB OnLine Reliability seal is based on the following standards.

Reliability Program Requirements:

- *Be a member of the Better Business Bureau where company is headquartered.*
- *Provide the BBB with information regarding company ownership and management and the street address and telephone number at which they do business, which may be verified by the BBB in a visit to the company's physical premises.*
- *Be in business a minimum of one year (an exception can be made if a new business is a spin-off or a division of an existing business, which is known to and has a positive track record with the BBB).*
- *Have a satisfactory complaint-handling record with the BBB.*
- *Agree to participate in the BBB's advertising self-regulation program, and correct or withdraw online advertising when challenged by the BBB and found not to be substantiated or not in compliance with children's advertising guidelines.*
- *Agree to abide by the **BBB Code of Online Business Practices**, and to cooperate with any BBB request for modification of a Web site to bring it into accordance with the Code.*
- *Respond promptly to all consumer complaints.*
- *Agree to dispute resolution, at the consumer's request, for unresolved disputes involving consumer products or services.*

Source: Better Business Bureau, www.bbbonline.org, March 2002. Used by permission.

Business-to-Business Assurance

The previous chapter outlined various ways a company can mitigate the risks inherent in an e-business environment. These approaches to mitigating risks, however, are limited in that they limit only the e-business risks within the enterprise itself. As discussed in the previous chapter, one of the characteristics of the e-business environment is an increased interdependency between organizations. An example discussed in Chapter 2 is that of Wal-Mart and its electronic partnership with its major inventory supplier, Procter & Gamble (P&G). Under the agreement, P&G has access to certain portions of Wal-Mart's inventory data. When Wal-Mart's inventory of P&G goods reaches a certain level, P&G automatically arranges for shipment of additional inventory.

As we can see from this example, Wal-Mart depends on P&G's ability to respond accurately and quickly to Wal-Mart's needs. Effective internal controls at Wal-Mart will not provide assurance that its business partners and associates, such as P&G, have implemented equally effective controls into their systems. Like a weak link in a chain, an unreliable system in an e-business partnership can be the source of a disastrous outcome for all parties involved. The CPA profession currently offers two services to meet the resulting demand for B2B assurance—SysTrust and SAS 70 Reviews.

SysTrust

To meet the demand for assurance on system reliability, the AICPA joined with the CICA to formulate a new assurance service called SysTrust. SysTrust is a service in which a CPA performs certain procedures to determine the reliability of a company's system according to a set of specified criteria. A reliable system is defined as "one that operates without material impairment during a specified period in a specified environment." To determine the reliability of a company's system, the CPA reviews the system and evaluates it according to the following four principles:[8]

1. **Availability**. *The system is available during times specified by the entity.*
2. **Security**. *Adequate protection is provided against unwanted logical or physical entrance into the system.*
3. **Integrity**. *Processes within the system are executed in a complete, accurate, timely, and authorized manner.*
4. **Maintainability**. *Updates (upgrades) to the system can be performed when needed without disabling the other three principles.*

To be reliable, a system must satisfy the all four of these principles by complying with corresponding documentation, procedures, and monitoring criteria under each principle (see Table 5.3, pp. 136-137). To obtain evidence that a system is reliable, a CPA follows procedures similar to the testing of controls in a financial statement audit. The CPA reviews the controls in place and tests them to see if they are functioning in accordance with the principles and criteria set forth by the SysTrust service.

Based on the four principles stated above and their corresponding criteria, CPAs can perform a number of services. Possible engagements include (but are not limited to) system reliability attestation, selected principle compliance, and consultation services.

System Attestation. Following the examination and testing of the system's controls, the CPA issues a description of the system examined and an attestation report that includes the CPAs opinion as to the reliability of the system during the period covered by the attestation report. This report can be relied upon internally by management, and can be used to provide assurance to an e-business' potential partners that the enterprises' information systems are reliable and can be trusted in an interdependent business relationship. There is no SysTrust seal, like the one marking WebTrust attestation, but management may choose to post the SysTrust attestation report online if public accreditation is desired.

Selected Principle Compliance. If a client does not need attestation as to the overall reliability of a system, but rather is concerned about compliance with a specific SysTrust principle, a CPA may perform tests to assure compliance with that principle.

Consultation Services. CPAs may provide consultation services relating to the SysTrust Principles in accordance with the AICPA Standards for Consulting Services. For example, consultation services may be provided to help a client prepare for a system attestation engagement.

SAS 70 Reviews of Service Organizations

SAS 70, *Reports on the Processing of Transactions by Service Organizations*, is an auditing standard issued by the AICPA that provides a standardized format in which service organizations can disclose their system controls to their clients or to their clients' auditors. "Service organizations" are any companies or organizations that provide data processing services such as paycheck processing, Internet data processing, or claims processing, to client organizations.

While SAS 70 reviews have a fairly narrow focus and were designed primarily to provide assistance in financial statement auditing, they can facilitate the conduct of e-business by alleviating some of the risks inherent in B2B transactions. For example, third-party service entities such as EDP service centers and value added networks (VANs), which, as explained in Chapter 2, are EDI facilitators, can demonstrate the effectiveness of established controls to customers through a SAS 70 report (discussed below). SAS 70 provides guidance to the auditor or to the auditor of the entity providing the service (service auditor) in designing a report that can be relied upon by the entity using the service (user auditor).

In the ordinary course of an audit, the user auditor is required to gain an understanding of the client's internal controls to effectively plan the audit. When a company outsources essential data processing activities that affect financial statement assertions to a third-party, the auditor is also required to gain an understanding of the portion of the client's system that resides at the service organization.

If the organization offers highly standardized services, the "service auditor" may be best suited to provide assurance: however, when the third-party offers many customized services, the "third-party auditor" may be unable to provide sufficient assurance regarding a specific client, and a SAS 70 report may be insufficient for the user auditor to rely upon.

Table 5.3 SysTrust Principles and Criteria

Availability

Documentation

- The system availability (SA) requirements of authorized users, and system availability objectives, policies, and standards are identified and documented.
- SA objectives, policies, and standards have been communicated to authorized users.
- SA objectives, policies, and standards are consistent with SA requirements specified in contractual, legal, and other service level agreements and applicable laws and regulations.
- Responsibility and accountability for SA have been assigned.
- SA objectives, policies, standards are communicated to personnel responsible for implementing them.

Procedures

- The acquisition, implementation, configuration and management of system components related to SA are consistent with SA objectives, policies, and standards.
- There are procedures to protect the system against risks that might disrupt system operations and impair SA.
- Continuity provisions address minor processing errors, minor destruction of records, and major disruptions of system processing that might impair SA.
- There are procedures to ensure that personnel responsible for the design, development, implementation and operation of SA features are qualified to fulfill their responsibilities.

Monitoring

- SA performance is periodically reviewed and compared with SA requirements of authorized users and contractual, legal, and other service-level agreements.
- There is a process to identify potential impairments to the system's ongoing ability to address SA objectives, policies, and standards and to take appropriate action.
- Environmental/technological changes are monitored; impact on SA is periodically assessed on a timely basis.

Security

Documentation

- The system security (SS) requirements of authorized users, and SS objectives, policies, and standards, are identified and documented.
- SS objectives, policies, and standards have been communicated to authorized users.
- SS objectives, policies, and standards are consistent with SS requirements defined in contractual, legal, and other service-level agreements and applicable laws and regulations.
- Responsibility and accountability for SS have been assigned.
- SS objectives, policies, standards are communicated to entity personnel responsible for implementing them.

Procedures

- The acquisition, implementation, configuration, and management of system components related to SS are consistent with documented system security objectives, policies, and standards.
- Threats of sabotage, terrorism, vandalism, and other attacks have been considered when locating the system.
- There are procedures to:
  - identify and authenticate all users authorized to access the system
  - grant access privileges to users in accordance with the policies and standards for granting such privileges
  - restrict access to computer processing output to authorized users
  - restrict access to files on off-line storage media to authorized users
  - protect external access points against unauthorized logical access
  - protect the system against infection by computer viruses, malicious codes, and unauthorized software
  - segregate incompatible functions within the system through security authorizations
  - protect the system against unauthorized physical access
  - ensure that personnel responsible for design, development, implementation, and operation of SS are qualified.

Monitoring

- SS performance is periodically reviewed and compared with documented system security requirements of authorized users and contractual, legal, and other service level agreements.
- There is a process to identify potential impairments to the system's ongoing ability to address SS objectives, policies, and standards, and to take appropriate action.
- Environmental/technological changes are monitored; impact on SS is periodically assessed on a timely basis.

Table 5.3 (cont.) SysTrust Principles and Criteria

Integrity

Documentation
- The system processing integrity (SPI) requirements of authorized users and the SPI objectives, policies, and standards are identified and documented.
- SPI objectives, policies, and standards have been communicated to authorized users.
- SPI objectives, policies, and standards are consistent with system processing integrity requirements defined in contractual, legal, and other service level agreements and applicable laws and regulations.
- Responsibility and accountability for SPI have been assigned.
- SPI objectives, policies, standards are communicated to entity personnel responsible for implementing them.

Procedures
- The acquisition, implementation, configuration, and management of system components related to SPI are consistent with documented SPI objectives, policies, and standards.
- Information processing integrity (IPI) procedures related to information inputs are consistent with the documented SPI requirements.
- There are procedures to ensure that system processing is complete, accurate, timely, and authorized.
- IPI procedures related to information outputs are consistent with SPI requirements.
- There are procedures to ensure that personnel responsible for the design, development, implementation, and operation of the system are qualified to fulfill their responsibilities.
- There are procedures to enable tracing of information inputs from source to final disposition and vice versa.

Monitoring
- SPI performance is periodically reviewed and compared to SPI requirements of authorized users and contractual, legal, and other service-level agreements.
- There is a process to identify potential impairments to the system's ongoing ability to address SPI objectives, policies, and standards and take appropriate action.
- Environmental/technological changes are monitored; impact on SPI is assessed on a timely basis.

Maintainability

Documentation
- Documented system maintainability (SM) objectives, policies, standards address all areas affected by system changes.
- SM objectives, policies, and standards have been communicated to authorized users.
- SM objectives, policies, and standards are consistent with system maintainability requirements defined in contractual, legal, and other service level agreements and applicable laws and regulations.
- Responsibility and accountability for SM have been assigned.
- SM performance objectives, policies, standards are communicated to those responsible to implement them.

Procedures
- Resources available to maintain the system are consistent with the documented requirements of authorized users and objectives, policies, and standards.
- Procedures to manage, schedule, and document all planned changes to the system are applied to modifications of system components to maintain documented system availability, security, and integrity consistent with documented objectives, policies, and standards.
- There are procedures to ensure that only authorized, tested, and documented changes are made to the system and related data.
- There are procedures to communicate planned and completed system changes to information systems management and to authorized users.
- There are procedures to allow for and to control emergency changes.

Monitoring
- SM performance is periodically reviewed and compared with SM requirements of authorized users and contractual, legal, and other service-level agreements.
- There is a process to identify potential impairments to the system's ongoing ability to address SM objectives, policies, and standards and to take appropriate action.
- Environmental/technological changes are monitored; impact on SM is assessed on a timely basis.

Adapted from: AICPA, www.aicpa.org. Used by permission.

SAS 70 provides for two types of reports that service auditor can provide to user auditors concerning the policies and procedures of the service organization:

- Reports on policies and procedures placed in operation.
- Reports on policies and procedures placed in operation and tests of operating effectiveness.

The first report provides the user auditor with an understanding of the service provider's internal policies and procedures that may be relevant to the user organization's internal control, whether or not such policies and procedures were in place covering the period of the audit, and whether the policies and procedures are suitably designed to achieve specified internal control objectives.

The second report not only provides the information from the first report, but also goes beyond to provide results of tests regarding the effectiveness of policies and procedures. This report is designed to convey reasonable assurance that the internal control objectives of the user organization were met during the audit period.

Although SAS 70 provides much needed guidance to auditors, some criticisms of the standard have surfaced. At least two potential problems exist with the service auditor reports. First, the service auditor's report provides a single overall evaluation and conclusion, whereas the user auditor might in some cases be better served by a control-by-control evaluation. Second, a disparity may exist between what is considered effective by each auditor. What is deemed to be effective by the service auditor may not be sufficient for user auditor to set control risk at a minimum.

The existence of SAS 70 does not eliminate the need for the SysTrust assurance service. Because SAS 70 lacks recognized measurement criteria for reporting and, because a service auditor's report is designed for auditor-to-auditor communication, SAS 70 reports are not particularly well suited for a broad range of third parties beyond data processing service organizations.

Other Potential New Services to Facilitate E-Business

E-business provides several other possible new service opportunities for CPAs. We briefly summarize some of the desired services that the AICPA believes could be provided by accountants. These include providing assurance for Value Added Networks (VANs), trusted key and signature providers, and makers of software that enables e-business. CPAs may also be able to play an important role in creating criteria for measurement systems that facilitate e-business. Finally, CPAs will likely be able to leverage the knowledge and business contacts they acquire through e-business assurance services to continue to be providers of choice for high-margin consulting services.

Value-Added Network (VAN) Service Provider Assurance

This potential new service is similar to the above-mentioned SAS 70 review in that a CPA reviews, tests, and evaluates the controls, integrity, and security of the value-added network provider. Thus, the CPA is able to provide assurance to user organizations. The main difference is that the SAS 70 review is primarily for auditor-to-auditor communication. This service supports assurance to a broad range of external third parties and is suited specifically to their individual needs. In addition, assurance can be provided as to the compliance of both parties with established trading criteria. Because of the CPAs reputation as an independent assurance provider, they are potentially excellent candidates for providing such services.

Evaluation of Electronic Commerce Software Packages

The advent of e-business has created demand for the creation of software packages that companies can use to bring their businesses online. Companies that provide such software, such as IBM and Novell, are some of the e-business infrastructure providers discussed in Chapter 3. Companies considering implementation of these software packages need assurance that the software contains necessary controls to facilitate their operations and to protect them from undue risks. CPAs can review and test the control and security features of these software packages.

Trusted Key and Signature Provider Assurance

One of the most important prerequisites in conducting e-business is to build trust effectively and efficiently between the parties that plan to conduct transactions. The required level of security to establish the needed trust is typically achieved through public key infrastructure or encryption, as discussed earlier in this chapter. Encryption technology is used to establish a trustworthy network environment through which e-business transactions can be reliably conducted. For public-key cryptography to be effective, however, users must be assured that their identities and keys—as well as those of the parties with whom they communicate—are valid and reliable. This assurance is achieved through the services provided by **trusted third parties (TTPs)**.

You may have noticed that the CPA WebTrust seal includes the name "Verisign." Verisign, Inc., based in Mountain View, California, is one such **trusted key** and **digital signature** provider. The company essentially distributes the electronic equivalent of identification cards to help customers and companies prove they are who they say they are. In other words, Verisign distributes digital certificates that work with security features built into Web browser programs to authenticate merchants and customers. Verisign's logo is part of the CPA WebTrust seal because Verisign is a CPA WebTrust partner that helps authenticate and prevent false usage of the WebTrust seal. Companies like Verisign may want to communicate their reliability and integrity to companies using their services. The effective communication of reliability and integrity to prospective business partners or customers may require trusted third-party assurance to increase the credibility of their representations. (See Text Box 5.10, p. 140.)

CPA firms are designing and offering services to meet a need for assurance by these companies by assessing the reliability and integrity of the trusted key provider, or even by acting as a trusted third-party key provider. For example, PricewaterhouseCoopers, LLP, offers comprehensive audit and consulting services to TTPs. They also offer their services by actually acting as a TTP, providing trusted security management services to their clients.

Text Box 5.10 Sign On the Digital Line

Will digital signatures ever be as widely accepted as pen-on-paper signatures? Legislation from Congress is making digital signatures more and more legally binding.

In April 2000, The United States General Services Administration (GSA) gave permission to Digital Signature Trust Co. (DST) to issue Access Certificates for Electronic Services (ACES) to the public. DST provides certificates that give positive identification in electronic transactions. The certificates guarantee the recognition of digital signatures by the federal government and will enhance electronic access to government information. The federal government is striving to make information more accessible to the public, and ACES is one way of achieving this goal.

Adapted from: Max Knudson, "Feds OK Digital Signature Operation," *Deseret News*, April 4, 2000.

Criteria Establishment

Sets of criteria are important parts of both WebTrust and SysTrust. In fact, any time assurance is to be provided, criteria for that assurance must either already exist, or must be developed. For example, if a Web site earns the CPA WebTrust seal, what does that seal represent? The meaning of the assurance provided by the seal must be defined by specific criteria against which e-businesses are measured.

Often, the developer of a set of criteria that becomes widely adopted and utilized has a significant first-mover advantage. Thus, if CPAs are to be significant providers of assurance in the e-business world, it will likely be in their interest to invest in the development of sets of criteria like those found in the WebTrust and SysTrust services.

Consulting Services

Assurance providers have long had an advantage in leveraging existing services to provide further lucrative consulting services. At one point, many believed that consulting opportunities represented the largest potential growth in revenues for CPAs with experience in e-business. As CPAs work with clients with existing e-business systems, they gain a wider knowledge base of best practices and necessary controls. This expertise naturally creates rich and varied consulting opportunities, helping clients develop more secure and effective e-business systems.

Recent events have encouraged CPA firms to divest their separate consulting practices.[9] With the collapse of Enron and the associated allegations of CPA wrongdoing at big accounting firm Arthur Andersen, LLP, questions have risen as to the sustainability of auditor independence when CPAs provide both consulting and auditing services to the same companies. However, CPAs will very likely continue to provide significant consulting services, at least to non-audit clients. One notion to keep in mind is that consulting services associated with the selection and implementation of information systems is a much different service than the systems reliability and e-commerce assurance services described here. As of this writing, the major national accounting firms are in the process of divesting themselves from the business of systems implementation and consulting.

At this point it is unclear what the ultimate effects of the Enron debacle will be on the consulting services offered by public accounting firms, but we believe that the closer a service is to the core audit, the more likely the firms will retain that service. We also believe that the firms should not and cannot remove themselves completely from the business of IT-related assurance for their audit clients because the quality of financial statements and the very health of so many clients depend so heavily on it.

What E-Business Means for Accounting Professionals

As has been discussed and illustrated throughout this book, the emergence of e-business has several important implications for accountants, particularly CPAs. Opportunities abound, but CPAs will need to leverage existing competencies and develop new ones, especially in the area of technology-related risk and control. They will need to be more entrepreneurial and customer-focused to compete effectively with a host of new competitors, and they will need to be mindful of new legal liability exposure.

Application of Current CPA Competencies

CPAs have long been considered to be independent professionals with expertise in assessing risks, evaluating evidence, and making professional judgments concerning the reliability and truthfulness of assertions made by their clients. These core competencies of CPAs naturally lend themselves to assurance services where such objective inspection and judgment are necessary.

CPAs are well positioned to take advantage of the new assurance and consulting opportunities created by the emergence of e-business. Table 5.4 (p. 142) outlines some of the core values, services, and competencies expected of CPAs. As they gain more experience with e-business, CPAs can combine their new knowledge with their existing competencies to emerge as the most qualified providers of the services mentioned.

New Competencies Required of CPAs

As assurance services become more high-tech in nature, CPAs need to ensure they are up-to-date on their IT understanding and ability. CPAs providing assurance in an e-business environment cannot continue to rely on the same processes and tests used in more traditional business environments if they are to remain competitive. The CPA of the future need to be well versed in the basic concepts and risks associated with information technology and e-business, as well as with the evolving methods to measure and control those risks.

Although CPAs today already possess many of the skills and attributes needed to excel in an e-business environment, many professionals will find it necessary to develop new competencies. Most importantly, many CPAs will need to strengthen their understanding of the nature and risks of e-business as well as of the enabling technologies underlying it. For example, CPAs will have to develop at least a broad level of understanding of technological issues such as data security, data encryption, and digital data communication. While an appropriate focus on the "information value chain" discussed in Chapter 1 is important, a more in-depth knowledge of e-business risks, measurements, and controls will make the CPA more competent to provide the emerging services designed to conduct e-business. Furthermore, it will be critical for CPAs wishing to offer services to develop new or enhance existing competencies, such as decision modeling, risk analysis, meas-

Table 5.4 Core Values, Services, and Competencies for CPAs

Core Values	Core Services	Core Competencies
Continuing Education and Life-Long Learning CPAs highly value continuing education beyond certification and believe it is important to continuously acquire new skills and knowledge. ***Competence*** CPAs are able to perform high quality work in a capable, efficient, and appropriate manner. ***Integrity*** CPAs conduct themselves with honesty and professional ethics. ***Attuned to Broad Business Issues*** CPAs are in tune with the overall realities of the business environment. ***Objectivity*** CPAs are able to deal with information free of distortions, personal bias, or conflicts of interest.	***Assurance and Information Integrity*** Provide a variety of services that improve and assure the quality of information, or its context, for business decision-making. ***Technology Services*** Services that leverage technology to improve objectives and decision-making including business application processes, system integrity, knowledge management, system security, and integration of new business processes and practices. ***Management Consulting and Performance Management*** Provide advice and insight on the financial and non-financial performance of an organization's operational and strategic processes through broad business knowledge and judgment. ***Financial Planning*** Provide a variety of services to organizations and individuals that interpret and add value by utilizing a wide range of financial information. These include everything from tax planning and financial statement analysis to structuring investment portfolios and complex financial transactions. ***International Services*** Provide services to support and facilitate commerce in the global marketplace.	***Communications and Leadership Skills*** Able to give and exchange information within meaningful context and with appropriate delivery and interpersonal skills. Able to influence, inspire, and motivate others to achieve results. ***Strategic and Critical Thinking Skills*** Able to link data, knowledge, and insight together to provide quality advice for strategic decision-making. ***Focus on the Customer, Client, and Market*** Able to anticipate and meet the changing needs of clients, employers, customers, and markets better than competitors. ***Interpretation of Converging Information*** Able to interpret and provide a broader context using financial and non-financial information. ***Technologically Adept*** Able to utilize and leverage technology in ways that add value to clients, customers, and employers.

Source: AICPA from **www.cpavision.org/vision.htm**. Used by permission.

urement, reporting, research, and the ability to leverage technology to enhance functional competencies. Finally, CPAs will need a broad e-business perspective in order to effectively meet the needs of clients. Such a perspective includes most of the topics covered in this book, for example the potential impact of technology, the various types of business models being employed, and the risks and risk management techniques involved in e-business.

Competitive Environment

As CPAs enter the market in providing new "e-assurance" services, they enter a competitive assurance arena that, unlike the financial statement audit, is not exclusively reserved to their profession. The profession essentially has a legislated monopoly over financial statement audits—no one but CPAs can legitimately perform them. Such is not the case for e-business or systems reliability assurance lines, or for any of the other new assurance services the CPA profession is developing. CPAs must compete in this market both with fellow CPAs and with other assurance providers such as the Better Business Bureau (see Text Box 5.9, p. 133).

CPAs are well positioned to capitalize on the new assurance opportunities provided by e-business. However, in considering their need for various kinds of e-business assurance, many people do not think of accountants as the people best suited to provide them. CPAs will have to become more entrepreneurial. They will have to work hard to enhance their image and gain marketplace "permission" to be able to provide these services. By marketing themselves as capable and willing, and by building on their reputation and existing client relationships, CPAs may be able to establish themselves as first-choice providers of these assurance services.

Legal Liability Issues

In addition to considering marketplace permission, new competencies needed, and competition, CPAs must always be aware of the ever-present possibility of litigation. In fact, a spate of lawsuits revolving around dot-com revenue recognition and other accounting issues may be just around the corner. Whenever CPAs provide assurance of any kind, the primary beneficiary of the assurance will likely rely on that assurance to improve their own information environment, and will often use the independent assurance to increase the credibility of their representations to other third parties. Thus, CPAs owe both an ethical and a legal duty to those who rely on their assurance. When subsequent events appear to contradict the nature of the assurance, or when CPAs are negligent, they are exposed to potential litigation. This risk should not by itself prevent CPAs from taking advantage of the new assurance opportunities being opened up by the emergence of e-business, but it certainly must be a carefully considered factor in deciding what portfolio of services to provide.

Summary

This book illustrates how e-business is changing the way business is conducted and how these changes are impacting the CPA profession. As discussed in this chapter, e-business has important implications for existing services, including financial statement assurance, but also creates new demands for other kinds of assurance that will facilitate the level of trust and confidence necessary to the conduct of e-business transactions. To adapt to these changes and take full advantage of these new e-business opportunities, CPAs need to acquire new competencies and leverage their existing competencies in creative and entrepreneurial ways. They also need to become more customer-oriented, designing services that directly meet the needs of their individual clients in order to be competitive both with other CPAs and non-CPA assurance providers.

This book makes it clear that the infrastructure that supports and enables e-business is highly technological in nature. However, as accountants invest in acquiring new competencies, they need to be cognizant of where their investments fall along the information value chain. CPAs do not have a comparative advantage in working directly with bits and bytes of information, or in software development. Therefore, it is not a wise long-term investment for someone targeting the upper-end of the value chain to focus large amounts of energy and resources at the lower end of the chain. However, there is great demand for professionals who can be information intermediaries—professionals who can bridge the gap between data and decisions by intelligently conversing with both IT technicians and business decision-makers. It is essential that CPAs understand the market opportunities, risks, controls, and assurance needs associated with e-business in order to thrive in the new online economy.

 For more information, please visit the Companion Website at www.prenhall.com/glover.

Review Questions

5-1   Identify the five most important implications of e-business for assurance services offered by CPAs.

5-2   What are the implications of CPAs assisting in the implementation of a company's internal e-business controls and performing audits in today's environment?

5-3   What might an auditor do to better understand an e-business enterprise's IT internal control system, and why is it important for an auditor to do so?

5-4   In e-business environments, auditors are likely to encounter clients who store information only in electronic form. Some of that information may be critical to the auditor as audit evidence. What are the implications for the audit if the client does not have adequate controls in place to protect the integrity of that electronic information?

5-5   What services might an auditor offer to facilitate electronic commerce? How would these services facilitate e-business? Who or what are the major competitors or roadblocks to CPAs capturing this assurance market?

5-6   What are the principles behind the SysTrust assurance service? Briefly explain the meaning of each principle and why it is an important part of the assurance offered. (Hint: What are the criteria behind the principles?)

5-7   What qualities, skills, and competitive advantages does the CPA have to offer in the new e-business assurance market? Why should CPAs play a role facilitating e-business? Although we have discussed many of the benefits, are there any deterrents or reasons CPAs should be cautious in offering e-business assurance?

Discussion Case

5-7   Peabody and Fisk, CPAs, recently finished the standard financial statement audit for Pack-It-In, a client engaged in the retail sales of outdoor equipment. Recently, Pack-It-In has developed a Web presence that allows the company to sell equipment directly to consumers over the Web. The company has developed a partnering relationship with Evergreen Accessories, a retailer of outdoor clothing, and is presenting Evergreen's goods through Pack-It-In's Web site. All sales of outdoor clothing are communicated to Evergreen, who ships the product directly to the customer. Of course, all outdoor equipment products are shipped by Pack-It-In, with help from a newly hired logistics outsourcer. Pack-It-In and Evergreen have established open communication between portions of their systems such that Pack-It-In is able to monitor the quantities on hand of Evergreen's merchandise. Evergreen is also able to monitor its Web sales through Pack-It-In's Web site. (1) What new risks does the company's move into e-business bring about? (2) What additional audit procedures, driven by Pack-It-In's move to becoming a Web e-tailer, should Peabody and Fisk, CPAs, have performed during the regular financial statement audit? (3) What additional audit procedures driven by Pack-It-In's partnership with Evergreen should Peabody and Fisk, CPAs, have performed during the regular financial statement audit? (4) What new demands for assurance by Pack-It-In or its business partners arise due to the introduction of e-business into Pack-It-In's business strategy? (5) Discuss the additional value-added assurance services that Peabody and Fisk, CPAs, could present to their client.

Research Cases

5-8 Finlay and Gleason, CPAs, have never offered the CPA WebTrust assurance to a client before. Presently, they have a client who has requested this service. What should the firm do to prepare to offer this service? Should they offer this service at the present time without any prior experience? Visit the AICPA Web site (www.aicpa.org/webtrust) to find the answers to these questions.

5-9 Meryll's Imports is engaging in a significant e-business partnering arrangement with foreign suppliers. The company is concerned with the reliability of its partners' systems. The company decides to take the lead and have its system certified with the CPA SysTrust assurance service. The company's desire is to show its partners its willingness to have its system certified and then ask the company's partners to do the same. Meryll's Imports contacts Nelson, Hardwick, and Moore, CPAs, to learn more of the requirements for a SysTrust certification. Unfortunately the CPA firm has never offered the SysTrust service to a client before. Help the firm determine if they can offer this service. Outline the requirements for providing such a service. Visit the AICPA Web site to gather information (www.aicpa.org/webtrust).

5-10 You are the controller and chief information officer of a new startup e-business company. Discuss the advantages and the disadvantages of obtaining a SysTrust cite seal in a memo to your CEO. Why would you choose to implement or not implement.

Notes

1. See Statement on Auditing Standards [SAS] 80, *Evidential Matter*, and SAS 94, *The Effect of Information Technology on the Auditor's Consideration of Internal Control in a Financial Statement Audit.*
2. Deutsche Bank, one of the world's largest financial services institutions, has begun using XBRL to process loan information and streamline its credit analysis process. Bank of America is piloting XBRL for the same purpose in the United States. In addition, Reuters and Microsoft both recently announced that they have published their financial statements using XBRL. General Electric has announced that its Corporate Tax Department will use XBRL to simplify and speed its tax reporting processes.
3. It should be noted, however, that traditional valuation models based on assets and expected cash flows are just as applicable to e-business enterprises as they are to conventional ones. As the crash of the "dot-com" stocks in 2000 fully illustrates, to be successful, e-businesses must generate cash and turn a profit just like any other business. In fact, a March 2000 study by John Hand indicated that economic fundamentals, such as current book equity, forecasted one-year ahead earnings, and forecasted long-run earnings growth, were the primary factors explaining Internet stock prices even at that time. See John R.M. Hand, "The Role of Economic Fundamentals, Web Traffic, and Supply and Demand in the Pricing of U.S. Internet Stocks," Kenan-Flagler Business School, UNC Chapel Hill, March 28, 2000.
4. FASB news release, www.fasb.org, January 14, 2002.
5. AICPA Web site, "Assurance Services," www.aicpa.org.
6. You can access these at the AICPA Web site, http://www.aicpa.org.
7. All AICPA material in this chapter is used by persmission. WebTrust material adapted from www.aicpa.org/webtrust.
8. SysTrust material adapted from www.aicpa.org/systrust.
9. Legislation pending as of the writing of this edition would in fact prohibit firms from offering consulting services to publicly traded audit clients.

Appendix A: Internet Technology

Any electronic network has two main components: hardware and software. The hardware side of a network is composed of computers connected together using **networking gear**. The software side consists of **protocols** for communication with operating systems and applications that implement those protocols. In this appendix, we describe some of the technology on which the Internet is built.

Networks are built by connecting **nodes** through some transmission medium. A node can be a PC, printer, or some other device. The most common transmission medium is a bundle of copper wires packaged in a **twisted-pair** configuration, but other media include fiber optics, coaxial cable (like cable TV), and wireless transmissions (e.g., radio or microwave). Nodes are typically connected to a transmission medium using a **network interface controller** (**NIC**) card.

At the smallest level, a **local-area network** (**LAN**) connects two or more machines in a single office or building. Typically, all the machines in a LAN must be relatively close to one another. The most common LAN technology, and the workhorse of the Internet, is **Ethernet**, also known as IEEE 802.3. In an Ethernet LAN, nodes attach to a common wire in a **bus** configuration. This means that all nodes in an Ethernet LAN are directly connected with one another, so that when a node transmits a **packet** of information, all other nodes receive the packet simultaneously. If two nodes attempt to transmit simultaneously, a **collision** occurs, and the nodes must attempt retransmission. Part of the Ethernet standard describes how nodes perform conflict resolution in the event of a collision.

Networking Gear

A typical Ethernet LAN uses an 8-wire cable organized into four pairs twisted around each other for more reliable transmission (wires carrying signals can interfere with each other, creating "crosstalk," and straight wires are noisier than twisted pairs). These cables use modular RJ-45 connectors on each end that look like a wide version of the RJ-11 telephone connectors you see in your home. The most common type of Ethernet cabling is called **category 5** wire. It can handle transmission speeds of 10 or 100 megabits per seconds (Mbps). **Gigabit** Ethernet is a newer standard that transmits 1,000 megabits, or 1 gigabit, per second. Most category 5 wire will handle gigabit speeds, but sometimes higher-performance **category 5e** wire may be needed.

LANs are often divided into multiple **segments** for better performance or manageability (see Figure A.1, p. 148). Segments can be connected using hubs, bridges, switches, and routers. In a twisted-pair network, **hubs** are commonly used to connect nodes. Hubs usually have between 4 and 32 **ports** for receiving RJ-45 connections. Hubs forward all traffic to all attached nodes. To reduce the possibility of collisions, a **switched hub**, or **switch**, is used to isolate network segments from one another, forwarding packets only when they are destined for one of the nodes on the segment. When the cabling between two segments is incompatible (e.g., twisted pair vs. coaxial), a **bridge** may be used to forward packets between two segments. Bridges, like switches, only forward packets intended for the other side of the network. A **router** is an intelligent and powerful **gateway**

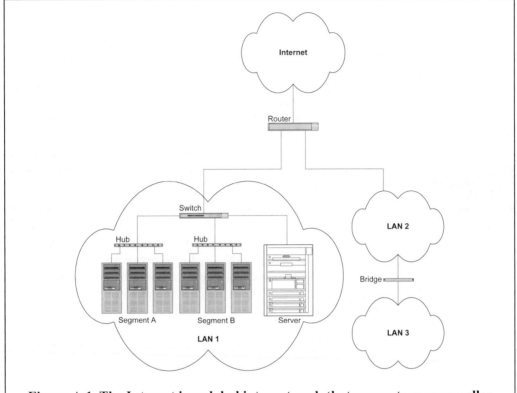

Figure A.1   The Internet is a global internetwork that connects many smaller networks located around the world.

device that routes or forwards packets to their proper segments. Besides interconnecting networks, routers also can implement firewalls (see Appendix D) and other security measures.

LANs in different buildings are often assembled into **campus networks**. In Figure A.1, LANs 1, 2, and 3, plus the router, correspond to a campus network. Within LAN 1, a switch increases performance by separating traffic within Segment A from traffic within Segment B. The server is on a separate switched segment so it can ignore intrasegment traffic in both Segments A and B. The switch guarantees that the server will only see packets addressed to it. A bridge connects LAN 2 with LAN 3, perhaps because both are in the same building and there is only one path from the building to the campus-wide router.

For more geographically dispersed organizations, a **wide-area network (WAN)** covers greater distances. To set up a WAN, you generally need to involve the services of a tele-communications company (telco). But as networking gear becomes less expensive and more sophisticated, the distinctions are blurring between LANs, WANs, and other forms of networks. For example, a company with a direct line-of-sight view between two distant buildings in the same metropolitan area might choose to install its own microwave transmission link rather than pay a telco for its services. Such an arrangement has characteristics of both a LAN and a WAN.

We finish our discussion of network hardware by comparing the Internet to the United States road system. Consider the interstate highway network. There are relatively few high-speed, high-capacity interstate highways that carry traffic across the country. These highways are designed to traverse long distances relatively quickly. The interstate system is fed by state, county, and city roads of various capacities that are designed to accommodate different needs and usage patterns. The road that leads to the driveway of your home is likely a fairly low-capacity road. The Internet is similar. The telcos provide a high-capacity, high-speed **backbone** that connects major metropolitan areas. In this backbone, fiber-optic and copper cables carry large quantities of Internet traffic between major cities. Submarine cables cross oceans to connect continents and countries. Sometimes wireless techniques like satellite, microwave, and radio are used. The backbone is fed by local systems of various capacities, designed for different conditions. Local systems are also supported by the telcos, though some are also privately owned and operated. At the end-user connection point, the capacity is usually low compared to the capacity of the backbone; most home users connect via **dial-up modem**, **digital subscriber line** (**DSL**), or **cable modem**. Business users tend to have higher-capacity permanent connections, such as **T1** (a service that can send about 1.5 megabits per second, or Mbps), **fractional T1** (a fraction of T1 capacity), DSL (up to hundreds of Mbps), **T3** (45 Mbps), and many other options.

Packets of data traveling on the Internet are like vehicles on the road system. Just as there are many ways to drive from Los Angeles to New York, different packets traveling the Internet might follow many different paths. The fastest or most reliable path from one point to another is not always the shortest physical distance. Just as you might travel from one side of a city to another by following a major highway that circles the city instead of surface streets that pass directly through the city, so also an Internet data packet might take a relatively circuitous path to reach its destination. For example, Internet traffic from Los Angeles might "backtrack" north and west to San Jose before heading east to Denver if San Jose has a faster backbone connection to Denver than does Los Angeles. Also, network "storms" of heavy usage can arise, temporarily clogging certain segments of the Internet. In these cases, traffic can be rerouted to increase performance. For maps of the Internet, visit http://www.cybergeography.org/atlas/more_isp_maps.html, which shows the backbone structures provided by various telcos. Many of the Internet service providers also post a map on their Web site. For example, WorldCom's UUNET gives a nice map of their global network structure at http://www.uu.net/network/maps/.

Internet Protocols

A **protocol** is a set of rules that governs how a system operates or communicates. Standard Internet protocols allow the global and ubiquitous interconnections on which the Net is built. Protocols are organized in layers. **Internet Protocol** (IP) is the lowest level protocol used in the Internet, and **Transmission Control Protocol** (TCP) works hand-in-hand with IP to make sure messages that are divided into packets are reliably transported from one machine to another. Together, **TCP/IP** is the networking foundation on which higher-level services are built. These higher-level services include such protocols as **File Transfer Protocol** (FTP) for uploading and downloading files, **Simple Mail Transfer Protocol** (SMTP) for sending e-mail, and **TELNET** for network terminal emulation. (See Appendix B for a discussion of HTTP, the **Hypertext Transfer Protocol**.)

In Chapter 2, we described the **Domain Name Service**, or DNS. One aspect of IP is that each node is assigned a numerical IP address like 255.100.7.42. DNS provides a distributed, hierarchical directory of **host names** or **domain names** for Internet-attached computers. Host names are placed within a hierarchy of domains. Three-letter **top-level domains** (**TLDs**) are listed in Table A.1. The first three, .com, .net, and .org are available to any interested party on a commercial basis. To protect names, it is a good idea to register domain names in all three top-level domains (e.g., Amazon.com should also register amazon.org and amazon.net). The last four three-letter top-level domains are restricted to organizations within the corresponding category. A special domain .arpa contains a few Internet infrastructure databases. Each country also has a two-letter top-level domain, such as .ac (Ascension Island), .br (Brazil), and .ch (Switzerland). Each country controls domain names registered within its own two-letter top-level domain. There has been discussion for some time about whether to add more top-level domains, and in November 2000, after considerable discussion, ICANN agreed to add the new TLDs described in Table A.2. We expect over time to see additional TLDs approved.

Table A.1 Three-Letter Top-Level Domains

Domain	Description
.com	Commercial entities
.net	Network service providers
.org	Organizations
.edu	4-year degree-granting institutions in North America
.int	Organizations established by international treaty
.mil	United States military
.gov	United States government

Originally, the **Internet Assigned Numbers Authority** (IANA), a United States government–controlled entity, was responsible for controlling how Internet names and numbers were assigned. Now the more open and international **Internet Corporation for Assigned Names and Numbers** (ICANN) controls these functions, though ICANN still uses IANA for many of these functions. An organization or an individual can register a domain name using one of the ICANN-accredited **registrars** such as Network Solutions in the United States or Council of Internet Registrars in Switzerland. However, registering a domain name is not enough—you also need to register an IP address to go with your domain name(s). Since all this can be a complicated process, there are many **Internet service providers** (ISPs) who will handle name registration, DNS services, and Web hosting for individuals and companies. Small companies tend to outsource this task, while larger companies tend to control the process in-house.

Table A.2 New Top-Level Domains

Domain	Description
.aero	Air-transport industry
.biz	Businesses
.coop	Cooperatives
.info	Unrestricted use
.museum	Museums
.name	For registration by individuals
.pro	Accountants, lawyers, doctors, other professionals

Source: ICANN, www.icann.org/tlds, May 2002.

Static vs. Dynamic IP Addresses

As discussed in Chapter 2, in order to join the Internet, a computer must have a unique IP address. This is true whether the machine is a server publishing Web pages or a PC used to send e-mail from home. There are two general ways of assigning IP addresses: statically and dynamically. A static assignment means that a computer is given a specific IP address that remains the same all the time. For example, most Web servers are given static IP addresses. The reason is because it is important for servers to be located at a known, stable address. (Imagine trying to deliver the mail if addresses were continually changing; stable addresses are important to message delivery.) Dynamic IP address assignment is more typical for machines that act as clients, not servers. For example, when you dial in to the Internet using a modem, your Internet Service Provider will probably temporarily assign you an IP address from a pool of several hundred possible addresses. The fact that you might receive a different IP address each time you dial in is not important, because your PC is acting as a client (e.g., for browsing the Web), not as a server. Each time you request a Web page, your PC sends the (dynamically assigned) IP address to which the Web server should respond.

The most common method for assigning IP addresses dynamically is called **Dynamic Host Configuration Protocol** (**DHCP**). Under DHCP, a client machine **leases** an IP address from a DHCP server. When a new computer (a DHCP client) joins a network, it broadcasts a configuration request. A DHCP server receives the request, allocates an IP address from its pool of reserved addresses, and sends the necessary information back to the client. When the client's lease on the IP address expires, the server reclaims the IP address and returns it to the pool of available IP addresses. This negotiation happens automatically, without involving the end-user.

Wireless Internet Technology

Radio transmissions have long been part of the Internet, but in recent years, wireless network technology has become increasingly popular. Most readers are familiar with cell phones, typically used for voice communications. As digital technologies replaced analog technologies, cell phones achieved sufficient quality to become ubiquitous. Now cellular phone providers are rapidly moving to deploy faster digital networks, called third generation networks (**3G**). Because 3G technology is incompatible with certain existing cellular networks, some telecom providers are using an incremental strategy (dubbed **2.5G**) to increase the speed of existing networks without moving all the way to 3G in a single, difficult step. The next decade will see continued advances in cellular networks. NTT DoCoMo, Inc. is one of the leaders in 3G technology, providing an advanced service dubbed **i-mode** over a high-speed 3G network in Japan. With i-mode, customers have access not only to the Web pages and e-mail, but also to streaming video.

Another important wireless technology is **Bluetooth**. With a range of about 10 meters and bandwidth just under 1Mbps, Bluetooth is a technology that could be useful for such applications as interconnecting a wireless handset with a telephone, or allowing a Personal Digital Assistant (PDA) to synchronize its calendar with a desktop computer without placing the PDA in a cradle connected by physical wires. Bluetooth has also been slow to get rolling, but it is picking up steam. Microsoft announced it would include Bluetooth support in its next version of Windows XP.

The **IEEE 802.11b** wireless communication standard known as **WiFi** has become quite popular recently. WiFi operates at a speed of 11Mbps over a range of dozens to hundreds of meters (range is shorter indoors, where radio signals have to pass through obstacles like walls and floors). WiFi is increasingly economical. To use WiFi, you need an **access point** (a receiver that listens for WiFi connections) and a WiFi-capable NIC (a card that allows your computer to talk to the access point). As this edition goes to press, a WiFi access point and network card can be purchased for less than $200. Many notebook computers currently ship with a WiFi NIC built in. A newer, faster (and more expensive) standard, **IEEE 802.11a**, increases bandwidth to more than 54Mbps, over a range similar to WiFi. Since 802.11a uses a different frequency than 802.11b, new hardware is required to implement the faster standard.

Another exciting wireless technology called **Ultra Wideband** (**UWB**) is poised to make a splash as well. UWB may find its first widespread applications in cars as miniature radar systems used for automatic collision avoidance. But Internet use is surely not far behind. UWB is capable of very high-speed communications (400 to 500MBps) over short ranges. Importantly, UWB has relatively low power requirements and is easy to integrate with computer chips. For these reasons, some observers expect UWB to displace Bluetooth at some point in the future.

Security is a major concern for all wireless technologies. Encryption and access controls are vital to establishing secure wireless communications. Radio interference is also a concern. For example, if my next-door neighbor and I both install WiFi, what happens? But despite these sorts of challenges, the trend toward wireless networking technologies will continue to grow significantly over the next decade. As wireless techniques are used more, the number of network-attached devices will explode. As an example, perhaps in the future it will be common for wristwatches to be network-attached, so they could automatically synchronize with an atomic clock (for accuracy) and tap into your event calendar to remind you of upcoming appointments. As we gaze into our crystal ball, we see major parts of the network of the near future operating without wires.

Appendix B: Web Technology

The **World Wide Web** (also, **WWW**, **W3**, or simply the **Web**), is a multimedia information system that uses the Internet to publish information in a wide variety of formats, including text, images, sound, motion video, and many others. Web documents are usually **hyperlinked**, so that clicking on a text or image **link** in one page brings you to another document elsewhere in the Web.

Hypertext documents are stored on Internet hosts called Web **servers** such as Apache (www.apache.org), Internet Information Server (www.microsoft.com), and iPlanet (www.iplanet.com). Users read hypertext documents using a Web **browser** like Microsoft Internet Explorer (www.microsoft.com) and Netscape Navigator (www.netscape.com).

Although some people use the two terms synonymously, the "Web" is different from the "Internet." As described in Appendix A, the Internet is the interconnected network that circles the globe; the Web is a hyperlinked multimedia information system layered on top of the Internet. Non-Web aspects of the Internet include e-mail, FTP, TELNET, and many other services.

Two key Web technologies are HTTP and HTML. Hypertext Transfer Protocol (HTTP) is the language that browsers and servers use to communicate. Hypertext Markup Language (HTML) is the language used to specify the content and structure of Web pages. Other important Web technologies include JavaScript, Cascaded Style Sheets, Extensible Markup Language (XML), dynamic Web pages, and cookies. We discuss these in turn below.

Hypertext Transfer Protocol

The **Hypertext Transfer Protocol**, or **HTTP**, is the set of rules Web servers and browsers use to communicate. Thus, when a browser accesses a page from a Web server, the two interact according to the HTTP protocol. We briefly examine this process. Each Web page has an address, called a **uniform resource locator** (**URL**). To load a page, the user must first indicate the URL, either by typing it into the browser's address box or clicking on a link that has the URL embedded in a Web page. Suppose the user chooses http://ebusiness.byu.edu/index.html. First, the Web browser breaks apart the URL to determine what is being asked. The prefix http: indicates that the URL is to be accessed using the HTTP protocol. (There are other possibilities, such as ftp:, gopher:, and mailto:, but those prefixes indicate that the URL references a different protocol, not HTTP). Next, // introduces the server name, in this case ebusiness.byu.edu. Finally, "/index.html" is the location of the document on the Web server. After breaking apart the URL, the Web browser contacts the server at ebusiness.byu.edu and issues the HTTP command "GET /index.html HTTP/1.1" (get the "/index.html" document using HTTP protocol version 1.1). The server responds either with the requested document content or with an error message such as "404" (indicating that the request page is not found on the server) or "403" (access to the document is forbidden).

When you fill in a form on a Web page and then click a button to submit it, your browser uses the HTTP "POST" command to send data to the Web server. Besides being able to download Web pages and files to your computer, HTTP also supports uploading files to the Web server. There are many other HTTP commands as well. The complete HTTP 1.1 specification is available at http://www.ics.uci.edu/pub/ietf/http/rfc2068.txt.

Markup Languages

In the days before **WYSIWYG** (What You See Is What You Get) word processors were commonplace, typesetting was generally done using **markup languages**. A markup language uses special characters to separate document text from document formatting information—hence the document is "marked up" with formatting instructions. For example, the sequence .B definition might cause the word **definition** to appear in boldface. Or the sequence \section{Introduction} might produce a new section in the document titled **1.0 Introduction**. A formatting program is used to generate a typeset document from the marked-up text.

Web pages are also written using a markup language, **Hypertext Markup Language** (**HTML**). Most markup elements are **tags** surrounded by angle brackets. For example, the following code defines a simple HTML document:

```
<HTML>
  <HEAD>
    <TITLE>A Simple Web Page</TITLE>
  </HEAD>
  <BODY BGCOLOR="white">
    <H1 ALIGN="CENTER">Section One</H1>
    <HR>
    <P>This is a simple Web page with a <B>single</B> paragraph. &copy;</P>
  </BODY>
</HTML>
```

Most browsers would render this HTML in the following manner:

```
A Simple Web Page
┌─────────────────────────────────────┐
│                                      │
│            Section One               │
│  ──────────────────────────────────  │
│                                      │
│  This is a simple Web page with a single │
│  paragraph. ©                        │
│                                      │
└─────────────────────────────────────┘
```

An HTML document is divided into a header and a body. The header usually contains the page title and other information that typically is not visible on the page (such as key words describing the document, inserted to help search engines find the page more easily). The body contains the information that is displayed in the main browser window.

Notice that the title, which is displayed in the browser's title bar, is distinguished by the tags <TITLE> ... </TITLE>. Most HTML tags are paired, with a forward slash designating the closing tag. But some tags, like <HR> (horizontal rule or dividing line), stand alone and are not paired.

Tags may also have **attributes**, such as BGCOLOR="white". An attribute modifies the behavior of a tag. In this case, BGCOLOR="white" tells the browser to use white as the background color for the Web page. The attribute ALIGN="CENTER" on the <H1> tag tells the browser to center "**Section One**" on the line. The <H1> tag indicates a level-one header; <H2>, <H3>, etc. indicate subheaders and are usually rendered in successively smaller font sizes.

Not all markup commands are represented as tags. Symbols can be inserted into an HTML document using another technique: © tells the browser to display the copyright symbol (©). Another commonly used nontag element is the nonbreaking space,   which tells the browser to insert an extra space.

There are many more elements to HTML that we cannot cover here. For those who are interested in the complete HTML specification, see www.w3.org for definitive information from the World Wide Web Consortium. We also recommend the Netscape developer site, developer.netscape.com. Look for the documentation section, then technical manuals, and there you can find a handy HTML tag reference.

One of the original design principles of HTML was that it should be a "logical" (not "physical") markup language. This meant that HTML should identify elements in the document and then let the browser decide how to render them. For example, to specify a section title, rather than telling the browser to use 18-point Times Roman boldface font centered on the line, you might instead say <H1> ... </H1>. The browser would determine how to render a level-one header. In fact, each user might customize browser settings to his or her own preferences (perhaps Sally would prefer all text to be shown in Arial instead of Times font).

However, this principle did not work as well in commercial applications as it did in the research environment where HTML was first designed. Graphics designers of commercial home pages wanted greater control over the layout of their pages, and they had to go to extraordinary lengths sometimes to achieve the effects they desired. Often, they would just render the whole page as a holistic image, getting around the problem of different browsers rendering the same page differently.

As Web-page designers clamored for greater control over the page rendering process, HTML became increasingly complex, adding more "physical" markup commands over time. In order to preserve some aspect of the separation between logical document elements and physical rendering information, the idea of **Cascading Style Sheets** (**CSS**) was introduced. Styles may be familiar to those who have used word processors like WordPerfect and Word. In a modern word processor, you can define **styles** that indicate font, paragraph formatting, and many other features. Then you apply these styles to different sections of a document, such as section headers, footnotes, or figures. The reason for doing this is to maintain uniformity across a document, and also so that if you make changes to a particular document element's representation, you do not have to go through the whole document looking for items to change. For example, suppose you decide you want all your section headers to be in 16-point font instead of 18-point font. If you had used a physical setting in the document, you would have to find each section header, select it, and apply a font size change to the text. If you had used a section header style, you could instead simply update the style, and then it would apply the change to all parts of the document marked as section headers. CSS is the same concept applied to Web pages. A CSS style description can be specified for each different tag, such as the following example for the H1 tag, defining the characteristics of a first-level heading:

H1 { font-size: 12pt; font-weight: bold; color: blue; }

HTML and CSS continue to evolve fairly rapidly (see www.w3.org). But it is likely that in the future a new generation of markup language will take over; **XML**, the **Extensible Markup Language**, is the most likely candidate. For a description of XML, see Text Box 2.6 in Chapter 2 (p. 32). A major difference between XML and HTML is that HTML has a limited set of predefined tags (e.g., TITLE, H1, BODY), but XML supports user-defined tags. This is extremely important for applications like EDI where data must be exchanged and interpreted automatically, without human intervention.

Interactive, Dynamic Web Elements

In its original form, the Web displayed essentially static documents, which could be quite dull (especially in the Web's original default gray background color). The market was soon clamoring for interactive capabilities in Web pages. **Animated GIF** images were among the first dynamic elements to show up on the Web. It was not long before sophisticated methods for programming Web pages were introduced as well.

Interactivity and dynamism are introduced in two general ways: client-side techniques and server-side techniques. On the client side (i.e., within the user's browser), there are HTML forms, plug-ins, embedded scripts, and applets. On the server side we find CGI form processing, dynamic Web-page generation using scripting languages, database connectivity, and Java technology. We now describe these elements in more detail.

Client-Side Interactive and Dynamic Techniques

One of the earliest mechanisms for creating dynamic Web applications was the use of HTML **forms**. A form can contain text boxes, drop-down lists, selectable list boxes, check boxes, radio buttons, push buttons, and other elements that allow for data-entry forms to be built within Web pages. When a user selects a push button, the form's content is usually sent to a Web server for further processing (see the next section, p. 57). Forms are a vital component in the dynamic Web arsenal.

Web browsers are designed with a modular architecture that allows for **plug-ins** to be added, to display special document types (other than HTML). For example, Adobe distributes the popular Acrobat Reader plug-in to display PDF files within a browser window. PDF is Adobe's proprietary Portable Document Format, and is useful for displaying typeset documents that are rendered identically on all platforms (getting around the HTML problem of the same page appearing different to different users). Another pair of popular plug-ins is MacroMedia's Shockwave and Flash players, which display rich, animated multimedia content (graphics, sound, motion video). There are hundreds of other browser plug-ins available. When you try to download a type of file that your browser does not understand, but for which a plug-in is available, most of the popular browsers offer to automatically download and install the corresponding plug-in.

Besides using plug-ins to display other file types, you can also configure your browser to launch particular file types in an application outside the browser. For example, if you download a compressed .ZIP file, your browser might open the file in WinZip, which can decompress files from the .ZIP archive.

Microsoft has been a leader in bringing power to the end-user's desktop. Each application in the Microsoft Office suite has a programming language built in; this macro programming capability is usually based on the Visual Basic language. While this also causes security problems, developers and users have generally come to rely on these powerful facilities. It did not take long for Web pages to acquire the same capability. Programming **scripts** can be embedded within HTML using a client-side Web **scripting language**. These scripts are instructions to the Web browser that are executed when certain events take place. For example, suppose you want a Web page that highlights the button over which the mouse is currently hovering. You can embed a script that waits for the mouse to enter the image, and then switches it to a highlighted version. Another script waits for the mouse to leave the image, and switches it back to the original version. Scripts can also respond to keyboard events, mouse clicks, and other events.

Various companies proposed several different Web scripting languages, but the best ideas were quickly gathered into a single scripting language, **JavaScript** (Microsoft's similar **VBScript** is also popular in certain circles). In the autumn of 1996, Netscape offered its JavaScript language to the standards community for adoption as an international standard. In 1997 the European standards body ECMA approved standard ECMA-262, which created the official **ECMAScript** language (see www.ecma.ch), effectively standardizing JavaScript. (Note: Microsoft calls its implementation of ECMAScript **JScript**.)

Besides embedding scripts directly in HTML pages, another approach for displaying attractive graphics or advanced interactivity in a Web page is to use **Java applets**. An applet is a small application (such as a scrolling marquee displaying news headlines or stock price quotes) that resides within a Web page. In 1995, Sun Microsystems introduced the Java programming language as a portable, Web-aware programming tool. Unlike scripts, which are interpreted directly by a Web browser, Java programs are compiled into instructions called **Java byte code**, which are then executed by a program called a **Java virtual machine** (**JVM**). The popular Web browsers come bundled with a JVM. You have probably loaded a Web page containing a Java applet, perhaps without even knowing it! For a variety of reasons, Java on the client side is less popular than the Sun marketing machine led the world to believe it would be. However, Java is becoming increasingly popular for server-side software development.

Server-Side Dynamic Generation

On the server side of the Web equation, there are two main technologies to understand: **CGI** and **dynamic page generation**. The **Common Gateway Interface** (CGI) specifies a mechanism for executing programs on Web servers. Sometimes it is useful to map a Web-page request into a command to run a program on a Web server. For example, suppose you want to have a "guest book" on your Web site for visitors to sign. When they enter their name and e-mail address, you need to store them in your database; you can do this by executing a program on the Web server. CGI is the mechanism that allows data in HTML forms to be passed to a program that runs on your Web server. Recall that one of the HTTP commands is POST. When a visitor fills in a form and selects the "Submit" button, the Web browser issues a POST command to the server, and passes along all the data in the form (e.g., which check boxes are selected, what text is in the text boxes). When a Web server receives a POST command, instead of loading the requested URL as an HTML page and returning it to the browser, it loads the requested URL as a program and executes it on the server. Data that accompanies the POST command is also given to the executing program. Any output from the program is returned to the browser. So the CGI program that receives a guest book entry could update the database, then print the message "<B>Thanks for signing my guest book!</B>." In this case, the CGI program generates HTML coding as output, but in general, CGI programs can generate any kind of output.

Based on the CGI interface, there are many different technologies used to generate Web pages dynamically. We briefly mention a few. The earliest CGI programs were usually written in the "C" programming language (or its close cousin C++), but C/C++ programming is fairly difficult compared to some of the alternatives. However, since C/C++ is one of the fastest languages available, Web applications that require high performance are still written in C/C++. C/C++ programs are compiled into machine instructions that execute directly on a computer processor without further translation or interpretation by another program.

In contrast, another popular class of server-side programming languages is the scripting languages. Like their client-side counterparts, scripting languages on the server are sequences of high-level instructions that are interpreted by another program. This interpretation process can be relatively slow, and so it is best for simple programs that do not require complex computations. Many CGI programs, such as those that interact with database management systems, tend to be good candidates for scripting languages.

Popular scripting languages include **Perl** (the Practical Extraction and Reporting Language), Microsoft's Active Server Pages (**ASP**), **PHP**, and Sun Microsystems' Java Server Pages (**JSP**). Because Perl and PHP are open source software, they can be downloaded from the Internet at no charge. They are both available on most popular Web server platforms, as is JSP (which is based on Java technology). ASP is a Microsoft technology that generally requires the Microsoft IIS Web server and Windows operating system.

The way a typical scripting language works is to embed instructions (scripts) within an HTML file. When a browser requests the file, the Web server first recognizes that it contains scripts that need to be interpreted, then it runs the file through the appropriate interpreter. Output from each script is written into the HTML file in place of the script instructions, and the result is finally downloaded to the browser. Consider the following HTML code with embedded PHP instructions, which might appear at the bottom of a file called index.php:

```
<HR>
<I>Last updated <? print date("D d M Y H:i:s", filemtime("index.php")); ?></I>
Copyright 2000, Acme Web Sites, Inc.
</BODY>
</HTML>
```

Since the file name ends in .php, the Web server knows that it must pass this file through the PHP interpreter before returning it to the browser. The PHP interpreter would generate output like the following:

```
<HR>
<I>Last updated Fri 12 May 2000 12:06:26</I>
Copyright 2000, Acme Web Sites, Inc.
</BODY>
</HTML>
```

The only difference is that PHP has executed the script inside the <? … ?> markers, and has substituted the output of that script (the underlined text) into the HTML code. This HTML coding is what the server sends to the browser that requested the file. This particular script is useful to identify when the file was last changed. Without a scripting capability, the HTML author would have to remember to manually update the "Last updated …" message each time the file is edited.

Server-side scripts are also particularly good at processing HTML forms and assembling pages dynamically based on the contents of a database. Suppose you want every Web page in your site to have a common header and footer. You can store the header and footer in a database, and then in every Web page place a script near the top to read the header from the database, and likewise place a script near the bottom to read the footer. Then whenever you change the header or footer, you only have to update the database once rather than updating each Web page individually. Scripts are also used to customize Web pages for each individual visitor. If a database of visitor preferences is available, a script might be used to decide which banner ads from the database to display each time a page is loaded.

For complex applications, JSP and ASP scripts can be helpful because they interact with objects that have been programmed and compiled on the server. (Recall that compiled code is faster than interpreted scripts.) For JSP, such objects are written in the Java language, and for ASP these objects are usually written in C++ or Visual Basic. There are many other technology choices as well, but regardless of the particular approach, it is clear that dynamic Web-page generation is a crucial aspect of the modern Web development toolbox.

Cookies

A **cookie** is a piece of information that is generated by a Web server and then stored on your computer by your Web browser (see Chapter 4). Web servers typically use cookies to identify returning visitors so the server can customize the pages displayed. Without cookies, these Web sites would have to wait until you "logged in" before they could identify you. With cookies, every time you return to the site, your browser automatically identifies you to the Web server.

The following scenario illustrates how cookies work. Jesse decides to open an account with Ebiz.com and buy some widgets; she is assigned customer ID 23859437. The Ebiz.com server stores Jesse's account information in the Ebiz database and also gives Jesse's browser a cookie with her account number inside. The cookie is actually stored on Jesse's hard drive. The next time Jesse's browser requests a page from Ebiz.com, it first checks its cookie file on Jesse's machine. The browser knows that every time it wants to load an Ebiz.com page it is supposed to hand over the cookie. So the browser gets the data associated with the cookie (Jesse's account number) and sends it back to the Web server. Before sending the requested page, the Web server in essence says, "Oh, you still have that cookie I gave you. Hello, customer 23859437." Then it looks up the account number in its database, and discovers that Jesse likes to buy widgets. After consulting the marketing database, it finds an advertisement related to widgets. The Web server inserts this ad into Jesse's page and sends it to her browser.

Each cookie has a name, value, expiration date, domain, path, and security flag (for the gory details, see http://www.netscape.com/newsref/std/cookie_spec.html). Servers can store several cookies on your computer, and so the cookie name is used to distinguish between multiple cookies. The value is whatever the Web server chooses to store, but most commonly it is some kind of unique identification number. The expiration date tells the Web browser when to delete the cookie. Most Web servers set expiration dates years into the future, making them effectively permanent. The domain indicates which Web servers should receive the cookie ("www.ebiz.com" for our example above). The path specifies which page requests will cause the cookie to be sent back to the server. A path of "/" indicates the cookie should be sent for all pages requested from the server. A path of "/store/" would cause the browser to send the cookie only when loading a page that begins with "http://www.ebiz.com/store/". The security flag indicates whether the cookie can be sent to a server that is not secure (i.e., not running SSL, see Appendix C). The reason a security flag is necessary is because a Web server might choose to store confidential information in your cookie, like a password or a credit card number. You would only want such a cookie sent across a secure connection.

Many privacy advocates despise cookies because of the security and privacy threats they cause. So the popular browsers give you some control over whether to accept cookies. But cookies are extremely useful, and many e-business sites require their customers to use them. You may want to examine the cookies stored on your computer to get a better feel for how they are used. If you use the Netscape browser, look for a file called cookies.txt; all your cookies are stored in this file. If you use the Microsoft browser, search for a directory called Cookies; each cookie is stored in its own file. These are ordinary text files that can be viewed with any text editor or word processor.

Wireless Access Protocol

In Appendix A we described several wireless technologies that are becoming an important part of the Internet. The Web is also becoming increasingly wireless-aware. **Wireless Access Protocol (WAP)** is a technology designed to make it easier for handheld computer users to access Web information more easily, by avoiding the graphics and superfluous text that simply do not fit on a small phone or PDA display screen. A Web site that supports WAP provides an alternate interface that sends far less data between the client and server. You can think of WAP as an alternative to HTTP designed for handheld computers using a relatively slow network connection.

Consider the task of choosing a restaurant in an unfamiliar city. A typical cell phone would be sufficient to accomplish this task if you could navigate a simple list of restaurants organized by food types, ratings, and cost. A smart application could also use location information (derived from data about the radio cell you use to communicate with the network). Perhaps some restaurants would generate an electronic coupon to try to entice you to visit. These are the kinds of scenarios used by the proponents of WAP.

You could implement a restaurant search application using a more traditional Web site (e.g. www.zagat.com), but imagine the kinds of high-bandwidth extra graphics you would expect to see on a traditional Web site. There would be pictures of the cuisine and the buildings, links to "how-to-get-there" maps, and so on. Such information is helpful if you have a large computer display and a fast network connection, but cell phones have neither of these. WAP meets the needs of low-bandwidth, small-display applications.

As with many technologies, the marketing folks and technology reporters got overly excited about it, and WAP has not been able to deliver on the initial hype surrounding its introduction. Nonetheless WAP fills a necessary niche in the wireless Web.

Postscript

For a fascinating look at an early vision of how the information revolution could impact the way we work and even think, see Vannevar Bush, "As We May Think," *The Atlantic Monthly*, July 1945 (on the Web at http://www.w3.org/History/1945/vbush). Bush describes a device he calls the "memex" which is used to retrieve and cross-reference virtually limitless quantities of information. In the modern world, the Web has in large measure taken the role of the memex envisioned by Bush over half a century ago. The Web is weak at supporting annotations, but there are "knowledge management consoles" and other software to help serve this function. The "digerati" often refer to "As We May Think" for inspiration on how best to develop the Web in the future.

Appendix C: Encryption—Privacy and Authenticity

Because the Internet community, like most communities, is made up of all kinds of people, both virtuous and villainous, it is necessary to safeguard personal information from those who might misuse it. This is especially the case in e-business, where financial transactions are broadcast and bounced from one computer to another across the Internet. As a result, the Internet relies on complex and ever-evolving methods of **encryption** to scramble data sent over the public network.

Until recently, the most common encryption technique was **symmetric encryption**, where messages are encrypted and decrypted using a single **secret key**. Since both parties are required to know the secret key, it must be transmitted somehow. Transmission of secret keys is an inherently risky process; keys can be stolen, even without the knowledge of the communicating parties. This happened to the Germans in World War II when the United States and Britain surreptitiously intercepted an Enigma encoding/decoding device. The Germans wondered why all their U-boats were being sunk, which was a direct result of intercepted intelligence about German operations.

Encryption was greatly improved with the development of **public-key cryptography**. A public-key process was first patented by Diffie and Helman in 1974 and was later refined into an architecture patented by Rivest, Shamir, and Adelman (**RSA**) in 1983. With public-key cryptography there are two separate keys used to encrypt and decrypt a message. The private key is kept secret and is never transmitted, while the public key is, suitably, public. The complex mathematical algorithm used to create the two keys makes it virtually impossible to use one key to discover the other, so it is safe to give out the public key to any third party, trustworthy or not. The public key can be transmitted to the receiver or maintained in a directory where people can find it, much like a telephone number. This two-key system makes public-key cryptography much more secure and thus today it is the generally accepted method for securing electronic transmissions.

Here is how it works: When a message is locked with a public key, it can only be unlocked using the corresponding private key. This ensures that encrypted messages can be decrypted only by the intended receivers (i.e., those who hold the private key). Thus, public-key encryption can be used to guarantee **privacy** of a message.

In the same way, when a message is locked using a private key, it can only be unlocked using the corresponding public key. Suppose you receive an encrypted message that can be unlocked by a particular *public* key. This means that the message originator must be the holder of the corresponding *private* key, or else the public key would not have unlocked the message. Assuming the message sender has kept the private key truly secret, you can verify the identity of the author or **authenticity** of the message with reasonable certainty. Encrypting something with your private key puts your personal stamp on it. It acts as **digital signature** that is actually much more difficult to forge than a traditional signature.

Here is an example of how the digital signature process works: Say Alice wants to send a message to Bob and include a digital signature so Bob knows the message actually came from Alice and that the message has not been altered along the way. First, a mathemati-

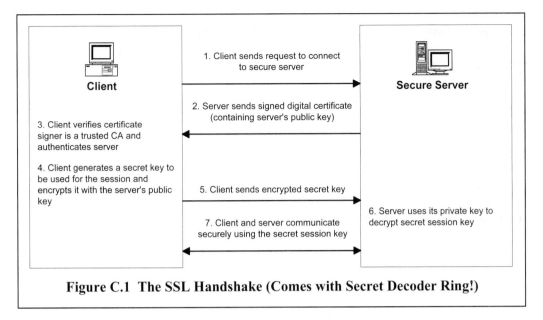

Figure C.1 The SSL Handshake (Comes with Secret Decoder Ring!)

cally condensed version of the message called a **message digest** or **hash value** is produced. This digest is then encrypted by the author's private key and is attached to the original message as a digital signature. Anyone with the author's public key can decrypt the signature and compare the hash value with the received message to make sure it has not been altered since the author signed it. Thus, public-key encryption and digital signatures can be used ensure message **integrity**.

In order to prove that a public key really belongs to the person you think it does requires the use of a **trusted third party** (TTP), such as a **certificate authority** (**CA**) to verify the source of the public key (see Chapter 5). A trusted CA, like Verisign or CyberTrust, issues **digital certificates** to individuals and organizations, which associate a given public key with an individual identity. A digital certificate contains the holder's name (or other identifying information) and their public key. It also contains the name of the CA and the certificate's expiration date, number, and **class**. There are four different classes of digital certificates, depending on how much client information the CA has verified in the certificate-issuing process. To guarantee integrity and authenticity, each certificate is digitally signed using the CA's private key. These certificates, also called digital IDs, act like electronic passports, proving the identity of the holder and verifying the holder's public key.

Public key encryption and digital certificates make it possible to communicate privately and securely across an open network such as the Internet. This is done smoothly by establishing a **secure session** between two computers. Netscape developed a secure session technology called **Secure Sockets Layer** (**SSL),** an open protocol for establishing authenticated encrypted sessions between clients and servers. SSL is layered between high-level protocols such as HTTP, SMTP, TELNET, and FTP, and the low-level TCP/IP protocol. SSL uses digital certificates to authenticate the server and public-key cryptography to encrypt communication. Public and private keys could be used to encrypt sessions, but they require considerably more mathematical calculation than a symmetric key. For efficiency, SSL uses public keys during an initial **handshake** to encrypt and securely transmit a unique symmetrical key that is then used by both client and server for the duration of the session (see Figure C.1, p. 147). **HTTPS (Secure Hypertext Transfer Protocol)** marries SSL with HTTP to encrypt Web transactions. Though there are competing approaches such as S-HTTP, by now HTTPS has become the de facto standard for secure Web transactions.

For more information on public-key encryption and SSL, see:

http://developer.netscape.com/docs/manuals/security/pkin/index.htm

Appendix D: Firewalls and Proxy Servers

Firewalls

A **firewall** is a system of hardware and software that monitors and controls the flow of computer communication between two networks and acts to protect the resources of a private network from users on other networks. Most frequently, a firewall is located at a network gateway to intercept data packets between the Internet and a LAN (see Appendix A). A firewall is often installed as the only connection between a network and the outside world, creating a single point through which all external traffic must pass (see Figure D.1). This "choke point" makes it easier to audit the security of the system. Also, system administrators can focus their efforts on a single access point.

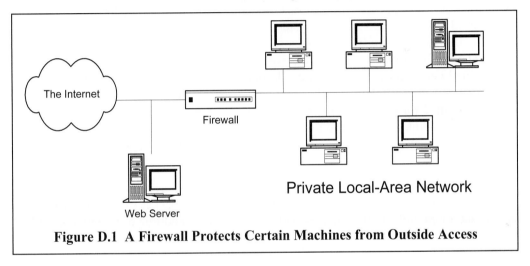

The Internet

Firewall

Private Local-Area Network

Web Server

Figure D.1 A Firewall Protects Certain Machines from Outside Access

A firewall decides whether to allow data to pass based on a **security policy**. A security policy is a list of rules set by the system administrator or security officer that defines and controls access for a network. The firewall compares each packet it receives to a security rule and decides if the packet should be allowed, blocked, or altered. For example, a firewall could be configured to drop all incoming FTP packets, effectively blocking all FTP services that try to cross the firewall.

A firewall acts to reduce security risks to a network by restricting access from outside networks. Often, a firewall acts as a one-way valve, allowing its local users to access the Internet but preventing outsiders from accessing the private LAN. A firewall can also be used to hide the structure of an internal network from the outside. Keeping internal structure hidden from potential intruders is important to network security because it is difficult for a hacker to attack an unmapped territory. Additionally, a firewall may include functions such as logging and reporting network traffic. These functions are crucial for auditing and network administration support.

Types and Configurations of Firewalls

A firewall can be configured in a wide variety of ways depending on the security policy it intends to enforce. The policy could be as extreme as restricting all outside access or as limited as just passively monitoring traffic flow across the firewall. There are two main types of firewalls: **packet filters**, which forward or discard data packets based on characteristics of each packet, and **proxy firewalls**, which act as intermediaries and prevent traffic from passing directly between networks.

Packet Filters

A packet filter is the simplest of firewall configurations. A packet filter firewall examines properties of each data packet it receives and decides to drop or forward the packet based on filtering criteria set by the system administrator. The packet filter firewall does not examine the data itself, but makes its decision based on the packet's **IP header**, which contains information such as the type of packet, its source and destination IP addresses, and port number. If the source, destination, or port of a data packet is unacceptable, it is discarded by the firewall. The administrator may, for example, filter out all packets destined for port 6699, the port typically used by the controversial Napster program. Or the administrator could allow data communication only from a trusted address or domain (e.g., accept all packets from the 192.150 domain except those coming from 192.150.2.63).

Because it operates on the network level and does not examine the data in the packet, a filtering firewall is typically very fast. The problem with a packet filter firewall is that it is possible to circumvent the filter by forging a source IP address, a deception called **IP spoofing** (see Chapter 4).

Proxy Firewalls

A proxy firewall, also known as a **proxy server,** is named as such because it "acts on behalf of" computers on either side of the firewall. The proxy server receives Internet access requests from machines within the protected network. After some manipulation of the data packet, the proxy forwards these requests to the public Internet. Results of these requests come back to the proxy, which then returns them to the appropriate client within the firewall. Under this scheme, traffic cannot pass directly between networks. Instead traffic must pass through the firewall that links the networks together.

Proxy servers completely hide the protected private network by altering outgoing packets to use different return addresses. Each IP packet has a source address and a destination address. By substituting the proxy server's IP address in place of the client's IP address, the proxy server ensures that replies from the public Internet will be returned directly to the proxy server. As far as the Internet is concerned, the request came directly from the proxy server, not from the private client computer. When the proxy server receives response packets, it must then reverse the process and forward each packet to the correct client machine within the protected network.

Because the proxy server performs address substitution within all packets, the public Internet has no knowledge of how many individual computers might reside behind the firewall. Again, this provides better security against hackers. Additionally, proxy firewalls can provide other features, such as advanced logging capabilities, access control, and document caching. For example, a proxy server might **cache** pages from frequently accessed Web sites in order to speed up access time and reduce strain on the network's bandwidth. Maintaining sufficient bandwidth for an organization's legitimate and growing needs is a continual challenge.

The main difference between a proxy firewall and a filtering firewall is the level at which the firewall examines data packets. A proxy firewall operates on an application protocol level, so it can make application specific decisions to block, permit, or alter the data. This requires a proxy server to be configured for each network application (e.g., e-mail, HTTP, FTP) that will be running on the local network.

While proxy servers are considered very secure, they can be quite slow. Also, a proxy server is not as transparent as a filtering firewall. With a proxy firewall, every client program needs to be set up to use a proxy, and not all can do so. This can cause a delay in implementing new protocols. As is usually the case, complexity and security must be balanced against speed and convenience.

Demilitarized Zone

A more secure firewall and proxy server configuration is called a **demilitarized zone** (**DMZ**). As diagrammed in Figure D.2, a DMZ applies several layers of firewall protection to a network to give different levels of protection to different portions of a company's network. A DMZ is a computer or small network of computers that runs in an area between a company's private network and the outside public Internet. Computers from an outside network can access only hosts in the demilitarized zone; it is neither part of the internal network nor directly part of the Internet. Like a proxy server, a DMZ host

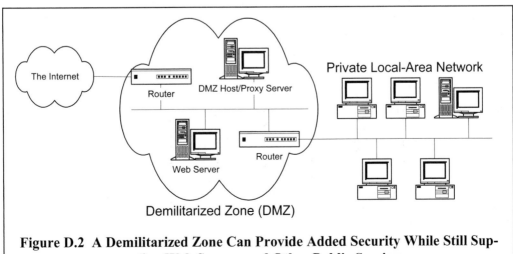

Figure D.2 A Demilitarized Zone Can Provide Added Security While Still Supporting Web Servers and Other Public Services

proxies requests from the private network to access the public network. But the DMZ host cannot initiate a session back into the private network—the DMZ can only forward data packets back into the private network if those packets correspond to a previous request. Often a Web server is located in a demilitarized zone so that a company's public Web pages can be served to the outside world.

This configuration protects the internal network. For example, an intruder who breaks into a Web server in the DMZ might be able to corrupt Web pages, but would be unable to access the internal network from the demilitarized zone. The only devices the intruder can access are those in the DMZ.

A Word of Caution

Although using a firewall between the Internet and a private network can significantly enhance network security, it does not eliminate the need for sound security practices on the systems inside the private network. Firewalls cannot protect against attacks that do not go through the firewall, such as insider attacks or attacks through Internet connections that bypass the firewall (in a large organization, verifying that there is only one connection to the Internet can be a daunting task, particularly when dial-up modem connections are so easy to establish). Often, organizations implement elaborate firewalls but neglect the security holes within their private network.

For more information on firewalls, see http://www.cs.purdue.edu/coast/firewalls/. For general security issues we also recommend Simson Garfinkel and Gene Spafford, *Practical Unix & Internet Security*, 2nd ed. (Sebastapol, CA: O'Reilly & Associates, 1996).

Appendix E: Getting a Small Business Online

In today's economy there are thousands of entrepreneurs starting new e-businesses and taking current businesses online. What does it take to get a small business connected? It turns out to be relatively simple and inexpensive. Text Box E.1 provides an illustrated profile of Paul and Marilyn Murray's business.

Text Box E.1 Selling Magnets on the Web

The Murrays own and operate SMBF LLC, a small business that sells magnets decorated with college basketball and football team logos. Started as a mail order business from their home, total sales for the first nine months were $2,000–$3,000. Then the Murrays decided to take their magnet business to the Internet. There are many Internet service providers that help businesses get online. SMBF decided to go with Netopia Inc. Netopia provided the Murrays easy to use point-and-click software tools to build their Web site. For about $100 per month Netopia provides software, technical support, hosting services, and real-time online credit card processing. SMBF also contracted with Web Site Garage for about $40 per month to put SMBF's Web site address and description on over 400 Internet directories and search engines. SMBG's retail sales for the first three months on the Web were almost $26,000.

Adapted from: "Small Investment, Big Results," *Wall Street Journal*, November 22, 1999.

Low-cost Internet service providers with cookie-cutter Web site designs are a good option for small "mom-and-pop" businesses, but usually these solutions are too simplistic for larger, more complex companies. Customized e-business Web sites that can efficiently and effectively handle large volumes of visitors and transactions come at significant costs. According to the Gartner Group, the average new e-business site costs $1 million to build. Eighty percent of the costs are for labor. The decision to outsource Internet services must be considered very carefully. However, even for large companies, there is ultimately some aspect of the Web site that is best handled by consultants or third-party service providers.

We note with interest that Borders Group, Inc. decided to partner with Amazon.com to salvage an ailing Web effort. Amazon, which has gained tremendous expertise in logistics and e-commerce, now manages the much more successful co-branded "Borders teamed with Amazon.com" Web site. Of course, you have to be a pretty big firm to get Amazon's attention. Small and medium enterprises can find numerous Web hosting services like Netopia, Inc. that will do a good job managing a smaller e-commerce initiative.

Appendix F: Electronic Payment Methods

All payment methods involve three parties: a **payee** who receives the payment, a **payer** who originates the payment, and a **third-party mediator**. Even in cash transactions, the government acts as a third party by backing the value of the currency and ensuring the integrity of the cash in circulation. The electronic payment methods described here vary in the extent to which a third party is involved and the extent to which a transaction's validity depends on the payer.

Electronic payment systems can be classified into two different types: **stored account** systems, similar to credit- and debit-card transactions; and **stored value** systems, where value is built into an electronic currency that is then transferred between parties.

Stored Account Payment

The most commonly used stored account transaction today is a standard **paper check** drawn on a bank account. In 1993, 96 percent of all noncash transactions in the United States were made by check, while only 0.2 percent were processed electronically. The cost of a paper check transaction is ten times the cost of an electronic funds transfer; therefore, there is a large opportunity for electronic commerce to replace the use of checks.

One promising replacement growing in popularity is the **electronic check**. An electronic check is a version of a paper check that is sent electronically. It contains the same information as paper checks (date, amount, account number, etc.), and can include additional information to enhance functionality and increase security (e.g., customer's ID number within the payee's database, customer's digital signature).

An electronic check works the same way a traditional check does and uses the same infrastructure as do existing banking systems. A payer "writes" an electronic check and gives it to a payee electronically. The payee deposits the electronic check, receives credit, and the payee's bank clears it to the paying bank, which charges the payer's account for the check. This is essentially the same process as a paper check but without the paper.

Because it works like a paper check but is in pure electronic form, the electronic check fits within current business practices, eliminating the need for expensive process re-engineering. Thus, it is easier to adopt than many other technologies. Electronic checks are also more secure than traditional checks, which are easily subject to fraud or error. Electronic checks can be **digitally signed** for added security, meaning that a mathematically strong digital signature is applied to the check using the payer's private key (see Appendix C).

Credit card payments are most popular for transactions that are not done in person or where there is not an established relationship between the payer and payee. Thus, credit card transactions are well suited for the Internet. However, many consumers do not feel their credit card number is secure in cyberspace. To address this concern, Visa and

MasterCard developed the **Secure Electronic Transaction** (**SET**) protocol to keep credit card numbers and transaction information private when sent over a network. While SSL encrypts data only while in transit (see Chapter 4), SET separately encrypts customer information intended for the merchant and the bank, thus securing data on the server level.

Prior to a transaction, SET authenticates the identification of the cardholder, merchant, and bank, and confirms the validity of the purchaser's card. Next, merchant information (such as items ordered) is encrypted using the merchant's public key. Information for the bank, such as the credit card number, is encrypted with the bank's public key. This way only the bank has access to the credit card details, eliminating a possible source of fraud. The entire transaction is then digitally signed to prevent the transaction from being altered.

SET has been slow to catch on because of its complexity and cost. It requires special software and digital certificates for the buyers, sellers, and merchant banks. Because of its complexity and the difficulty of getting consumers to use unfamiliar and complex technology, we expect SET will continue to be largely ignored in the coming years. SSL, on the other hand, has received broad acceptance, and today is used in most Internet transactions.

Beyond security, however, there are other obstacles to the use of credit cards. According to the Payment Systems Survey Association, half the U.S. shopping public cannot qualify for a credit card, and only one in four checking account customers hold credit cards with available credit. For checking account holders, **debit cards** are more widely available, though only 30 percent of those surveyed use their debit card for retail purchases. Despite these obstacles, credit and debit cards seem to be the most immediate solution for Internet transactions. In fact, the Coca-Cola Company plans to spend $100 million on software that will connect their vending machines to the Internet, allowing them accept credit and debit cards.

Some companies, such as CyberCash (www.cybercash.com), offer merchants a suite of stored account payment solutions for the Internet, including secure credit card processing and authorization, automatic checking account withdrawal, and Internet check transactions. Other organizations, such as the Financial Services Technology Consortium, work with banks, government agencies, universities, and technology companies to sponsor research and development on payment systems and leveraging new technologies.

One implementation of stored account electronic payment that has been growing in popularity is **Electronic Bill Presentment and Payment** (**EBPP**), also known as **online bill payment**. EBPP is the process that allows bills to be created, delivered, and paid online. EBPP over the Internet is exploding: worldwide revenues jumped 540 percent to $32 million in 1999. Consumers will be paying bills online in greater numbers, which could bring market revenues to $1 billion by 2004. This growth is fueled by the potential use of EBPP to replace the 1.5 billion paper transactions sent to U.S. consumers every month, costing nearly $6 billion. (Source: International Data Corp.)

The United States Postal Service is aware the potential for EBPP to erode its annual $17 billion in first-class mail revenues from delivering bills and bill payments between companies and customers. This represents almost 25 percent of the Postal Service's business! (The Postal Service is also under pressure from e-mail and courier services.) Fearful of losing this substantial revenue source to online bill payment, the United States Postal Service launched eBillPay, an online service similar to PayMyBills.com, which allows consumers to collect and pay all their bills online.

Fueled by the online auction community, e-mail payment services, such as PayPal, have become some of the most heavily trafficked financial sites on the Internet. PayPal enables any person with an e-mail address to effectively accept credit cards by brokering funds transfers through online accounts. For example, PayPal establishes online accounts for each of its customers. To make a payment, a customer simply indicates the amount and the PayPal identity of the recipient. If the customer does not have a sufficient balance in the PayPal account, PayPal charges the customer's credit card for the funds. At any time a customer can retrieve money by initiating an electronic funds transfer (EFT) or requesting a paper check. Customers can also deposit funds in PayPal accounts by EFT from a bank account. So far PayPal provides these services at no fee. Interest in such services is growing significantly.

Stored Value

The archetype stored value instrument is **cash**. The value of "legal tender" is in the currency itself (or the public trust in the currency), and has the same value regardless of the bearer. The advantage of a stored value payment system over a stored account system is its independence from the payee. Since the identities of the parties involved in a cash transaction are irrelevant to its value, cash transactions can be anonymous. Contrast this to checks, instruments whose validity not only requires reference to the issuer, but whose value is dependent on the issuer's solvency. Stored value transactions are particularly useful for **micropayments**, low-value transactions (under $10) that are too small to justify the cost of stored account transactions.

Since cash cannot be stuffed through a telephone line, online stored value payment methods are a form of digital cash equivalents that may be authenticated independently of the issuer. eCash Technologies (acquired by InfoSpace, Inc. in February 2002) provides such a method using **digital tokens** or **coins**. The digital coins have predetermined values and are digitally signed by the issuing bank (see Appendix C). Digital coins are purchased by a bank and then downloaded to a computer. These digital coins can then be spent as virtual cash (**e-cash**) on the Internet. A merchant receiving an e-cash payment can verify the authenticity of the digital coins with the issuing bank, and later redeem them for money. This method, like cash, provides a measure of anonymity and value-independence for the parties involved.

While eCash Technologies supplies software to download electronic cash onto a computer hard drive, a more popular implementation of e-cash storage is with stored value cards or **smart cards**. Smart cards contain a computer chip to store information and provide the higher level of security needed for stored value applications. With a stored value card, the consumer pays up front, gets a card to authorize a certain amount of purchasing power, and spends that value over time. Smart cards may be disposable or rechargeable. In some instances, smart card technology is being placed on ATM cards or credit cards. Most smart cards available today permit users to pay for long-distance telephone calls, public transportation, and other single-purpose transactions. Smart cards are currently more popular in Europe than in the United States.

Though it received much hype in the mid-90's, the use of electronic cash has not been widespread. One problem is incompatibility between e-cash services. If a merchant supports only one e-cash service, each customer also has to use that particular service in order to transact with the merchant. Furthermore, because of the cost involved, not all merchants are willing to support e-cash payments. Such incompatibilities are unacceptable to consumers; e-cash will have to be nearly universal in order to achieve widespread acceptance. Also, many governmental and financial institutions are unwilling to support a completely anonymous electronic currency system. According to the Institute for Technology Assessment, governments worldwide may clamp down on the use of digital money if it finally does become popular because of risks to national monetary systems and the relative ease of committing financial crimes, such as money laundering.

In sum, credit cards and electronic funds transfers are likely to maintain their dominant position in electronic payment methods for some time to come.

Index

Aastrom Biosciences, Inc., 92–93
Abacus Direct, 96
Accounting, impact of e-business on, 15–18, 19, 141–143
ACL, 120
Active Server Pages (ASP), 158, 158
Addresses, IP, 151
Advertising banners, 67, 97
Aggregation/aggregators, 41, 68–70
Agora, 41
Akamai, 71
Aladdin Knowledge Systems, 88
Alliance, 41
AltaVista, 70
Amazon.com, 2, 11, 12, 14, 24, 41, 52–56, 66, 68, 124
    cookies used by, 97
    gross revenues, 126
    privacy issues, 95
    security problems, 77, 89
American Institute of Certified Public Accountants (AICPA), 16, 19–20, 95, 108
    Special Committee on Assurance Services, 127–128
America Online (AOL), 4, 70, 71
Ameritrade, 60
Andersen Consulting, 71, 72
Andreessen, Mark, 25
Animated GIF images, 156
Apple Computer, 71
Application controls, 118
Ariba, 71
Arthur Andersen, 140
Assurance services, 19–20
    business-to-business (B2B) model and, 134–138
    business-to-consumer (B2C) model and, 130–133
    certified public accountants and, 113
    defined, 113
    electronic commerce, 129
    Elliott Committee, 20, 127–128
    financial statements and, 114–115
    information systems reliability, 129
    new, 138–141
AT&T, 70, 71
Auctions, 53, 56–59, 62–63
Authenticity, 88, 106, 162–164
Automobile industry, 63–64

Backbone, 29, 149
Banner advertising, 67, 97
Barnesandnoble.com, 28, 55
Barnes & Noble Inc., 28
L.L. Bean, 2
Benford's Law, 121
Better Business Bureau (BBB), 133
Bezos, Jeff, 52
Biometrics, 94–95
Bluetooth, 152
Boeing Corp., 6
Boot virus, 101
Borders, 53
Bridges, 147
Britannica.com, 69
BroadVision, 71
Bus, 147
Bush, Vannevar, 161
Business advisory services, 19
Business model(s)
    categories of, 41–42
    defined, 41
Business risk, 78–80
Business-to-business (B2B) model, 42, 43, 45–47
    See also under category of
    assurance and, 134–138
    auctions, 62–63
    supply-chain management, 61–64
Business-to-consumer (B2C) model, 42–43
    See also Online stores
    assurance and, 130–133
Buy.com, 11, 77, 83

Cables, 147
California HealthCare Foundation, 96
Campus networks, 148
Canadian Institute of Chartered Accountants, 120
Carnivore, 85
Cascading Style Sheets (CSS), 155–156
CD Universe, 84
Certificate authority (CA), 163
Certified Public Accountants (CPAs)
    assurance services and role of, 113
    impact of e-business on, 141–143
    non-CPA firm seals, 132–133
    proprietary firm seals, 132
    Vision Process, 15
    WebTrust, 130–132
Checks, paper and electronic, 170

Chemdex, 64
Chicago Board of Trade, 83
Christensen, Clayton M., 27
Cigital, 107
Circuit City, 2, 53
Cisco Systems, 70, 71
Citibank, 97
Citicorp, 115
Clark, Jim, 25
Clicks-and-mortar business, 60
Click trails, 70
CloudNine Communications, 83
CNET.com, 68
Coca-Cola Co., 171
Cold site, 86
Comcast Corp., 97
Comdisco Inc., 10–11
CommerceOne, 71
Commodity auctions, 62
Common Gateway Interface (CGI), 158
Compaq Computer, 70, 71
Computer controls, 117
Computer Emergency Response Team Coordina-
    tion Center (CERT/CC), 82
Computer Sciences Corp. (CSC), 87
Confidentiality, 106
Consulting services, 140
Consumer Reports, 66
Consumer-to-consumer (C2C) marketplace, 56,
    57
Content aggregators, 26, 69–70
Content providers, 64–68
Cookies, 96, 97–98, 160–161
COPS, 87
Copyright issues, 67
Costs, impact of e-business on, 8–9, 45, 46,
    65–66
Covisint, 9, 63, 64
CPAs. *See* Certified Public Accountants
CPA WebTrust, 130–132
Cracker, 87
Credit cards, 170–171
Customer impersonation, 92
Customer service, impact of e-business on, 6–8,
    11–12
Customer surveys, 9
Customization, 26
CyberCash, 171
Cybercop Scanner, 118
CyBerCorp, 60
CyberSource, 83

DaimlerChrysler, 9, 63, 64
DATAS (Digital Analysis Tests and Statistics),
    121
Data theft, 84
Datek, 60
DCS1000, 85
DealTime.com, 11
Debit cards, 171
Defense Advanced Research Projects Agency
    (DARPA), 28
Degradation-of-service attacks, 83
Dell, Michael, 49
Dell Computer, 2, 5, 11, 41, 43, 49–52, 61, 65,
    70, 71
Deloitte and Touche, 79
Delta Air Lines, 9
Demilitarized zone (DMZ), 167–168
Denial-of-service attacks, 14, 82–83
Digex, 71
Digital certificates, 94, 163
Digital signatures, 94, 139–140, 162–163, 170
Digital Signature Trust Co. (DST), 140
Digital subscriber line (DSL), 149
Digital tokens or coins, 172
DirectAg.com, 64
Directory, 69
Disaster recovery plans, 85–86
Disruptive technology, 23–24
Distributed denial-of-service attacks, 83
Distributive network, 41
Divine, 71
Domain Name Service (DNS), 31, 150–151
DoubleClick.com, 71, 96, 97
Drugstore.com, 53, 122–126
Dumpster diving, 103–104
Dutch auctions, 62
Dynamic Host Configuration Protocol (DHCP),
    151

EarthLink, 70
eBay.com, 11, 14, 41, 56–59
    security problems, 77, 82, 83, 90, 93
E-billing, 9
E-business (electronic business)
    affects on accounting professionals, 15–18
    benefits of, 4–12
    defined, 2–4
    development of, 30–32
    implementation of, 12–14
    risks of, 14–15
    starting, 169

strategies, 26–28
eCash Technologies, 171
ECMAScript, 157
E-commerce, defined, 3
Edmunds.com, 26, 66
Egghead.com, 81
Electronic Bill Presentment and Payment
    (EBPP), 171–172
Electronic business. *See* E-business
Electronic data interchange (EDI), 28, 32–36, 47,
    61–62
Electronic Disturbance Theater (EDT), 82
Elliott, Robert K., 127
Elliott Committee, 20, 127–128
E-mail
    hijacking, 93
    spoofing, 91
Emergent risks, 107
Encryption, 85, 88–89, 162–164
Encyclopaedia Britannica, 69
English, Kevin W., 64
English auctions, 62
Enron, 140
Environmental outages, 84
Ernst & Young, 19, 61, 71, 72, 77, 85, 95, 117
eSafe Protect, 88
E-Steel, 64
e-tailers, 49
Ethernet protocol, 29, 147
eToys, 1
E*Trade, 14, 60–61, 77
Exodus Communications, 71
Extensible Business Reporting Language
    (XBRL), 23, 120–121
Extensible Markup Language (XML), 37–38,
    120, 156
Extranets, 51, 61–62

False storefronts, 92
False Web sites, 92–93
Falsified identities, 90–95
FBI, 85
Federal Trade Commission (FTC), 96
FedEx, 71
Fidelity Investments, 60
File Transfer Protocol (FTP), 31, 150
File virus, 101
Financial Accounting Standards Board (FASB),
    124
Financial fraud, 115
Financial Services Technology Consortium, 171

Financial statements
    See also Information technology auditing
    assurance and, 114–115
    risk factors, 121–127
Firewalls, 86–87, 165–168
First-mover advantage, 79
First-price auctions, 62
Flying start site, 86
Ford Motor Co., 9, 63–64
Freemarkets, 62

Gap, 54
Garden.com, 106
Gates, Bill, 25, 107
General Electric (GE), 1, 9, 10, 27
Generally accepted accounting principles
    (GAAP), 113, 115
General Mills Inc., 9
General Motors (GM), 9, 26, 63–64
General Services Administration (GSA), 140
Geron Corp., 92–93
W.W. Grainger, 12, 43
Grainer.com, 12
Gramm-Leach-Bliley Act, 99

Hacking/hackers, 81, 84
Half.com, 58
Hallmark, 7
Hardened facilities, 89
Hardware layer, 33
Health care industry, 68
Healtheon/WebMD, 68
Hershey, 84
Hewlett-Packard, 27, 71
Hijacking, 93
Hiring, impact of e-business on, 11
Hoax, 102
Home Depot, 11
Host name, 93, 150
HotHotHot, 48
Hot site, 86
Hubs, 147
Human factors, risk and, 103–105
Hypertext documents, 30
Hypertext Markup Language (HTML), 30, 37,
    152, 154–156
Hypertext Transfer Protocol (HTTP), 30, 150,
    153–154, 164

IBM, 6, 8–9, 11, 71, 84, 139
IDC Research, 9

IDEA (Interactive Data Extraction and Analysis), 120
Identities, falsified, 90–95
IEEE 802.11a, 152
IEEE 802.11b, 152
IEEE 802.3, 147
i-mode, 152
Independent auctions, 62
InfoBeat, 95–96
Infomediaries, 26, 69
Information
    risk, 114
    timeliness of, 45
    value chain, 16–18
Information technology (IT)
    financial statements and, 115–121
    risk and, 80–90
Information technology auditing
    assessing control risk, 116–117
    control systems, internal, 116
    evaluation of evidence, 119
    performance of substantive tests, 119–121
    purpose of, 115
    software, 118
    specialists, 117
    testing controls, 117–119
Infrastructure, risk and, 80–90
Infrastructure providers, 70–72
Ingram Micro, 43
Inktomi, 71
Innovator's Dilemma, The (Christensen), 27
Integrated test facility (ITF), 119
Integrity, 106
Intel, 71
International Computer Security Association, 86
Internet
    addresses, 151
    benefits of using, 65–66
    development of, 28–29
    domains, 31
    early reactions to, 24–25
    terminology, 29–32, 147–151
    time, 78
Internet Assigned Numbers Authority (IANA), 150
Internet Corporation for Assigned Names and Numbers (ICANN), 150
Internet Fraud Complaint Center (IFCC), 77
Internet Information Server (IIS), 81, 88
Internet Protocol (IP), 29, 149
Internet Scanner, 118

Internet service providers (ISPs), 150
Intranet, 9
Intrusion detection software, 87
Inventory, impact of e-business on managing, 9–11
IP spoofing, 92
i2 Technologies, 71

Java applets, 157
Java byte code, 157
JavaScript, 157
Java Server Pages (JSP), 158, 159
Java virtual machine (JVM), 157
JScript, 157
Jupiter Communications, 7
Jupiter Media Metrix, 71

Kaiser Permanente, 9, 10
KPMG, 86
Kraft, 9

Lands' End Inc., 4, 7
Landsend.com, 4, 7, 12
Legal issues, 143
Levin, Vladimir L., 115
Levi Strauss, 54
Linux, 41
Living.com, 53
Local area networks (LANs), 29, 147, 148, 149
Logic bomb, 102
Love Bug virus, 99, 101
Lucent, 71

Macro virus, 99
Manugistics, 71
Markup languages, 154–156
Marriott.com, 6
Marriott International, 6
Marshall Industries, 43
MasterCard, 171
McAfee.com, 101
Melissa virus, 99
Merrill Lynch & Co., Inc., 27, 60
Meta-search engines, 69
Microsoft, 24–25, 65, 66, 71, 107, 157, 158
    Internet Information Server (IIS), 81, 88
MicroStrategy, 126
Miller Brewing Co., 9
Mitnick, Kevin, 91, 104
Modems, dial-up and cable, 149
Motorola, 71, 104

Movie industry, 67, 68
MSN, 70
Music industry, 67
MyAirplane.com, 64
MySimon.com, 11

Napster, 67
NASDAQ, 83
NECX, 43
Netscape Communications Corp., 25, 71
Network effect, 25
Networking gear, 147–149
Network interface controller (NIC), 147
Newbies, 55
New York Times, 67
Nexus, 126
Nielsen Netratings, 71
Nigeria, 92
Nodes, 147
Non-repudiation, 106
Nortel, 71
Novell, 139
NTT DoCoMo, 152

Office Depot, 4
OfficeDepot.com, 4
Omidyar, Pierre, 56
Online bill payment, 171
Online stores, 47
    advantages of, 48–49
    Amazon.com example, 52–56
    categories of, 48
    Dell Computer example, 49–52
    eBay example, 56–59
    lessons learned, 49
    Schwab example, 59–61
Oracle, 71

Packet filters, 166
Packets, 29, 147
Passwords
    cracking programs, 87
    selecting and/or changing, 89–90, 91
    unauthorized access to, 85
Patches, 81
Patents, 55
Payments, electronic, 57, 170–173
PayPal.com, 57
Perl (Practical Extraction and Reporting Language), 158
Pets.com, 1

PHP, 158
Physical controls, 89
Physical outages, 83
Pillsbury, 6, 8
Plug-ins, 156–157
Portals, 26, 70
Ports, 147
Pottruck, David, 59
Priceline.com, 11, 58, 125
Pricewatch.com, 11
PricewaterhouseCoopers, 7, 71–72, 139
Privacy, 88, 162–164
    compromised, 95–99
    policies, 98–99
Private auctions, 63
Procter & Gamble, 8, 12, 106, 134
Product reviews, 68
Prosumers, 41
Protocols, 147, 149–150
Proxy servers, 166–167
PSINet, 70
Public key encryption, 88, 162
Publishing industry, 66–68
Pure Internet play, 60

Quality control, 9, 46
Qwest, 70, 71
QXL.com, 58

RealNetworks, 25, 95–96
Reconfiguration, 84
Reebok, 54
Reliability issues, 45
Reports on the Processing of Transactions by Service Organizations, 135, 138
Research/surveys, electronic, 9
Reuters, 7
Revenue Recognition in the Financial Statements, 124, 125, 126
ReverseAuction, 95–96
Ricardo.de, 58
Right Aid Corp., 122, 123
Risks, 14–15
    See also Security
    anticipating and managing, 107–108
    categories of, 79–80
    characteristics of, 79
    compromised privacy, 95–99
    data theft, 84
    defined, 78–80
    denial-of-service attacks, 14, 82–83

e-mail problems, 91, 93
emergent, 107
false Web sites, 92–93
falsified identities, 90–95
financial statements and, 121–127
human factors, 103–105
information, 114
information technology and, 80–90
passwords and, 85
premium, 78
service interruptions, 82–84
sniffing/sniffers, 85
statistics, 77
system interdependencies and, 105–106
viruses, 99, 101–103
Risks, methods for controlling
cookie screening, 98
digital signatures/certificates, 94
disaster recovery plans, 85–86
encryption, 88–89
firewalls, 86, 165–168
intrusion detection, 87
password selection and change, 89–90
physical, 89
privacy policies, 98–99
scanners/security probes, 87–88
security suites, 88
for software, 86–88
tokens and biometrics, 94–95
Robertson, Paul, 81
Rocknob, 48
Rollins, Kevin B., 51
Routers, 29, 147–148
Royal Doulton, 84
Royal Dutch/Shell, 8
RSA Security, 71

Sales, impact of e-business on, 4–5
SAS. *See* Statement on Auditing Standards
SATAN, 87
Scanners, 87–88
Schultze, Eric, 85
Charles Schwab & Co., 7, 27, 59–61
Schwab.com (e.Schwab), 59–61
Screen It, 68
Scripting languages, 156
Sealed-bid auctions, 62
Search engines, 68–70
Sears, Roebuck & Co., 14
Second-price auctions, 62
Secure Electronic Transaction (SET), 171

Secure Sockets Layer (SSL), 85, 88, 89, 163–164
Securities and Exchange Commission (SEC), 124–126
Security
See also Risks
probes, 87–88
software, 118, 120, 121
suites, 88
Service interruptions, 82–84
Shadow mode, 86
Signatures, digital, 94, 139–140, 162–163, 170
Silent auctions, 62
Simple Mail Transfer Protocol (SMTP), 150
Simulation, parallel, 118–119
Smart cards, 172–173
Sniffing/sniffers, 85
Social engineering, 103
Software
intrusion detection, 87
outages due to, 83
security, 86–88, 118, 120, 121
Sony Music Entertainment, 96
Southwest Airlines, 9
Spam/spammers, 91
Spiders, 70
Spoofing
e-mail, 91
IP, 91
Sprint, 70, 71
Staff Accounting Bulletins (SABs), 124–126
Standish Group, 83
Statement on Auditing Standards (SAS) 70, 135, 138
Stickiness, 70
Stored accounts, 170–172
Stored values, 172–173
Sun Microsystems Inc., 4, 70, 71, 157
Supplies, impact of e-business on the management of, 9–11
Supply-chain management, 61–64
Sustaining technology, 23–24
Switches, 147
Symantec NetRecon, 118
SysTrust, 134–135, 136–137

Target, 2
Taxes, 126–127
TCP/IP (Transmission Control Protocol/ Internet Protocol), 29–30, 150
Tech Data, 43

Technology
   See also Information technology
   disruptive versus sustaining, 23–24
TELNET, 150
Tesco, 4, 5
Teseco.com, 5
Test data method, 118
3Com, 70, 71
Ticketmaster.com, 6, 12
Time Warner, 4
Tokens, 94
Top-level domains (TLDs), 150, 151
Toys "R" Us, 2, 53
Tradeout.com, 58
Tradescape, 60
Transmission Control Protocol (TCP), 29,
   149–150
Trap door, 102
Triak, John S., 80
Trojan Horse, 92, 101, 102
TruSecure Corp., 81
TRUSTe, 133
Trusted third parties (TTPs), 130–131, 139, 163
Twentieth Century Fox, 6–7
Twisted-pair wires, 147
Ultra Wideband (UWB), 152
Uniform resource locator (URL), 153
UPS, 41, 71
U.S. Department of Defense (DOD), 10, 82
U.S. Postal Service, 45, 71, 171–172
UUNet, 71

Value added networks (VANs), 33, 138–139
Value chain
   defined, 41
   information, 16–18
VBScript, 157
Vecna Technologies, 65
Verisign, Inc., 139

VerticalNet, 43
Virtual private networks (VPNs), 47
Viruses, 99, 101–103
Visa, 170–171

Wall Street Journal, 66, 96, 101
Wal-Mart, 2, 106, 134
Walton, Kenneth A., 93
TD Waterhouse, 60
Web sites, false, 92–93
Webvan, 1, 5
Welch, Jack, 1
Wells Fargo Bank, 57
Weyerhaeuser Co., 3
Whitman, Meg, 58
Wide area networks (WANs), 148–149
WiFi (IEEE 802.11b), 152
Wireless Access Protocol (WAP), 161
WorldCom, 6, 9, 41, 70, 71, 83
World Economic Forum (WEF), 82
World Wide Web (WWW/Web)
   browsers, 153
   client-side techniques, 156–157
   defined, 30–32, 153
   servers, 153
   server-side techniques, 158–160
Worms, 102

XBRL (Extensible Business Reporting Language), 23, 120–121
XML (Extensible Markup Language), 37–38,
   120, 156

Yahoo!, 14, 18, 70, 77, 82, 83
Yankee auctions, 62

Zagat, 161
Ziff-Davis, 67, 77
Zombies, 83